Whisper In The Heart

Whisper In The Heart

THE ONGOING PRESENCE
OF NEEM KAROLI BABA

PARVATI MARKUS

MANDALA
PUBLISHING

SAN RAFAEL LOS ANGELES LONDON

Neem Karoli Baba is a being who transcends all boundaries – religious classification, preconceived notions of a yogic path, even death – so why wouldn't he be as real to those of us who never physically met him as our own most beloved family members? In this magical and evocative collection of stories, we meet the one Ram Dass called Maharajji in all his variegated beauty, his unconventional holiness, his deep humanity and sublime transmission, his wildness and rootedness. If you didn't already love this baba before picking up this book, I promise you will fall in love right here, and that such a love will change everything, everything.

—MIRABAI STARR
author of *Caravan of No Despair* and *Wild Mercy*

People all over the world have had interactions with Neem Karoli Baba since he died in 1973. These stories remind us that the hereafter is here and now, and that love transcends death. That presence and love are never really distant. The influence of such a being is always available, no matter our limited concepts of time and space. The wind of grace is always blowing!

—RAMESHWAR DAS
co-author of *Being Ram Dass*

Years ago, after hearing me complain about not having the sort of karma that allows you to meet a being like Maharajji in person, Krishna Das put his hand on my shoulder and said, "The Longing is the grace." This book will fill you up with that kind of grace. Stories of Maharajji are somehow more than just stories. They reach through time and allow you a taste of the sweetness that drew so many people to India just to spend a few moments at his feet.

—DUNCAN TRUSSELL
comedian, writer, podcaster, actor

Parvati has birthed a beautiful blessing for our world. Listen! This book will amplify the whispers of hope, inspiration, courage, and kindness in your heart.

—Trudy Goodman
PhD, Vipassana teacher and founding teacher of InsightLA

When I first "met" Neem Karoli Baba through chanting with Krishna Das, reading stories of him by the old devotees was the way I learned to understand the feelings that arose. Stories about saints fortify our faith, so I thank Parvati for widening the circle by including these stories of Maharajji's contact with our hearts through infinite time and space.

—Nina Rao
musical artist and chant leader

In each lifetime, in each moment, He finds us and brings us back home to ourselves…to Himself. Out of His love for us, He wakes us up again and again… life after life. He is the one who is HERE! We are dreamers, asleep in our inner darkness. He turns on the light for us to give us a glimpse of what we truly are.

—Krishna Das
chant master

For many of us who didn't have the good fortune of being with Maharajji in the physical body, it is the stories that bring us his presence and love. We are always thirsty for the devotees' memories and stories of him and this book is yet another well of grace to quench our hearts.

—Trevor Hall
singer/songwriter

"This wonderful collection of stories about encounters with Neem Karoli Baba is a feast for the Soul. These stories embody the essence of Grace . . . that indefinable blessing of connection with the Divine . . . mystical events that have happened to so many of us, in which we find ourselves stepping briefly out of the mundane and into the Sacred. The experiences so beautifully portrayed in this book will help to stretch your awareness and to see through the very thin veil that separates ordinary experience from the miraculous. Neem Karoli Baba reminds us that every moment is a miracle . . . no matter how mundane it may seem . . . and that miracles often happen through simple events we might overlook if we're not paying attention . . . with a quiet mind and an open heart tuned to Love."

—RAMANANDA JOHN E. WELSHONS
author of *One Soul, One Love, One Heart*, and *Awakening from Grief*

In *Whisper in the Heart* we learn that the veil of death is just that, and that a great being like Neem Karoli Baba removes that veil and touches the hearts and minds of people all over the world. Both while sleeping and waking, he reaches into the mindstreams of people of many ages and nationalities and lights them up with love, wisdom, and humor. What originally impressed Ram Dass, then Richard Alpert, was Maharajji's omniscience about the death of his mother. But until the birth of this book, we might not have known that Maharajji's omniscience goes beyond time and space and can still be accessed. What a valuable gift Parvati Markus has skillfully given us, to know this is possible and to bring these stories to the world in these challenging times!

—LAMA TSULTRIM ALLIONE
author of *Wisdom Rising* and founder of Tara Mandala

It has been so hard for me to put this book down and return to attending to my daily life. Maharajji's transmission flows through all of it, with an enormous flood right out of the gate. I found myself in tears many times. I love every one of the shared stories, and there is a sweet flow to all of it. Maharajji just comes through the book.

—MELINDA EDWARDS, MD
psychiatrist and founder of Living Darshan

From the point of view of a devotee, it reassured me tremendously that there are so many others who have experienced Maharajji since he left his body; though each person's experience was their own, there was a thread that connected all of us. I think that for others who have not been so fortunate as to experience Maharajji yet, this book may very well serve as his invitation!

—GAYATRI WAGLE
Bach Flower practitioner

DEDICATION

To the One Who Whispers in Our Hearts
Neem Karoli Baba Maharaj

TABLE OF CONTENTS

Foreword

BY PETE HOLMES, AUTHOR OF *COMEDY SEX GOD*

Like 99.999 percent of the population, I never met Maharajji. In fact, until I was thirty-five, I had never even heard of him. If you had shown me his photo, I would've thought it was Sean Connery. Or maybe a bald Tom Selleck. I had no clue as to what an earth-shattering spiritual figure he was. But that all changed when I was a guest on a fellow comedian's podcast, *The Duncan Trussell Family Hour.*

Most comedians are atheists, which makes sense. First of all, atheism looks so cool. It's the cigarette of beliefs. Just leaning on your Dodge Charger, smoking away, scoffing, "You think there's a *God?* GET REAL!" Comedians don't want to belong to any group or belief system. We prefer to be in the back of the room, huddled together and making fun of the people dumb enough to sit up front and participate.

Duncan, however, is the exception to most rules. Not only is he a hilarious comedian, he also, from what I could tell that day, believed in whatever God crossed his path—Buddha, Krishna, even Christ, the faith I was raised with. I was surprised and delighted when Duncan would go on and on about his love of Jesus, even if it was after licking three drops of liquid THC off the back of his hand. Still. To use the language of the church I grew up in, he seemed pretty "on fire for the Lord." As we chatted about myth, metaphor, symbol, and LSD, I noticed behind his wide-smiling, Jim-Henson-looking head, a photo of a bald man in a blanket in front of which Duncan had left a bunch of bananas.

I had never seen someone leave fruit for a photograph before.

Duncan explained that the man wasn't Magnum P.I. but was in fact the guru of another man I had never heard of, a man who would go on to change my life, Richard Alpert, aka Ram Dass. Story after story followed of miracles, lessons, and transformations of heart that shook something loose in me. Like Richard Alpert, a heady Harvard professor before his pilgrimage to India, I knew that I, too, needed to move down from my head and into the more gracious and loving space of my heart.

The bananas never magically disappeared (at least not that I saw) but I knew I had found a new path that might lead me closer to God.

The following months I devoured everything I could find by Ram Dass. His lectures, his videos. I even managed to get my evangelical mind through *Be Here Now*, which to this day I tell everyone is far too trippy to be people's first introduction to the man. It looks like someone hand-stamped an acid trip. But I managed. I even started going to the retreats on Maui. It was great singing kirtan and eating fried rice in the same room as the now wheelchair-bound Ram Dass. But as lovely as it was, I couldn't help but feel something unexpected: Spiritual FOMO.

FOMO, for those of you over fifty, is *Fear Of Missing Out*.

Spiritual FOMO is the feeling you get while watching a YouTube video of hippies and their teacher laughing and crying on a grassy hill in Portugal while you're stuck working the drive-through at a Coffee Bean in Pennsylvania. Or the *why-not-me?* feeling you get meeting people who worked with Mother Theresa or ate brunch with Thich Nhat Hanh. It's a hot, secret jealous feeling. And it sucks. There I was in Hawaii, supposed to be having a religious experience, and all

I could think was how lucky all these old hippies were to have gotten to hang out with Maharajji – *the* guy – and all I got was white folks with Hindu names rehashing stories of the man who changed their lives but not mine. It was too much.

I felt like I had missed the boat. No matter how many times the older people reassured us young folks that "Big Maharajji" (the term they use for the cosmic, body-less continuing energy of the deceased guru) was still available to change and shape us, I couldn't help but think that sounded like a load of crap. I wanted the real guy. The real feet. The real eye-gaze. The real fruit tossed at my head.

Luckily, it turns out they were right.

After a few group retreats, I signed up for a private retreat with Ram Dass and learned that Ram Dass, my hero, wasn't just a great speaker, writer, and be-here-nower. He was also an amazing welcomer (dare I say conjurer?) of the Big Maharajji. Over the course of two private retreats and a few casual visits to his house, I experienced Ram Dass's biggest secret talent – welcoming his guru into the room.

He appeared to be able to do it on command because Ram Dass always saved it for the last of his visits during each retreat. It was, in show biz terms, his "closer." The big finish. The last number. And it was unbelievable. He'd sit quietly, eyes down, just letting the breeze and the birds become the only sounds in the world and, after a moment, this feeling would saturate the room. Each time I remember it feeling like snuggling into a sleeping bag filled with Love, or a snowsuit packed with bliss. Cozy, warm, and close to your skin. As close as the air. It shook, sort of like napping inside a subwoofer, but the gentle vibrations weren't a thumping bassline but an overwhelming sense that you were a vital part of *This*, cherished and deeply accepted.

After the feeling had arrived, Ram Dass would look at me and say, "Maharajji is here." Both times, as someone open to unexplainable phenomena, I glanced around the room just in case there was a translucent Maharajji standing in the corner like Yoda and Obi-Wan at the end of *Star Wars*. But no. There was nothing to "see" so much as the feeling of being seen.

It was a trip.

When I went back to my room, the photos of Maharajji stopped looking like photos of someone else's dead guru and started looking like photos of a beloved family member, someone who might pop by with a casserole at any moment.

A year or two later, my brother Ram Dass left his body. Shortly after, I started telling more and more of the newer devotees my story of visiting with him and feeling the Big Maharajji. And just like that, suddenly *I* was the old hippie at the retreats telling people *my* "I was with the guy" story, possibly causing a new generation of devotees to have some fresh cases of spiritual FOMO.

Maybe you can relate.

Maybe even reading this right now, you are feeling left out, too. Just as I had on my first retreat. Just like a lot of us have or still do.

And that's where this book comes in.

In the pages that follow, the kind-eyed, lovely, and talented Parvati Markus has compiled many, many stories of the Big Maharajji still at work in our human lives. Wild stories, small stories, and everything in between. I believe the accounts have the power to comfort and inspire and hopefully even squash any spiritual FOMO for many generations to come. Because it's true. Maharajji isn't gone; he's just changed.

As a friend once told Krishna Das, when he was devastated that Maharajji had died: "Your guru isn't gone. Your guru is what's looking out your eyes right now."

That's good news.

Maharajji isn't done with us. He's still at work or, perhaps more accurately, he's still at play. His dance continues in some surprising and unexpected ways.

But for more on that, you'll have to read on.

Introduction

BY PARVATI MARKUS

Over the last five decades, since my time with Neem Karoli Baba in India in the early '70s, I have loved to hear and share stories of Maharajji, as he is known. I heard about Maharajji in the summer of 1969 from Ram Dass, and three days after meeting him I became Ram Dass's secretary—typing up responses to the mail he was receiving after speaking across the country. Later I edited "History"—the opening section of *Be Here Now* in which Ram Dass describes his journey from Harvard professor to psychedelic explorer and finally to devotee of Maharajji.

Two years after meeting Ram Dass, I was sitting in front of Maharajji in India. Baba told me I was no longer Ram Dass's private secretary, I was *his*. He would call me over, shouting "private secretary" in English! Never had I thought I'd be so thrilled to be a secretary.

It turns out that my "private secretary" mission has meant helping to birth some of the other devotees' books that share stories of Maharajji's love. Dada Mukerjee's *By His Grace* and *The Near and the Dear*, *Chants of a Lifetime* (Krishna Das), *HeartSourcing* (Ram Giri Braun), and *Deva Bhumi* (K.K. Sah) all passed through my hands. That led to a desire to gather the stories of those of us from the West who had been with Maharajji in India, before we all take our leave for the big *bhandara* (a festival meal) in the sky. I interviewed over seventy Westerners about their journey to the East and their experience with Maharajji—and the book *Love Everyone* was born.

But the stories didn't stop after Maharajji left his body. Countless seekers, who never met Maharajji as a physical being, are experiencing his presence to this day. As you will read in the stories here, they are being called to him in so many different ways.

Many of us first went to India to be with Maharajji after meeting or hearing Ram Dass. Even after Maharajji's bodily form departed in 1973, Ram Dass continued to be the "bait" on the hook of Maharajji's fishing line, reeling many into the unconditional love that is Maharajji's presence. Others enter Baba's heart space through chanting the sacred names and the Hanuman Chalisa[1] with Krishna Das, Jai Uttal, Nina Rao, Trevor Hall, and other *kirtan wallahs* (chant masters) leading the way. Many read the books put out by Western and Indian devotees and connect through the written stories. Some have *darshan* dreams—lucid moments of being in the presence of a saint or divine being—or experiences and visions in meditation. Sometimes Maharajji appears "in person" to those who have never even heard of him.

When I interviewed Ram Dass for *Love Everyone*, he said, "I have a difficult time with the concept of some people who were with him and some who were not. Since I am in the public to talk about him, I find people who have met him through their dreams, visions, or through books, or through devotees' stories. Some of them have golden hearts and appreciate Maharajji even more than those who

---

1 The Hanuman Chalisa is a song of praise, reminding Hanuman, the monkey god who is one of the heroes of the *Ramayana*, of who he is and his mighty accomplishments. It is comprised of forty verses in Hindi, which, amazingly, thousands of Westerners now know by heart.

were 'with him.' He calls people, and certainly he calls people now that he is out of his body. I listen when people approach me, and I can hear when they have a Maharajji connection. They're looking at me, but they're really feeling Maharajji."

And as Dada Mukerjee, one of Maharajji's long-time Indian devotees, said: "Once he catches hold of you, he never lets go."

The Guru

Guru literally means the "remover of darkness"—whether that be the darkness that stems from hurtful thoughts, words, and deeds, or the darkness of ignorance that keeps us from loving others and ourselves. In the Upanishads, the ancient Vedic wisdom, it says:

asato mā sadgamaya,
tamaso mā jyotirgamaya,
mṛtyormā 'mṛtaṃ gamaya.

From the unreal lead me to the real!
From the darkness lead me to the light!
From death lead me to immortality!

You may have many *upagurus*—teachers who point the way— like a spiritual teacher who takes you far along the path or a difficult person who teaches you where you are not, but you have only one *satguru*, the "true" guru who takes you home. The satguru takes you from living in duality—the realm of pleasure and pain, good and evil, rich and poor—to *Sub Ek,* where it's All One, where form merges into the formless.

Someone once asked Maharajji, "How do I know if someone is my guru?"

Maharajji said, "Do you feel he can fulfill you in every way spiritually? Do you feel he can free you from all desires and attachments? Do you feel he can lead you to final liberation? When you feel all these things, perhaps then you've found your guru."

Those of us who are Maharajji devotees feel in our deepest hearts that he fulfills all these requirements. Others feel the same way about Jesus or Mary or Ramana Maharshi or Anandamayi Ma or another realized being. Those who have experienced Maharajji in the decades since he left his body, or any realized being that no longer walks the Earth, know that a physical connection is not necessary for the soul connection. That connection is love—unconditional, unreserved, unlimited love.

Guru Kripa

Ram Dass talks about the method of *guru kripa*—the form of *bhakti yoga* (the path of devotion) that focuses on the guru and the guru's blessing or grace (*kripa*). He says, "The essence of a relationship with a guru or spiritual teacher is love. The guru awakens incredible love in us, then uses that love to help us out of the illusion of duality."[2]

The relationship with a guru has nothing to do with intellectual concepts, and "surrender" to the love of the guru does not mean you give up your power or your individuality. You may *think* you're surrendering or that you are resisting, but there's really no mind involved at all, no decision to make or action to take. Your karma is simply unfolding, and you are drawn to your guru when the time is right for you.

That is no less true today than it was when Maharajji was

---

2 Ram Dass (with Rameshwar Das), *Polishing the Mirror: How to Live from Your Spiritual Heart* (Sounds True, 2014 paperback)

embodied in India. Maharajji himself said that the guru does not need to be in a body. As Swami Vivekananda[3] once noted, "It may be that I shall find it good to get out of my body—to cast it off like a used garment. But I shall not cease to work!"

When Dada Mukerjee visited Canada and the U.S., he said that the biggest miracle he had ever witnessed—and he had witnessed many with Maharajji—was meeting numberless Westerners who had not met Maharajji in the body, yet had the same spiritual connection to him as those who spent time with him in India.

During his trip to the States, one of the places Dada visited was Montauk, New York, the furthest point on Long Island with an all-encompassing view of the Atlantic Ocean. Dada gazed out into the boundless waters for some time without moving. When he finally came around, he was asked what he had been feeling as he stared at the ocean. He kept repeating, "He is so vast, he is so vast! When he was in a body, he was able to reach only so many, but now, now he is unlimited."

The guru's grace is available around the clock, 24/7, for your whole life and beyond.

Dealing with Doubt

It is often difficult to connect head and heart. You may wake from a dream in which you fully experience Maharajji's love in your heart, but your mind says, "It was only a dream." You may read the stories in *Miracle of Love* or *Love Everyone* and think, "But they met Baba in person!" You may see Maharajji driving past you in a car, or walking

---

3 Swami Vivekananda (1863-1902) was a disciple of Ramakrishna Paramahamsa, and a key figure in bringing Vedic teachings and practices to the West.

down the road, or standing on the corner and discount it as not possible. You may have looked at his picture and burst into tears, your heart overflowing, and yet doubted his presence.

That is one of the main reasons for this collection of stories, all from people who met Maharajji after he left his body: so that you will know that what you are experiencing is real. Yes, you *have* connected with Maharajji. Yes, that *is* his love you found in Ram Dass's eyes, felt in meditation or while chanting, or when you called out for his help and were comforted. Perhaps it isn't Maharajji who shows up. You may be connected to a different saint, a deity, another embodiment of divine love. The stories in this book can affirm for you, too, that what you are experiencing, dreaming, and sensing in your heart is real. No matter how extraordinary these experiences might be, the most miraculous aspect is the way your heart opens and your life changes.

This collection is arranged in ten broad categories, but please understand that these are very fluid. Unconditional love has no boundaries and the seed that was planted from a photo or a book or a dream can come to fruition in kirtan, at a retreat, or when you pick up a piece of sea glass on the beach. Some of these stories come from decades-old letters to Ram Dass or Krishna Das. Others come from interviews on Maui at the 2015 and 2019 retreats with Ram Dass, or virtual interviews during pandemic shutdown, so all together they span snail mail to Zoom.

Westerners grow up in a culture that often doesn't easily acknowledge or appreciate the realities that exist beyond the five physical senses. If you can't smell it, taste it, touch it, see it, or hear it, how can it exist? But it's that sixth sense—the one we usually call *intuition*—that reaches beyond time and space. You may know who's calling before you look at the name on your phone. You may feel the strong presence of your grandmother and later learn it was the exact time she passed. You may suddenly feel that one of your loved ones is having a hard time and reach out to discover this is true.

Maharajji is beyond time and space. He would show up in two places at once, escape from locked rooms, and do other miraculous things on a regular basis that confounded so-called physical reality. What's to stop him from coming to you from the beyond?

God, guru, and your deepest Self are One. Open your heart on the path of devotion and follow your inner guidance into the realm of unconditional love.

Listen to that whisper in your heart.

A Word

FROM ANNIE LEVITT

"If I don't meet you in this form,
I'll meet you in another form."
—NEEM KAROLI BABA MAHARAJ

In September of 1973, the being we call Neem Karoli Baba, or simply Maharajji, left his body. Known throughout northern India as a great saint, or *siddha*, Maharajji first became known in the West as Ram Dass's guru, but he was and is so much more. Since that September day so many decades ago, Maharajji has continued to reveal his presence, manifesting quite unexpectedly in various ways to people around the world through dreams, sightings, conversations, meditation experiences, unexplainable "coincidences," or a deep inner knowing of the heart.

Such encounters with divine beings are not unusual, occurring across cultures and religions, across time and place. Miraculous appearances and heart blessings of bodhisattvas, saints, and enlightened beings are apparently never far away. Fortunately, although we may often forget them, these great beings don't forget us, and are ever ready to guide and inspire. As the Bengali saint Sri Ramakrishna Paramahamsa said, "The winds of grace are always blowing."

I never met Maharajji in the body. I came to know about him first through Ram Dass in 1970, and then through the other Westerners and Indian devotees who spent time with Maharajji and shared their stories in books such as *Be Here Now*, *Miracle of Love*, *By His Grace*, *Love Everyone*, and *Chants of a Lifetime*. In 2015 I read a story on Facebook about a modern-day, miraculous encounter with Maharajji. I thought, oh, what a wonderful story! Wouldn't it be great if "somebody" would collect such stories for sharing?

Coincidentally, I saw that Parvati Markus was offering potential authors a complimentary consultation. I didn't know Parvati personally, but I felt pushed to connect with her about this idea of collecting stories about Maharajji's appearances. Parvati said, "Oh, I'm working on that project for the Love Serve Remember Foundation. I could pass some of that on to you." Although astonished by Parvati's response, and involved full time in challenging work, I wasn't going to say no to Maharajji's "private secretary!" She seemed to trust that I could do this. Soon afterwards I retired from my healthcare career. Between the two of us we collected many personal stories, resulting in the book you now hold in your hands. I no longer believe in coincidence.

Whisper in the Heart challenges our usual skepticism. But what may seem implausible is also a chance to open one's heart and connect to an inner reality, a guiding presence. As Maharajji assured us, "It is not necessary to meet your guru on the physical plane. The guru is not external."

I
Appearances

Kabir says: "Listen, my friend!
There is no other satisfaction,
save in the encounter with the Beloved."
—SONGS OF *KABIR*, LII
TRANSLATED BY RABINDRANATH TAGORE

No matter how often we Westerners sat before the *takhat* (wooden platform) on the porch at Kainchi (Maharajji's temple and *ashram*, his spiritual residence in the Himalayan foothills), waiting for darshan, it was always startling when Maharajji burst through the doors and suddenly there he was! The banging doors and his sudden appearance never failed to captivate and somehow surprise us.

Some days it was the Lion of God that settled onto the blanket-covered takhat and took wickedly accurate aim with an orange or apple or banana. Sometimes it was the tender Krishna, sweetly offering assurances and making us giggle with delight. Other times it was Shiva, unmoving and silent, impenetrable, as majestic and awe-inspiring as the Himalayas. Sometimes he felt like your grandfather, your beloved, or your child. He could be tall or short, fierce or gentle, or all "10,000 things" of the Tao at once—the portal to take you beyond time and space or deep into your own being, manifesting in whatever way the moment called for.

It's like that in the following stories. You're a frightened nine-year-old boy and a man appears and wraps you in a blanket. You catch a glimpse of him standing on a corner, riding a bike, or he shows up in your meditation. He dances for you while you're sitting on a beach or skips alongside you down city streets. He can be an ethereal presence, or you just might find his physical form lying at your doorstep.

There are no rules, no schedules, no guidelines for how and when he might appear, but show up he does!

Angela Strynkowski

About twenty years ago I was doing a yoga teacher training at Omega[4]. We had permission to go to other events at Omega while going through our month-long training. I got to sit in on some of Ram Dass's talks; I found him to be quite amazing, but I really didn't know who he was. Krishna Das was there doing kirtan. At some point Krishna Das said he was from Long Island. After the kirtan I went up to him and said, "Hi, I'm Angela from Babylon. I live on Long Island, too." He giggled.

I got hooked on kirtan and started to follow Krishna Das around. He had a nickname for me—the Bodhisattva from Babylon. That touched my heart. He used to do kirtan at Ananda Ashram[5] on weekends. One weekend, when I left the kirtan, I was exhausted, extremely high from the kirtan, and starving. I was driving in Monroe in the middle of nowhere and I needed food. I saw a gas station and stopped to buy some nuts and pretzels.

As I walked out the door, I saw Maharajji to the right of the building. I definitely saw his form; it wasn't like a ghost or anything. He was standing and smiling and just being. I looked again and he beamed this giant smile. I'd heard stories that masters can come back and show themselves to you. I was young in the yoga world, so I didn't know what to do. I literally just smiled and drove away. I didn't tell anybody.

I haven't been to Ananda in quite a while. I don't remember where that gas station is, but Maharajji grabbed me there. Now I've grown to have a relationship with him. When my life fell apart, I would sit with Maharajji's picture and talk with him, yell at him, cry

---

4 Omega Institute, in Rhinebeck, NY, is a nonprofit educational organization that hosts countless retreats and events.

5 Ananda Ashram, in Monroe, NY, is a yoga retreat and spiritual-educational center.

to him. I knew he was supporting me, and I knew that I needed to deal with whatever I was going through.

I feel him. I hear him. I know he's here.

ᚺᚢ

Bonnie Divina Maa

I was living what some would call the dream life in the Hudson Valley in upstate New York, but I was quite unhappy inside. I was going through a divorce in 2011 and a friend took me to see Krishna Das in Garrison, New York. I was blown away. It was in a church-like monastery, so it had this feeling of reverence. It was the first time I had ever been exposed to anything like that, and I thought, "I want to do this every week, like church." My friend gave me a "Flow of Grace" CD. I didn't know what the Hanuman Chalisa was, I just knew it felt great!

Then the divorce. We had these emotional and physically violent interactions with one another, and I was feeling quite shattered. This same friend said, "Well, why don't we go up to Kripalu[6]?" I had a wonderful time that weekend, but a week later I was in even more inner turmoil and hoped meditation might bring some answers. I was sitting there meditating when this bearded man in a blanket appeared. My eyes were closed, but there he was right in front of me, and he said, "Laugh!"

It jolted me out of the meditative space. I asked my friend, who was sitting nearby, "This guy in a blanket, a friendly-looking man, who is he?" I had seen his photo.

He said, "You mean Neem Karoli Baba?"

---

6 Kripalu Center for Yoga & Health, in Stockbridge, MA, is a nonprofit educational organization.

"I don't know, maybe. He's still here! He's like right here."

I walked outside, and there was Baba floating around me, laughing like Santa Claus with his belly shaking and tears of laughter. And I was laughing. Of course, I was the only one seeing him! I was skipping down the street, smiling and laughing, and I felt like he was right here. We were holding hands and having this wonderful laughter for over an hour.

He told me to laugh, to keep it light, not let it get too heavy. I went home and googled "laughter Hudson Valley." What came up was Laughter Yoga at Ananda Ashram. I signed up immediately. The ashram was only thirty minutes from my house. I went to the regular morning program of meditation at the ashram and stayed for the next day, then I stayed for lunch, and then I just stayed. Ananda became my home away from home, my refuge.

The path with Maharajji was a slow unfolding after that. I had photos of him all around my house; he was so real to me. I went to India, to Kainchi and Vrindavan. I found Ram Dass through the book *Be Love Now*. Not too many years later, here I am, still laughing! And I've been teaching Laughter Yoga all over the world.

ॐ

Clark Samson

In 1971, I had a music teacher at my university in Lubbock, Texas, the last place you'd think anything hip or new or modern would be taking place. He was one of the very first yoga teachers from Yogi Bhajan's[7] first teacher class and he introduced us to *Be Here*

---

7 Yogi Bhajan (Harbhajan Singh Khalsa) was an Indian-born American entrepreneur, yoga guru, and spiritual teacher, who brought his version of Kundalini Yoga to the West in the late '70s.

Now. I paid more attention to Ram Dass than Maharajji, who was just a picture on the brown pages of that book. In the decades that followed, I was in and out of spirituality, then around 2000 I started to read the books that were coming out about Maharajji. I thought how wonderful it would be to have a guru who would answer all my questions and make life easier. How come I didn't have one?

I'd spent about a year with my nieces and nephews, teaching them how to swim and being Uncle Clark. They were going to move away, and I was very upset. I remembered reading in *Miracle of Love* where Maharajji was asked what would happen to his devotees when he died. He said, "What could possibly happen? If you call, I'll come." I was very distraught. I said, "I have to know if you'll come."

So I called him.

I was sitting in the cab of my plumbing truck. A column of warm light came through the top of my truck and down into my forehead and filled my heart with love. I had waited my whole life for something like this to happen, then had difficulty really believing it when it did happen. All this love was pouring down through my head and overflowing out of the top of my heart. I didn't know what to make of it, but I was crying as I heard a voice say, "Would you like to become my *chela* (disciple)?"

I said, yes, yes, please. I knew that it was Maharajji because that's who I'd called. I sat there in tears for a while, then finally everything came back into normal focus. I thought, "Wow. Now I know I'm crazy, but maybe it'd be best if I never become sane again because that was so wonderful."

I told a friend about this incredible experience. She gave me Ram Dass's number and I called him. He said, "What did you want to talk about?" *Maharajji.* Then every month for about a year and a half, I got these one- or two-hour tutorials from Ram Dass, and the doors to this community opened wide. I met Jai Uttal, and I couldn't talk to him about this experience without having tears flooding down my face. He assured me that it was totally real and authentic and that I should trust in it.

I have a beautiful picture of Maharajji on my altar. I talk to him and get guidance about what I'm doing and how I'm doing it and what I'm clinging to and need to let go of. Since that day in my plumbing truck, my life's been about my relationship with Maharajji.

ॐ

Donna

FEBRUARY 1, 1987
Dear Ram Dass,

Miracle of Love is one of those books that I pick up from time to time and open it to no place in particular. I read a paragraph or two and then go to bed feeling good. Ha! Before I know it, I've read a couple of chapters and half the night has slipped away. One night I did just that. By the time I put down the book, I was so full to overflowing with Maharajji that I was weeping. I felt his presence so strongly I began talking aloud to him, scolding him for leaving his body before I could have darshan.

When I turned out the light and closed my eyes, the moment my head hit the pillow there was an explosion of glorious light, and there we were sitting together. He was positively aglow, with light coming out of him in all directions. Gone was the funny plaid blanket. He was draped in soft, shiny, ivory-colored cloth, and his light splashed and spilled into every atom of me until I, too, glowed. He appeared to be younger than in the pictures I have of him.

The communication was non-verbal, but it was crystal clear. He patted me on the head as if he were indulging a child. "Well, here we are," he said, "Isn't this what you wanted?" He never stopped

8

grinning at me with that impish grin. Of course, time was not, and I'll never know if we were sitting together for five minutes or five hours. When he got up to leave, he patted me on the head again, still grinning from ear to ear, walked a few steps and faded away.

But there was a residual of light that stayed for what seemed like a very long time.

卐

Dr. Ronald A. Alexander

In 1972 I was researching *kundalini* (the dormant force of spiritual energy) yoga and mindfulness meditation with the Veterans Hospital in Topeka, Kansas, and the Menninger Clinic. Dr. Green, who was doing meditation and biofeedback research, told me to look up Dan Goleman[8] at Harvard University. After spending an afternoon at his lab, I invited Dan to speak at the University of Massachusetts on the Tibetan "wheel of birth and death" and on meditation. Dan stayed at the farmhouse I was renting, and twice each day we practiced mindfulness for forty-five minutes. He put up several wonderful pictures of Maharajji. My heart felt a craving to meet Neem Karoli Baba, as Dan shared so many stories of Ram Dass and that first group of Westerners who found Maharajji. I said, "I must go meet him!" But at that time I had very little money, so I had to wait.

In 1973 I co-sponsored a conference at Amherst College and invited Ram Dass, along with other speakers in the field of consciousness studies. I was thrilled to hear Ram Dass share his

---

8 Dan Goleman (named Jagganath Das by Maharajji) is an author and science journalist who wrote the book *Emotional Intelligence* (among others) and has twice been nominated for a Pulitzer Prize.

personal story of meeting Maharajji. Sometime later I asked Ram Dass how I could meet Maharajji. He said that Maharajji had left his body, but you could meet him through your heart. I was devastated that I could not meet Maharajji in person.

Over the next seventeen years, I meditated on Maharajji's photo daily. In July of 1989, I was deep in sleep when I was awakened by hearing Maharajji's voice, in English not Hindi, saying, "Wake up! You must awaken." The clock read 3:20 a.m. I could see the stars through the skylight. I looked at the foot of my bed and there was a miniature-sized Maharajji in the etheric tones of deep purple and blue. I was aghast! I thought I was dreaming, then he said, "Look again at the clock. It's 3:22. You are awake and not dreaming."

I started to tell him how disappointed I was that I didn't meet him when Ram Dass, Danny Goleman, and Krishna Das all got to be with him in India. He started to yell, "WAKE UP, WAKE UP! It's now time to be with me. You must stay awake now and serve everyone. I haven't gone anywhere. I left that physical form and returned to the source. Keep your heart open, especially during difficult times, and deepen into the love."

That September I attended the ten-day meditation retreat in France with Ram Dass called the "Advanced Course." When I had one-on-one time with Ram Dass, I asked him why Maharajji showed up in the etheric and not in the physical. Ram Dass laughed and said, "You guys who receive him in the etheric must have greater faith than we did, as we needed to experience him in the body." I felt special for a moment, then Ram Dass immediately added, "Now don't let that get to your ego. How you meet Maharajji does not matter. Just keep opening and practice 'nobody' meditation."

Durga Julia Sánchez

The first week that I moved to Miami from Colombia, I went to this yoga studio that was near my architecture office. At the end of class, in *savasana* (corpse pose), the teacher played a kirtan by Krishna Das. Suddenly, I started to cry and cry; I didn't know why I was crying so deeply. The teacher said, "Are you okay?"

"I am, but what is that music? Who is that man singing?" That's how I found out about Krishna Das and music called kirtan in June of 2008. After class I got on the computer to check out who Krishna Das was. On his website I saw a photo of Maharajji, and whoa, he looked so much like my physical father! I started to cry again. After that, every night after I came back home from work, I'd sit at my computer and go through Maharajji's photos.

Soon after, a friend from work put *Be Here Now* on my desk. I opened the book and the first thing I saw was another photo of this man in the blanket. Okay, something's going on with this guru. I had found very little to alleviate my suffering and the traumas I experienced growing up. Somehow, looking at his photos soothed me a lot. I printed a photo of Maharajji and put it on my altar, a cardboard box inside my walk-in closet, and started to talk to Baba. "You are showing up in my life suddenly, and I want to ask you to help me, help me find answers, help me heal. Help me understand the suffering." I asked him for a teacher. There had to be somebody in this world who could guide me.

About seven or eight months after that, I was at a church where I used to sing with their kirtan mass—a Christian service but the music was kirtan. One Sunday this tall man came into the church, and my first thought was, "He's my teacher." I saw something in him that I had never seen in anybody else up to that point in my life. Two days later, a friend told me the tall guy was a devotee of Neem Karoli Baba and I went ballistic. "I have to meet him. I have to talk to him." Eventually he gave me Ram Giri's address and phone number.

When I came into the house to meet Ram Giri, it was filled with pictures of Maharajji and statues of Ganesh and Shiva and Hanuman. Was this a museum? He shared some stories of Maharajji. At some point I asked if he could be my teacher. Eventually everything else evolved—our marriage, our long pilgrimage in India, his death from pancreatic cancer.

Three months after I met Ram Giri, I started to ask Maharajji, "Are you really my guru? What are you supposed to do? What am I supposed to do in this relationship?" I believe I needed confirmation because I grew up in a very fanatical Catholic family and never had the blind faith that they had. To come back to feeling and believing in another figure that is not alive, or at least not in the body—I mean, he's more alive than anything else—but that I could see and touch and grab, it was difficult for me.

One weekend Krishna Das was in Miami doing a kirtan and a workshop. When the workshop was over, Ram Giri and I went to the beach and sat close to the water. I noticed a father with a little girl. He was holding her like she was the most precious jewel, bringing her up in the air and then down into the water. The girl was laughing and they were having a beautiful moment. I started to cry, wishing I had had that with my father.

I closed my eyes. Then the next thing I saw—with my eyes closed— was the horizon, very clear, and a distinct black point in the horizon that was coming closer and getting bigger. It was Maharajji and he was doing a dance that I grew up dancing, called *cumbia*. It's a very typical folklore rhythm from Colombia, and he's waving the blanket and going in circles and stepping one foot in front of the other one. This is a dance between a male and a female, and the female has a very long skirt that she flips from side to side and brings it all the way to the top of her head. Maharajji was doing the female movements, bringing the blanket to his head and moving his hips. I was describing this all to Ram Giri as I was seeing it. Then Maharajji came closer and closer to us. He asked me, "Am I doing it right? Am I doing it right?"

"Yes, Maharajji, you are doing it right."

The next thing he was sitting on my left, Ram Giri on my right. Baba opened the blanket and put it over my right shoulder; I felt the weight of the blanket. He grabbed my face like my father used to do when he'd turn it around to tell me something that I wasn't hearing. Maharajji did the same. He turned my face to his face and said, "Don't cry. I'm your father. Don't cry." Then he got up and entertained me a little more, like cheer up, cheer up. He came close again and grabbed my cheeks and jiggled them. He said the same thing again, "Don't cry. I'm your father. Don't cry." He approached me a third time, held my chin and head up with both of his hands, and told me again, "I am your father, don't cry." Of course, I couldn't stop crying—a mix of sadness and happiness all together. He started to dance again and slowly waved the blanket, went to the horizon, and disappeared.

ᵈᵉᵛ

Gayatri Wagle

I heard Krishna Das sing "Mere Gurudev" for the first time some sixteen years ago when I attended a Reiki seminar. My life was a mess. I felt sad, depressed, and anxious all the time, and I was consumed by anger from my childhood. When I heard his voice, I felt something shift in me for the first time in years. Of course, I attributed my feeling of relief to my Reiki teacher, but I kept listening to Krishna Das and suddenly chants from my childhood started coming back to me. I remembered that my grandma used to chant every day.

In January 2015, I attended a workshop that Krishna Das conducted in Mumbai. I had always seen a picture of Baba whenever Krishna Das sang, but I had no curiosity to know more about the man in the picture. A few days later, as is my practice each morning, I walked around a park while chanting along with Krishna Das on my phone. Suddenly my phone pinged and Maharajji's photo popped up. I could not stop looking at him. I felt like I had definitely seen him before.

A few days later I started getting attracted to the Hanuman Chalisa, which gave me such solace. I live with my husband and son. My mother-in-law, who was bedridden for the last five years of her life, also lived with us. She was the kindest, most loving person I had ever met, and I viewed her as my mother. I started chanting the Chalisa for her and she said that it brought her such peace. We chanted together every morning and evening.

One day I was walking in the morning, chanting as usual. The park in which I walk has a Hanuman Temple. I passed the temple and suddenly, from the opposite direction, there was a huge beautiful golden monkey walking right towards me, looking straight at me. His eyes were almost human. This is not the kind of monkey we see in a city like Mumbai. It didn't seem like the few people walking near me had registered this monkey, which kept walking straight at me. At about a hundred meters, the monkey moved sideways and disappeared into the bushes. I followed, but it was gone.

Then it dawned on me: Was this a darshan? Did Baba just appear to me? Did he grace me with his presence? I started to cry and could not stop. From that day on, I read every book I could find, watched every video I could find, and so many of the things that I read in Dada's books, in Parvati's book, in Krishna Das's book seemed familiar.

I finally managed to get to Kainchi with a few friends in 2018. I went to see my parents before I left Mumbai and, to my great joy, my father shared that when I was a little girl of six, we had visited his friend in Nainital when Baba was in Bhumiadhar, and my dad had taken me to see that temple. He remembered Baba blessing me!

I have no recollection of this at all and my dad never spoke of it before. At Kainchi I went to Baba's room, rested my head on his blanket, and wept and wept. The tears would not stop; my heart was bursting. Finally I went to sit opposite his *murti* (a sculpture that embodies a saint's or deity's essence) and said to him, "So, Baba, we finally meet!" Before I could even finish the sentence, from the corner of my right eye I saw the same golden monkey I had seen in Mumbai casually walk past on the wall.

I heard Baba laugh and say, "Nay, we have met before." I was overwhelmed.

When I was in Kainchi, the only thing I prayed for was that Baba free my mother-in-law from her suffering. She was very fearful about the process of death. When I returned to Mumbai, I shared pictures and stories of Baba with her. The next morning she was very excited to tell me her dream—Baba had held out his hand to her and said, "Come, I am here waiting for you; you are not alone." She was not afraid anymore. One evening, I knew she was transitioning. She opened her eyes and asked me to chant. As I finished the chant, she passed on.

ॐ

Grace Kripa

(TRANSLATED BY HANNAH SCHOEN)

I lived with X for twenty years. We did everything together: work, shopping, travels, hiking, even going to the doctor. My health was not very good, but doctors didn't know what was wrong with me. I was planning to go to the hospital in Paris for three days. I thought that he would come with me as usual, but he said he was feeling tired, and I believed him. He accompanied me to the train station and stayed there sending kisses as the train departed. During the three days I was at the hospital, he called me several times during the day to see how I was doing.

The day of my return home, I called in the morning to tell him the arrival time of my train. The message on the phone said that the number was no longer in service. I thought that something was wrong with the phone company. When I arrived at the train station, nobody was there to greet me. He knew that I was coming back that day. I arrived at my apartment with an indescribable feeling. I opened the door, and the first thing that caught my attention was the disappearance of a painting that his mother had given us. His desk was empty, his closet was empty, his toothbrush was gone. There was nothing, nothing, nothing . . . it looked as if he had never existed.

My legs couldn't support me. I called my daughter to see if she had seen him. She said, "Yes, he took the children to school." I called his mother, and she told me that she didn't know anything, but hearing the strained tone of her voice, I started to understand. I couldn't stop crying. I went to my bank to get some money and was told that he had closed our account. Even though I am a proud person, I fell apart and cried, "What am I supposed to do?" I went to the garage to see if my car was there. Yes, it was, but in bad shape. I realized that I had nothing left, not even enough money to pay the rent.

Back in my apartment, I closed all the windows and told myself that it was here my life would end. I took lots of medications and went to bed all dressed.

I don't know how many days and nights went by until I heard a noise at the front door. I walked over hesitantly and noticed that the door was slightly open. I was sure that I had closed it properly. There on my front doormat was an old man lying down, with a blanket covering his body. With his hand on his head, he spoke to me in a language that I didn't understand, but strangely I came to understand that he was telling me, "Go, go sing." There was a certain anger, even contempt in his voice.

I got scared and asked myself, "How did this tramp get in without the code of the building?" I was shaking. I went to my computer, and as I often do, put some classical music on YouTube. But a different page opened to where someone was singing strange songs that I had never heard, and to my surprise behind the singer was a huge portrait of the tramp that was at my front door. I learned through YouTube that the singer was Krishna Das.

I went to the kitchen with the intention of eating an orange, but then decided to give it to the tramp. I opened the door, but he was gone. I ate the orange and at that moment I felt strong and in a fantastic mood.

I told my daughter calmly what I thought had happened with X. She lent me some money and I did all the necessary legal paperwork. As I was packing everything, I listened to the chants of Krishna Das and glanced at the picture of Baba without knowing who he was. I was not tired at all with all the work I had to do . . . forty-five boxes just for books! I gave all my furniture and other possessions to my daughter. I even sold my car to reimburse her.

I went back to Paris and lived on very little. I did lots of research. I learned that the man with the blanket was Maharajji Neem Karoli Baba. I learned about the many good things he has done and of all the young Americans he has taken under his wing. In France, the main religion is Christianity, mainly Catholic, and people believe in the Church. The only person with whom I could share the songs of Krishna Das was my granddaughter. In France, they call it a cult. I translated word by word Baba Ram Dass's books. I read everything about Gurudev Baba and, I have to tell you, since 2014 I am not the same person.

I told myself, "I, Grâce Ezzine, will come to see you, Maharajji Gurudev." I saved money and in 2017 I flew to India. I traveled all alone by taxi; I knew that with Baba's protection, I could see all the good things that he had done and what he had left for us.

After a warm welcome at Kainchi Dham, I visited all the cities where Maharajji had gone: Mathura, Agra, Vrindavan, Benares . . . I didn't speak English, but my faith had no borders. I visited Rishikesh, Mother Ganga, and Baba's temples. It was in Nainital that I met Ram Rani (who speaks French). I broke down and told her everything that had happened to me.

I was at the feet of Gurudev Baba, and I cried a lot while I was thanking him. The night before my departure, I had a joyous dream. I was sitting on Kainchi Dham's first cupola. Maharajji was sitting there too. His arm reached toward mine and we climbed the cupola together. I was not afraid; on the contrary, my heart was filled with joy. I had become a new person, a bhakti.

I am very happy now. I live in a little studio apartment in Paris. I honor Maharajji Gurudev Baba. I honor Sri Hanuman. I sing every day the Chalisa with the precious help of Krishna Das. I don't suffer anymore, as my sickness is gone.

राम

Hanuman Das Kane

I was living at the Taos ashram and managing it. One morning I was getting ready to leave town when a devotee called and said, "Can you pick me up at the bus station?" I asked a friend to take my truck and go pick her up. On his way back, he ran a red light and the police stopped him. He didn't have a driver's license, so they did a check on the vehicle, my vehicle. I'm sitting at the dining room table in the ashram and suddenly this devotee comes running in and says, "The police are coming to arrest you." They had told him if he brought them to me, they would not give him a ticket.

The next thing I know, a policeman walked in and said, "Are you Jon Kane? I have a warrant for your arrest." I was in a *lungi* (a sarong-like cloth wrapped around the waist) and a t-shirt, so I asked if I could go put on my pants. When I came out, he was standing in front of the big picture of Neem Karoli Baba on the wall in the kitchen. He said, "Where is this guy?"

"He's our guru. He left his body in '73."

"Don't give me that shit," the policeman said. "I see him here all the time. I see this guy walking around with his plaid blanket. I go to see what he's up to and he turns a corner and disappears. That's happened to me three times in the last two weeks."

"Okay, but he really is not in his body."

The police officer took me to the station. It was about five o'clock in the afternoon, and I asked, "Well, do I have to spend the night in jail?"

"Yeah, the bail bondsmen are gone, so I'll have to put you in jail until you can see a judge." As he said that, a bondsman walked in and said he could write up a bond for my bail. For $125. This was in the late '80s before I ever thought about having a credit card. I didn't even think about bringing money with me. I reached in my pocket and there was exactly $125 in there. Okay, Maharajji, let's do this.

I went home. I had a flight scheduled for 8:30 that night. I was driving down the highway and suddenly I saw this specter of a skinny coyote. How was it even alive? It was in the middle of the road and wouldn't move, so I pulled off the road. As I pulled off the road, my engine exploded! It was snowing and I was ten miles from town. I hitchhiked back to the house. As I walked in, the phone rang. A devotee said she had a gun and was going to kill herself. I talked her down. She's good; she's still alive. I thought, okay Baba, you did all of that just so I would be here to get that phone call. As it turned out, the flight was canceled that night because of the snowstorm.

The next day I went to the police station to find out what I needed to do. They said, we don't know what happened, but there's no warrant for your arrest. There is nothing; we're very sorry. Here's your money back and please forgive us. We'll come and visit you." The following day, the policeman that arrested me brought five policemen to the ashram and introduced them to all of us. He kept telling all the other police that he sees this guru, this guy who has left his body, but he's still here, so take care of this place.

राम

Lorna Metcalfe

October 9, 1986
Dear Krishna Das,

I have only recently "met" Maharajji, mainly through a friend who lent me her copy of *Miracle of Love*. But despite not having the good fortune of meeting him in India, I have a tale to tell.

I had been living in a Buddhist community for about nine months, going through my usual sufferings. One night things seemed worse than usual and I couldn't sleep. After an hour or so, I decided to give up on sleep and lay there in the dark, crying because I couldn't get any peace of mind. I felt so bad about the things I had done wrong in my life. I got up and started to bow to the shrine I kept in the corner of my room, crying with regret.

The following day I was to serve food to the community. Standing with a pan of rice and a ladle, I started to serve each person. As I was doing this, I became aware of Maharajji. He seemed to be inside me, dishing out the food with me, and I knew that if we didn't have enough to go around, which happened from time to time, well, this time there *would* be enough because he would see to it.

I finally got my own plate of food and sat quietly in one corner and started to eat, but I couldn't . . . I was suddenly in India at Maharajji's feet, and he was feeding me rice, sweets, and fruits. This world was full of light, and I was full of love and bliss. I couldn't eat anything because I felt filled with love. In fact, I couldn't eat much the next day either. I felt completely taken over by this bliss and love. During the following days I tried to carry on as usual, but it was quite difficult. I was lovesick for Maharajji and so happy! All through spring and summer I felt this intoxication, and it really changed me.

Now I read *Miracle of Love* and feel closer to Maharajji as time passes. The feeling that I'm left with most of all is that Maharajji gives me everything I need spiritually; all questions are answered when I think on him. I don't have to search anymore. I've come home. I think it shows how far the blessings of his presence extend. His love and presence still spread from heart to heart, through no effort on our part. What a miracle this is.

ॐ

Lynn
(FROM A LETTER TO RAM DASS)

My dad died in January. Being an only child and having lost my mother five years previously, I was engulfed in grief. Luke, my son, and I went to Mississippi to settle things. When I returned home, I latched onto "Ram Dass is coming! Hurray, he'll say just the right things. Everything will be fine..." I was looking for another daddy to make it all better.

The big weekend arrived, two months to the day after my dad passed. I was an emotional wreck, praying to make it to the auditorium to hear THE WORDS! My babysitter had backed out and I was feeling nervous about having Luke there, not wanting him to distract me from my salvation. Ram Dass began his talk and Luke settled into nursing and sleep. He had spoken only for a minute or two when another mom from Lama Foundation[9] pushed her four-year-old daughter in at my feet and said, "I have to go," and quickly disappeared out the door! Luke immediately sat up and forgot sleep. They were noisy, of course, and I had to bring them outside. I was so angry, scared, and sure there was no hope of hearing THE WORDS that I was beside myself.

As I sat glumly on the steps, I kept hearing laughter, a kind of giggling. I knew it wasn't the kids; they were playing below me and this was coming from above. I was angry that someone dared detract from THE WORDS that I was having to miss. I jumped up to find the culprit, wheeled around, and there he was . . . that beloved man in the blanket at the top of the stairs. He was laughing at me with those twinkling eyes! He said, though not with words, "Your place is here; it is all here," and then was gone that fast.

I can't begin to tell you the healing those brief moments were in my life. I was so set on the FORM that my "salvation" had to take. Little did I know by *not* being in the auditorium with Ram Dass that I would be with Maharajji more deeply than I've ever known. It was my "miracle of love" thanks to Neem Karoli Baba, the ultimate LOVE.

जय

Mary G.

In 2010 I went to a kirtan at my local yoga studio. Kirtan had a surge in Cincinnati for a very short period, and then it quickly went

---

9 Lama Foundation is a spiritual community, educational facility, and retreat center near the Carson National Forest in northern New Mexico, with strong ties to Neem Karoli Baba and the Hanuman Temple in Taos, NM.

away. I was sitting off to one side against the wall. At one point during the chanting, I looked across the room and I could see an old guy; it was very clear to me that I could see him, but no one else could. I had no idea who it was. He was wrapped in a blanket and was there for a considerable amount of time. I was looking at him and checking him out. There was a woman I knew in Cincinnati who's a good medium, and I had taken her classes on working with your guides. I think that was what prepared me to see that old guy across the room.

After a while everyone moved closer together to concentrate the energy in the room because there weren't that many people there. As soon as everyone moved closer together, *whoosh*, the old guy across the room was gone. A little bit later we did a Hare Krishna chant, and I could feel all this energy pouring into me. After the kirtan finished, I told a friend that I thought I saw the kirtan wallah's guru and I was a little freaked out.

I had volunteered to work the desk, so I went into the lobby and not five feet away from me these two women I didn't know were having a conversation. One said to the other, "Who's his guru?" and the other one replied, "Neem Karoli Baba." I made a note of the name and went home to look him up. I didn't know who he was, didn't know who Ram Dass was, barely knew who Krishna Das was.

I read about Ram Dass online and thought, I can get into this stuff. That was back when Ram Dass used to do a monthly YouTube livestream video. I started watching those videos every month on Sunday nights. And that was how I got started on this path.

राम

Paul Pettit

Little Paul was born in Sydney, Australia, to what was a middle-class family with a middle-class suburban lifestyle. When I started attending school, I realized at some point that something wasn't quite right with Paul's life; things weren't quite the same for other kids as they were for me. When you're growing up, you only know what you know, right? I didn't know how to express to anyone what had been happening. From at least six onward, I had been systematically abused, both emotionally and sexually, by groups of men on many occasions and over multiple years. From the outside my family looked fine; it was behind the scenes that was not fine.

When I was nine, almost ten, it was coming to the close of winter in Australia, so it was still getting dark early. Mum and Dad were both working in those days, so the house was usually empty when I got home from school. On this day I had missed my usual train and bus rides home, so it was later and darker than usual. I went down the steps and turned to open the front door, but the whole security storm door had been ripped up and pushed outward. Danger! I got scared. I ran around the corner of the house to where my parents' bedroom was located. The window to their room had been blown out; it was like a bomb had exploded in the house.

As I was standing there, frozen on the spot, a gentleman showed up out of nowhere and put a blanket around me. I could feel the scratchy wool of the blanket; I can still feel it in my mind, and the smell of it. I heard him say, "It's all done," as in, it's all over. It's finished. I went blank after that.

My parents' ridiculous explanation regarding what had happened to the house was that the dog had caused the damage. Then the whole thing got swept under the carpet and nothing more was said. But from that moment on, little Paul was left alone. Never again was I touched.

I tried to process this, as we say here in the U.S., trying to come to grips with the abuse, but in truth I just repressed it. Little Paul thought, okay, I was either being punished or I'd deserved what had been happening. As time passed, I thought the abuse had never happened and continued through life in a "normal" way. Moments of joy were few. Moments of pain were many. By the time I was twelve, I was smoking marijuana and drinking alcohol.

Of course, I attracted people that abused me emotionally or physically, including a twenty-year marriage to a narcissist with a drinking problem. Externally, everything was portrayed as wonderful; Paul had grown up and believed that nothing could go wrong as long as I had money. I worked hard, built up a business, and had the dog, the cars, and the holidays. I also had two beautiful children. But behind closed doors, life was terrible.

In August 2015, I was in South Australia when my youngest son sent me a text message, "Dad, you need to come home. She's done it again." Referring to his mother. This time something in me clicked, and when I walked in, I said, "That's it, it's over." I left the marriage. The two boys, seventeen and fifteen years old, moved with me into a high-rise apartment I rented. It was a beautiful place; you could walk out on the balcony and enjoy an ocean view on one side and mountains on the other.

I was free from the dysfunctional relationship, but not free from the trauma. One day I found myself on the balcony with one foot hanging over the edge and the other one about to go over. I was going through the divorce; I was going through legal problems; I was a single parent; I was running a business; I was getting financially crippled. I thought, *this is it.* It's not that I wanted to die; I just didn't want to live anymore.

Suddenly, I heard a voice inside saying, "You are loved. You are loved." I felt an indescribable amount of overwhelming love . . . and I stepped back from the edge. I suddenly thought, wow, what about the boys? You can't leave them.

So that was the turning point, September 2015. It had started on the 11th of September in 1973—the day he put the blanket around me. I remember that day. To me, it's like asking, "Do you remember the day President Kennedy was shot?" It's etched into my brain—the 11th of September 1973.

[Parvati to Paul: "That's the day Maharajji left his body! September 11, 1973. You didn't know that? Wow. That's a date none of us will forget." Clearly overwhelmed with this new information, Paul could not speak for a bit.]

I didn't know of Babaji. I didn't know of Krishna Das or Ram Dass. I didn't know anything back then. I didn't know any of this, even in September of 2015 when I was on the balcony and knew I was loved and stepped away from the edge. And each step that's taken place since September 2015 has been a gift.

My story keeps getting better. In 2016 I started coming to the States on and off while I went through a courtship with my present wife. We met on a meditation app. Within a short period of time, I was here in the USA as a life coach, a reflexologist, and Reiki therapist, which is nothing like the thirty years I had spent grinding away in the construction supply industry. Now, well, not a heck of a lot of finances, but happy! We are now a blended family with five beautiful boys—her three and my two.

In 2017, it was either in a magazine, a book cover, an advert or something, but I saw a photo of Babaji for the first time. He had a brown-colored blanket around him. I burst into tears and said to Susie, "I saw the blanket! I saw the blanket!" I could feel it; I could smell it. Then I looked at the man and went, "Oh my gosh, that's him. That's the man that had the blanket and literally, not figuratively, wrapped it around me in 1973. This is the guy I've been talking about." There was his name: Neem Karoli Baba. I went on a discovery of who is Babaji.

Since then, what I do for a living, my life's work, and my life's passion have all aligned. I can close my eyes and I know that he is here, but it's actually *I am here*. He and I are slowly melting into each other. I understand that everything happened for a reason, and I'm grateful for my past. Grateful. It's not despite it, but because of it that I'm me. It's a whole new world that has opened up.

ॐ

Rajesh Kumar

I had visited an ashram not far from my home here in India where I saw a photo of Neem Karoli Baba. I thought, there seems to be *someone* sitting there. Then in March of 2019, I got the opportunity to go with a group on a *yatra* (pilgrimage) to Neem Karoli Maharajji's ashram in Kainchi Dham. As soon as I did *pranam*[10] to the takhat there, I felt as though there was a power of Maharajji that I felt deep in my heart—that even today Maharajji is still sitting there and that his hand has been put on my head. At that moment, the tears from my eyes couldn't stop. I can't tell you what that moment was like.

I finished the yatra a few days later and, when I came home, I put a photo of Neem Karoli Maharajji on my *puja* (altar) table. The next day my six-year-old daughter came to join the puja in the morning, which she normally does. She saw the photo and said, "Papa, this Baba came and ate at our house last week." She said he looked just like the photo. Had very little hair, same mustache and beard; he was wearing a *dhoti* (men's garment) and *kurta* (shirt). She said he asked, "Can I get some food?" My wife and daughter sat him down,

---

10 *Pranam* is a Sanskrit word meaning to bow forward or prostrate yourself in a respectful or reverential salutation. There are different types of pranam, from touching your forehead with hands in prayer position to bowing down and touching the ground with your forehead.

fed him, and gave him a little offering of fifty-one rupees and some wheat. Then he left.

I asked my wife, "Did you see him carefully?"

She said, "Yes, and he looked just like in the photo."

She started asking me stories about him, and I told her that he left his body many years ago, and that he has many devotees in America. I told her, "It could be that it was Maharajji that came to eat at our house! You're saying that he looked exactly the same." And kids don't lie; they'll say whatever truth is on their mind. I listened carefully inside myself and thought there is definitely some power here.

Suddenly, both my son and daughter started saying *Ram* as a greeting. My wife became very interested in the Hanuman Chalisa. All this sudden interest seemed to have come directly after the mysterious visit.

राम

Roberta Green

I never met Maharajji, but there was a time when his physical manifestation came to me directly and I feel so grateful for this experience. It was a blessing unlike any other I have received.

In the winter of 2017, I attended the Open Your Heart in Paradise Retreat in Maui. After spending some days listening to Ram Dass, Mirabai Bush, Jack Kornfeld, Trudy Goodman, Sharon Salzburg, chanting with Krishna Das and connecting with my beloved *satsang* (community of devotees), I was in a state of blissful contentment. It felt like heaven on Earth.

A couple of days into this retreat, I awoke early for a sunrise silent meditation led by Rameshwar Das. As I sat in the open-air tent with my eyes closed, I saw Maharajji come and put his hand on my head, right on the top of it, and then slowly walk away and put his hand on the heads of several other people who were sitting there in silent meditation. It was very quiet and very loving and very beautiful.

Whenever I think about this experience or relate it to others, I am overcome with tears of gratitude and joy. While I feel his presence so strongly through the stories of his devotees, looking at his picture, chanting, and sensing his love through so many brothers and sisters in my satsang, I never felt a concrete physical presence of him as strongly as I did that morning.

राम

Sruti Ram

I had gone to India, not to find Neem Karoli Baba, but to be with Satya Sai Baba[11]. When I returned to New York City, I got involved with a New York City teacher. In the course of events, Ram Dass got involved in that very same teaching. Then he was going on tour and asked me if I'd like to be a meditation master on his retreats. I agreed with delight and traveled with him. I was known as the Satya Sai Baba guy who traveled along with the Maharajji satsang.

Several years went by, and there was a party on Guru Purnima, which is the Indian celebration of Guru's Day. Forty or fifty people had gathered in one of the devotee's homes. There was a suggestion that we make a circle and everybody tell a guru story. When it came my turn, everybody's eyes rolled up, like here comes another Sai Baba miracle story. I said, "Well, as you all know, my guru is Neem Karoli Baba. No. Oh wait, I've been too influenced. My guru is . . .

---

11 Satya Sai Baba was a South Indian guru with a huge following who died in 2011. He was known for magically producing objects from thin air.

Neem Karoli Baba." I tried a third time and said, "Well, my guru is Neem Karoli Baba . . ." Everybody was looking at me, like what's going on with Sruti Ram? And then it dawned on me, my satguru, the main man in my life, *was* Neem Karoli Baba. From that day on, I was his. I went home, took down all my other pictures, and put up a picture of Neem Karoli Baba. And that's the way it's been ever since. You don't pick your guru, they find you. He found me.

He showed up during Christmas season. I wanted to put a large tree out in the field with Christmas lights on it. I thought it would be quite magical. I drove to Kingston to find a tree at Adam's Farms. They had just gotten in their Christmas trees and they had some really big ones. I said, "This is a very nice tree. How much is it?" When the attendant said $350, I said, "That's an awful lot of money for a cut tree. I'll think about it." I took out my pen and I put a Ram on the ticket in case I came back.

A few days went by, and I was really disgruntled because I wanted that tree, but $350 was exorbitant. I was driving back to Kingston on the back roads, and on the road ahead of me I saw a big fat man on a bicycle. It was December, and he was dressed in all white—white shoes, white pants, white coat, white hat—and he was unsteady on the bike. How peculiar. As I drove past him, I lowered my window. This person turned and looked at me—it was Maharajji on the bicycle! He looked right into my window and said, "Boy Scouts, Boy Scouts," and then went back to riding. I passed him, but I had to get another look, so I stopped. I looked for him, but he was gone. Bicycle gone, man gone.

I thought, "Boy Scouts? Boy Scouts? Oh, the Boy Scouts sell Christmas trees in Kingston for charity." I drove right there and was waiting in line when the man in front of me said, "Isn't it sad what happened here last night? Somebody broke in and stole fifteen trees from them. Christmas season and somebody's stealing Christmas trees. But there's a good part to the story. The local nurseries donated trees back to them."

I said, "Oh, that's a lovely Christmas story." When my turn came, I asked the fellow if they had any large trees. He said they had one, and he brought me over to this gorgeous, beautiful tree. I looked down at the tag and there was my Ram. I said, "How much is this tree?"

"It's expensive. Seventy-five dollars."

"Well, I'm not giving you $75 for that tree. I'll give you $108 for it." They put it on my car and I brought it home, put it up in the field, and it was Maharajji's Christmas tree.

राम

Steve Newmark

I was seeing a therapist when I was a sophomore in college, hoping he'd tell me what to do, but he just kept asking, "Well, what does your heart say?" I had an epiphany that if I listened to this voice in my heart, I was going to be in good shape. In 1972 I read *Be Here Now*—a monumental moment in my life. I didn't go to India to find Maharajji because we were told Maharajji didn't want to see anybody. Then Maharajji left his body in '73.

That summer I had a meeting with Ram Dass. Before I met with him, I meditated and felt Maharajji surrounding me. It was a special experience. I asked Ram Dass if this inner voice that I was listening to was Maharajji. He said, "Yes, Maharajji is your guru. And he is speaking to you through your heart. I can see him standing behind you."

A few years later, I went to India by myself and met K.C. Tewari. I knew he was one of Maharajji's closest devotees. We sat together and I told him everything—from the relationship with my manic-depressive mother to my disillusionment with the New York spiritual scene I'd been in. It was like talking to a great therapist who completely got me. He said, "Maharajji told me to wait for you."

Raghu's father (Dasaratha) and Chaitanya[12] had come to India and said to Tewari, "Hey, come with us and we'll travel around India together." Tewari said, no, I have to wait for this guy. India scared the hell out of me at that time, so traveling with Tewari and these Westerners was fantastic.

This trip was the first time Tewari had been back to Vrindavan since Maharajji left his body. Siddhi Ma[13] was there and she gave me a blessing, but I wanted to meet Maharajji, although I didn't know what that really meant. How could I meet Maharajji? I decided that I had to face him myself. I left the group and went to Kainchi. It was almost Christmas, so it was cold in the foothills. I was lonely and in a bad, bad way. Then I went to a Ramayana reading and something happened: my heart blew open. The people were so devotional and so much in their hearts that it broke all my resistance. The next day I was sitting in Maharajji's room at Kainchi and my heart blew open again. Everything I saw was love. I felt completely content that I'd gotten what I wanted.

The next day I was at the temple before leaving to connect with Tewari and the group again. I was sitting next to the takhat with my back against the wall, and I heard this voice say, "You wanted to talk to me." I swung my head to the right and there was Maharajji,

---

12 Raghu Markus (Director of the Love Serve Remember Foundation), his father Dasaratha, and Chaitanya Samways were Westerners who had been with Maharajji in the early '70s.

13 Siddhi Ma's name means "mother of spiritual power." A very close devotee of Maharajji, she was a great yogini and considered a saint in her own right. When Maharajji left his body in 1973, he left the running of his ashrams and spiritual leadership to Siddhi Ma, who took care of his devotees until she left her body in 2017.

leaning on the takhat towards me. Then he disappeared. But I had seen Maharajji clearly; there was no doubt in my mind. This voice continued talking to me for quite a long time. I had questions and the voice gave me answers.

Three or four years later, I was in Varanasi with Tewari; he was pretty old and he didn't have that many years left. One day I was with him and a friend on the river, and Tewari was doing prayers and chanting. We stopped the boat so my friend and I could go up to a temple at the top of a mountain. Then on the way back down the long flight of stairs, I saw three sadhus[14] sitting on a platform. One sadhu got up and it was Maharajji! Behind me, my friend said, "Hey, it's Maharajji!" He saw it too. But my mind couldn't deal with it. Here was something I'd always wanted and, when it happened, I was scared. Tewari called from the river. He had stayed on the boat and was ready to get going.

I asked Tewari later whether seeing Maharajji had been real. He said, "Oh, that used to happen to me all the time. I'd leave him at Kainchi and go straight to Delhi. I'd be walking and I'd see somebody who looked like Maharajji, and think, no, it couldn't be Maharajji. I just left him. He couldn't have gotten here this fast. And then the next time Maharajji saw me, he'd say, 'Hey, why didn't you say hello to me in Delhi?'" There was no doubt in Tewari's mind that it had really happened.

राम

---

14 *Sadhu*—a Hindu yogi or devotee who focuses on spiritual practice and often travels from place to place.

Trudy Goodman, PhD

Before I had met Ram Dass or really knew of Maharajji, I was a few weeks deep into sitting a meditation retreat at IMS[15] in Barre with Sharon Salzberg, practicing day and night. I liked to meditate outside, even in a New England winter. It was a beautiful snowy walk down to the frozen beaver pond in my parka, carrying my blankets. I positioned myself cross-legged on a wooden bench facing the pond, simply meditating in the cold. Suddenly—out of nowhere—I heard the loud, undeniable sound of harmonium music, but there was nobody around. There was a van parked down the road, but it was too far away for the sound to be coming from it. I looked around, puzzled.

I don't know what prompted me, but at that moment I looked up . . . and there was Maharajji in the sky! He was looking at me, laughing joyfully. I thought, *I must have slipped into Sharon Salzberg's mindstream.* There was no rational way I could understand why he appeared, but the moment was one of total joy and laughter. And then he vanished.

Back inside, I relayed the experience to Sharon since she was so close to Ram Dass and had a spiritual connection to Maharajji. Did I somehow slip into her mindstream? Did Maharajji slip into mine? Is there any sameness or difference there?

These are the kinds of mystical questions that arise in the presence of grace.

ॐ

---

15 Insight Meditation Society (IMS) in Barre, MA, is one of the West's oldest meditation retreat centers, founded by Sharon Salzberg, Jack Kornfield, and Joseph Goldstein. IMS offers Buddhist meditation teachings in *vipassana* (insight) and *metta* (lovingkindness) practices and a Forest Refuge for independent retreats.

Uma Reed

In the fall of 1973, I was working as a flight attendant for an international airline. On a layover in Rome one evening, another crew member and I struck up a conversation that changed my life. He had read many spiritual books, among them Ram Dass's *Be Here Now*. My friend filled my head with ideas that were totally new to me, and yet I knew in my heart that the words he spoke were true.

When I returned home, I immediately bought a copy of *Be Here Now* and it became my bible. I used it to begin my own humble *sadhana* (spiritual practice), and within a year I had quit my job and moved to California. I gave up drugs, ate an increasingly organic vegetarian diet, practiced *japa* (the repetition of a *mantra*, a sacred word or sound), a little hatha yoga, and awoke early every morning to meditate before going to work at the University of California. At lunch I would meet a friend to read holy books on the quad. I obtained a copy of the album *Love Serve Remember* and learned the songs and chants.

Two days before Thanksgiving in 1974, two friends had arranged to meet each other at my apartment before going to a movie. The first arrived with a joint of marijuana whose reputation as exceptional preceded it. Although I hadn't touched any drugs in several months, I couldn't resist trying this weed. I took one hit from the joint, maybe two. I immediately began to have a terrible wrenching pain in my heart. My thoughts became so chaotic and confused that I could not maintain a conversation with my friend. I was afraid I had done some damage to my body by smoking. I decided to go outside for some fresh air in the hopes it would clear my head and relax the incredible tension in my chest. It didn't.

My friend was still waiting, and I told him I had to go to bed. I went into my room and sat down on the bed with the intention of meditating. Then I realized that I hadn't ever understood what meditation was. I decided to repeat a mantra, and immediately my mind went blank; I couldn't think of a mantra. I began to grow frightened; the wrenching in my chest was becoming unbearable, and my thoughts were racing uncontrollably. Finally in desperation I screamed out loud, "I'LL DO ANYTHING FOR GOD!"

In the split second the words left my mouth, the wrenching in my heart peaked and felt as if it burst open. My entire body became filled with a vibrant peace. I opened my eyes; the room was filled with a blue light. And there in front of me sat Maharajji, wrapped in his blanket, with one hand in his lap, the other in *abhaya mudra* (dispelling fear). He was more alive and real than anything else in the room, and the sweetness of his presence was indescribable. The wrenching in my heart had turned to what I guessed had to be called love, though it seemed so inadequate a term.

I was strongly drawn to watch Maharajji's lips, which were silently moving. I realized he was repeating a phrase over and over, and I understood that I was to repeat it with him. As I watched his lips closely and mimed their shape with each syllable, I discovered we were saying "OM NAMAH SHIVAYA." I began saying the mantra over and over in synch with Maharajji, and as I did, I began to experience many lives; I lived them in vivid detail from beginning to end, hundreds and hundreds of them in the blink of an eye. As this went on, I began to be aware I was observing it all from within the reality of my "Self." And my Self was a field of pure consciousness, the Self of everything, within which all existence takes place. The sense of Self at that point was not that of a human being having an experience; "I" was simply loving awareness, uncontained and undefined.

At some point I became aware of myself sitting with Maharajji in my room again, still repeating the mantra. Maharajji then stood up, lifted his left arm, and held it perpendicular to his body. Beneath his arm, as if displayed on a movie screen, scenes from my current life began to play. There were about ten vignettes from various periods of time in my life. Somehow in each, a subconscious understanding of the meaning of the scene would occur, then it would be replaced with the next. After these scenes ended, Maharajji was standing there, changing identities rapidly. Among them, I recognized the man who had turned me on to the spiritual path in Rome. But it was clearly Maharajji's essence permeating them all.

The next thing I knew, I was waking up the next morning. Remembering Maharajji's visit, I was beside myself with joy. I immediately decided that I would work to save enough money to go to India so I could be with him. I pulled out my copy of *Be Here Now* to look at his picture. I was curious about the words beneath the picture: "Mahasamadhi September 11, 1973." I had never paid attention to those words before. I now suspected what they meant but suspended any reaction until I could look up the word *mahasamadhi*, which I learned meant the "great and final *samadhi*," the act of consciously leaving one's body. To say I was stunned to find out that Maharajji had left his body more than a year before I met him is a major understatement. But the experience of that short, sweet visit transformed my life forever.

ᴵᴿᵃᵐ

Victoria Sojourn Prince

DECEMBER 7, 1981
To Krishna Das

I was sitting in the hospital with my dying father chanting *Sri Ram Jai Ram Jai Ram* when I looked up and there was Maharajji dancing around my father's head. He was very tiny, as big as my thumb. I thought to myself, "I wonder what Ram Dass's guru is doing here?" I didn't even know his name. Somehow, when my father died, I felt comforted and knew that he was okay because Maharajji was there.

Seven months later I went to a Ram Dass retreat at the Lama Foundation in New Mexico. One beautiful afternoon, I was sitting quietly in the woods outside Ram Dass's little house waiting for my turn to meet with Ram Dass, when suddenly I looked up and saw Maharajji. This time he was huge; he took up the whole sky. My heart was torn wide open and I received his love and grace. I felt incredible bliss, like I had never experienced before. I saw that Maharajji was everything and that I was a part of him, no separation, no desires, completely fulfilled.

Ram Dass rang his bell and I staggered in for my interview. My eyes were red and puffy from crying. Ram Dass said, "Is something troubling you?"

I told him what happened. "What does this mean, Ram Dass? Does this mean I'm not Jewish anymore? What do I do now?"

Ram Dass handed me the photo book of Maharajji, autographed it, and told me to "hang out" with Maharajji. And I've been doing that ever since.

2

Books

*I do believe something very magical
can happen when you read a book.*
—J.K. ROWLING

Books are magical vessels that can transport us to another time and place and let us walk in another's shoes for several hundred pages. We can recognize ourselves in the thoughts and emotions of those of different races, genders, religions, and life experiences. They allow us to develop compassion by sharing in the suffering of humanity; they can lead us toward our personal life goals and guide us along the path of spirit.

Before going to India in 1971, many of us who were called to Maharajji's feet had devoured the "must-read" books for spiritual seekers that were available in the Sixties: Paramahansa Yogananda's *Autobiography of a Yogi*; *The Gospel of Sri Ramakrishna*; the novels of Herman Hesse, like *Journey to the East, Siddhartha*, and *The Glass Bead Game*; *The Teachings of Don Juan* by Carlos Castaneda; Gurdjieff's *Meetings with Remarkable Men*; Alan Watts' *The Way of Zen* and Philip Kapleau's *The Three Pillars of Zen*; and *The Doors of Perception* by Aldous Huxley. I'll never forget coming down from my first acid trip and being handed Evans-Wentz's *The Tibetan Book of the Dead* with its descriptions of what I had just experienced through a little orange pill. Many of us hippie/seekers carried a copy of the *Bhagavad Gita* in our backpacks on our way to the land of its origin.

Of course, you needn't look further than *Be Here Now* to recognize the impact of books on the spiritual journey. Think of the countless hearts that have been opened by the two million copies that have been in circulation since 1971. That book quickly became a portal—the Ram Dass gateway to Maharajji—and has since been followed by a hefty collection of Ram Dass books and those written by Maharajji's Indian and Western devotees. (See Resources.)

In this section, you'll see how books have provided an opening for Maharajji to come into hearts. They have been the lifeline for those who couldn't get to kirtans or retreats, acted as dear companions in times of need, and were spurs to further exploration of the bhakti path.

Anatta Blackmarr

Spiritual books are one of the treasures of my life. The books by Ram Dass, Dada, and others have given me a way to discover my connection to Baba and reinforce it. It's funny, my path to Baba is like that of many people in *Love Everyone*. First I got my Transcendental Meditation mantra, then spent some years in Ananda Marga[16], and then time with Swami Muktananda[17]. Nothing hit the bull's-eye.

Most of my life I've lived in the San Francisco Bay Area. A boon during my college years was when Ram Dass came to speak at a small church in Palo Alto, circa 1970. It wasn't until years later that I saw how a seed had been planted that night. By the end of the evening, I felt for the first time that my spiritual questions had been answered. I paid my dollar and signed up to receive "the box" (*From Bindu to Ojas*, the precursor to *Be Here Now*), which showed up around a year later.

It was decades afterwards that I began to recognize my connection to Baba. I realized my reaction to Ram Dass wasn't only about him but was also about Baba. One day I saw a photo of Baba on an acquaintance's car steering wheel and felt the urge to reread *Miracle of Love*, which I had previously enjoyed as just another nice spiritual book. That's when I got pulled in closer to Baba and started to relate to him as my guru. My practice became reading and rereading the books about him on a daily basis. Over time, the stories became

---

16 Ananda Marga, "The Path of Bliss," is a socio-spiritual organization founded by Shri Shri Anandamurti.

17 Swami Muktananda was a powerful Indian guru, a disciple of Bhagavan Nityananda and the founder of Siddha Yoga. He died in 1982.

so familiar that if I had a problem or a question, one of the stories would pop into my head, serving as an answer from him.

Books seemed to prompt dreams. In one, I was riding my bike through a small canyon. When I emerged, I was garlanded with flowering vines and chanting a mantra—a mantra I had come across in a Baba book. Another time, I woke up spontaneously saying to myself, "I don't just want to be in Baba's heart, I want to be stitched to the very center of it." I had been reading *Barefoot in the Heart* and *Chants of a Lifetime*.

I'm not around others who experience Neem Karoli Baba as their guru, although my husband and my friends are devoted seekers of one kind or another, so I have to extend my thanks to all those who share their Baba stories so generously and candidly. As far as service to others, this is one of the kindest examples I can think of. The value of the books about Neem Karoli Baba as an avenue for getting to him shouldn't be underestimated.

ॐ

Dave Groves

FEBRUARY 26, 1988
Dear Ram Dass,

In March of 1987 I had ended a course of psychological counseling that cleared up much of the confusion I was experiencing regarding problems of unworthiness, helplessness, etc., which made relations with my wife and children, with myself, with friends, all very difficult. At some point I asked myself, "How can I learn to truly feel my pains and fears and then let them go?" I read about a lot of different trips—psychodrama, Esalen[18], all kinds of possibilities—but I never tried them. What was I to do? Move to California or New York where those things were available?

During this limbo I happened across my old spiritual books in the attic. I found I was able to experience the message on a much more profound and meaningful level than before. For the first time, I was able to think, "Yeah, that could be me," rather than "Boy, these guys sure are lucky to be able to feel that." Paramahamsa Yogananda, Meher Baba, *The Only Dance... Grist... Lazy Man's Guide...* Patanjali. I ran out and bought all the new stuff, too—quite a binge. But my main connection was still with the *description* of these spaces, rather than being *in* the spaces themselves.

One day I saw the front of *Miracle of Love* in a bookstore and couldn't get the cover image out of my mind. I went back to the store, but the book was gone. I ordered it. Weeks later, I took the book home and have never been the same. Those stories of Maharajji affected me in a way that is difficult to describe. I had certainly read a lot of other "tales from India," but this was different. I tried to read it slowly and savor it, but I couldn't. My mind was reeling. When I read the story about Dr. America and the WHO campaign against smallpox, and I reached the part where Maharajji disappears under his blanket and obtains a security clearance at a Paris cocktail party, I experienced something akin to a hand reaching into my heart and pulling a plug. My whole mapping of the world started to dissolve.

That night around 3 a.m., I awoke to a feeling that every last cell in my body, head to toe, was awash in divine love and ecstasy. Simultaneously, the upper portion of my visual field was filled with an image of Maharajji in the form of the cover photo of the book. Nothing in my life up until then had prepared me for what I was feeling.

---

18 Esalen Institute, in Big Sur, CA, is a holistic learning and retreat center.

I was exalted and dumbfounded at the same time. My rational mind spun for answers. I said to my wife that next morning, "I don't quite believe this, but someone must love me."

During the next seven days or so, my heart center continued to be "zapped" at unexpected times. I would be awakened by the most incredible sensations, somewhat like vibrating longitudinal waves descending from heaven, energizing my heart center. The energy was incredible. There were several times when I became alarmed—like in the Biblical stories when the angel tells you to "fear not" because even when your mind is turned towards God, the experience tends to melt your old sense of reality.

One night I remembered the mantra you shared in *Grist*, "The Power of God is within me, the Grace of God surrounds me," and although heretofore it had left me unaffected, this time saying it shot what felt like a steel bar from my crown down to the base of my spine. These experiences gradually faded away and my sadhana continued. Although I missed all the excitement, my faith had been strengthened immeasurably.

On another night I was asleep, but this didn't feel like a dream. I was receiving darshan from Maharajji. He was sitting on his takhat, and there were twenty or thirty devotees there. He was throwing *prasad*[19] to some, talking with others, doing nothing with others, but at the same time he was addressing the karmic needs of each one. I was privileged to perceive that he was also fulfilling his obligations to devotees not in his presence, as well as tending to beings without bodies who were working off karma in other realms. And still, beyond that, he was working on something that had to do with maintaining the balance of creation on a level that included

---

19 *Prasad* is anything, usually vegetarian food, that is offered to a saint or deity and then distributed to the devotees as a gift or grace.

everyone and everything. And still further, he was firmly rooted in no-thing. All done in perfection, all simultaneously.

Humility came easier for me after this experience.

ॐ

Elizabeth Andree Quigley

SEPTEMBER 17, 1986
To Krishna Das

I was gifted with *Miracle of Love* by someone I met at the Omega Institute when Ram Dass was there in 1983. It has served as a handbook of inspiration and a guide to better living for me since then. If I reach an impasse in some life situation of health, money, anger, etc., I say to Maharajji, "Show me a sign…" Then I flip through the book to "The Stick That Heals" or "Take it to Delhi." Of course, there are no answers, just *leela* (divine play), and that's the best part.

For some strange reason I love this man I never met, and I think I understand the complexity of trying to explain him.

You don't know how far the huge boat has floated… far beyond those who knew Maharajji in his physical body. A picture of him and the wonderful Taos Hanuman grace my suburban kitchen counter, and he reaches so many others who ask me, who is he? Why is he here? It's the same at Middle Earth, the school where I teach delinquent kids. There's something about Maharajji's picture that makes them ask questions. Then I tell them stories from *Miracle of Love*.

ॐ

Eric Lang

When I was seventeen, I was in a very dark place. I was an atheist, a materialist, suicidal and depressed, then I had an LSD trip that changed me overnight. On that trip everything was filled with light, everything was one. Then I came down, but I had a sense that there was something more.

My uncle later said I should read *Be Here Now*. As I pulled it out of its Amazon packaging, the book sent energy all throughout my body, and Maharajji filled me. When I read the story where Maharajji said "spleen" to Ram Dass, my heart opened just like Ram Dass's had. I felt that pain in my chest, that confusion, that lightness. The middle brown section of the book was read to me by the most beautiful voice I'd ever heard, which I have never heard since then. I finished the whole book that night. Since then, everything has been part of my awakening.

But I didn't consider Maharajji my guru. I wondered, who is my guru? Who's going to take me through these practices? I went to see Ram Dass in Texas at an Omega retreat and asked him about who I should have as a guru. He recommended that I take his guru. That really affected me. But I still wasn't sure. I was like, maybe it's Amma[20]. When I went to receive her darshan and she hugged people, she whispered "*Ram Ram Ram*" in my ear . . . and from that moment on the blanket guy was my guru.

राम

---

20 Amma (Mata Amritanandamayi), known as the "hugging saint," is regarded as one of India's spiritual leaders; her religion is love.

Hank Grampp

AUGUST 6, 1986
Dear Ram Dass,

I became conscious of my spiritual journey about twenty years ago. Since then, I have been visiting Strands (a used bookstore in New York City) on a weekly basis to check out the books in the spiritual section. About a year ago I spotted *Miracle of Love* on the shelf. I opened it and started reading at random. Before I had read a single paragraph, tears started to stream down my face. In the past I have read many spiritual masters and have never had this intensity of emotion before. I was extremely surprised at my reaction and did not know what was happening, but I felt very strongly that this book was very important to my spiritual progress.

Since then, I have read it many times. Each time I pick it up, however, I can only read for a few minutes because I can't see the print through my tears! This is the *only* book I cannot read in public....

Why am I so uncontrollably emotional over this book?

ॐ

Jagadish

My childhood friend and I discovered LSD, and through it I experienced my first taste of the spiritual realm. We were at the mall in a bookstore and he said, "Hey, Jeff, look at this book. It's so cool!" He was holding *Be Here Now*. That weekend, armed with *Be Here Now* and some tabs of LSD, we tripped and read The Book! In due time we tripped with a larger crew of our friends and turned them onto the book, which became an icon in our circle of friends.

As time passed I was still obsessed with the book, but other friends were like, "Oh, that was last year's thing. Move on already." Hah, I couldn't.

In 1996, about four or five years after I first read the book, I was at the bottom. Years of empty drug addiction and chaos made me forget about *Be Here Now*. I sat on the old brown couch (the one on which all the old LSD trips took place) alone in an apartment that my roommates had bailed out on without paying rent. I had no place to go and was broke. Darcy, who had been part of our tripcapades, now lived in Dallas, Texas, and said he could get me a job with the moving company he worked for. I needed $100 for a one-way Greyhound bus ticket. Another problem was that I had a nasty heroin habit I was kicking. I cried and prayed to someone or something, trying to make a decision. Something compelled me to look inside the couch—to peel back the slightly ripped material under the cushions—and there was *Be Here Now*. I hadn't thought about or seen it in years! It was like a blinking neon sign saying, "Go to Dallas."

I begged my parents to give me $100 for the bus ticket. A day or two later I was on a three-day bus ride with a small bag of clothes, my guitar, and the book. Just long enough to withdraw from heroin and read *Be Here Now* again, really internalizing it with tears.

Dallas was good and life got much better, but I was feeling a little empty. Darcy and I were at a bookstore. I saw an orange book titled *It's Here Now, Are You?* Hah, I thought, a cheap takeoff on *Be Here Now*. But when I started to read, I realized this was the Western man named Bhagavan Das from the opening story of *Be Here Now*. He was the man who led Ram Dass to Neem Karoli Baba, the old man in the plaid blanket in the foothills of the Himalayas— the satguru. It so inspired me that I went crazy with Baba's *Ram* mantra.

I started ordering any book I could and soon read *Miracle of Love*. I was so moved by the stories of Maharajji that energy started moving in ways I'd never experienced. Bliss and peace overcame me.

It felt like the realest thing I had ever felt besides LSD experiences of Oneness. I went to community college and passed my classes with ease. I started chanting all the time. All it took to manage my life was to remember *Ram*. Jesus said, "First remember the kingdom of heaven and all else will be added unto you." I experienced this. I know it's All Here Now.

ᚦᚢ

Kate Gannon

JUNE 25, 1987
Dear Ram Dass,

When I was nearly eighteen in the spring of 1971, I got "turned on" to a refreshing little book costing $3.33, *Be Here Now*, but I paid very little attention to "your" guru, Neem Karoli Baba. I read your other books over the years and learned something from each and every one. Except *Miracle of Love: Stories About Neem Karoli Baba*. I was not aware of its existence until I found a copy at the Tucson Public Library, heavily scented with incense. By the end of the first chapter my heart belonged to Neem Karoli Baba. That sly old fox!

I got up at sunrise on the morning of the summer solstice to do puja and meditation. I placed *Miracle of Love* in my meditation space so I could contemplate Babaji's picture. I offered a small bowl of fruit and a tiny plate of honey to Babaji at the end of my ceremony. Then I ate the offering as prasad and went back to bed.

As I fell asleep, I silently did mantra and my thoughts jumped to Neem Karoli Baba. Then I had a dream dealing with the current issues of my life. At the conclusion of this dream, I found myself in astral form. As I "flew" past a door with a large glass panel, I decided to look at my reflection for the fun of it. I had done this before in astral form and found it quite amusing. I had a most unexpected surprise this time. Superimposed over my reflection was the face of Neem Karoli Baba! It was so funny and sweet to see his mustache on my upper lip. "Oh Babaji!" I cried out, then swooned into a place I had never been before. His love filled me totally. It was pure bliss. I dissolved into nothingness, a soft, healing nothing, free of anxiety, free of fear, free of form.

When I was awakened by my telephone, I seemed to come from somewhere far away, and I felt a great sense of wonder at what had happened to me.

राम

Mark S.

I was a very naive young school kid in Arizona in 1977, living alone for the first time in my life. A neighbor said, "Hey, you want to drop some acid?" So I did. After the acid trip I had trouble dealing with life on a day-to-day basis, and a couple of years later I got admitted to a hospital psych ward for about six weeks; I was hallucinating without taking any psychedelics. It gradually faded away.

Four years after the acid trip, I was drinking a lot. My drinking buddy pulled this book out, *Be Here Now*, and gave it to me. I've been carrying it around ever since. It gave me the feeling that I wasn't alone. I didn't necessarily have to look at my difficult acid experience as a problem; I could see it as an opening, just one that I didn't know how to handle. I started reading other Ram Dass books, and whenever he came into town, I'd go see him talk. When *By His Grace* came out, I made a large copy of the front cover photo, like three by four feet (I was in the business of large format printing). That's when I first got the sense that I wasn't just looking at a picture of him; I sensed his presence.

My drinking was problematic, so I went to AA for the sake of my child and for the sake of my marriage, not for my sake (part of the addictive problem). I stayed sober in AA from the first moment in 1985. Then fifteen years ago, my life started going south again. I lost my home, I lost my relationship, and I had health problems. I pulled *Be Here Now* out again and opened it to one of the pictures of Maharajji. I was woken up in the middle of the night, and some message of assistance clearly came from him along the lines of "here's the healthier way you've been asking for." But I disregarded it.

By the end of August 2019, I was in a dark place and again I pulled out *Be Here Now* and asked for help. This time Maharajji came in a more profound way. I was deeply suffering and looked at a picture of Maharajji on my computer screen in desperation. I closed my eyes and when I opened them again, I was aware of this profound sense of peace, like being immersed in a limitless ocean of peace. I'd never experienced that before in my whole life.

I reread *Miracle of Love* and everything I could find about Maharajji and Ram Dass. Chanting to Krishna Das and Nina Rao has become my primary spiritual practice, and I'm learning the Chalisa. I began talking to Maharajji because that was one of the things Ram Dass said to do. Maharajji has a daily, prominent presence in my life now.

Michael Blackburn

I was raised in an LDS[21] family, and my education with religion came from the Mormon angle, so I was a "child of God." We had a large family of eight kids, living in a small 900-square-foot house

---

21 LDS is The Church of Jesus Christ of Latter-day Saints—the Mormon church.

set on a rugged piece of property, all gravel. God's in the church, right? But I had negative experiences there; they scared the hell out of me! I was convinced God would never accept me. I decided, *that's the end of it . . . I'm no good, I might as well play this game as hard as I can.* And I did. I trashed this body out, and along the way I've had a difficult time.

I came upon a copy of *Be Here Now* when I first joined the military at the age of seventeen. I needed some discipline and structure, so the military was very good for me. At that point I was a lost child. I had dropped out of school. As we know, difficult times turn us to the Father. I cracked open *Be Here Now* and there was Maharajji.

Fast forward twenty years, alcoholic, huge, three children, three marriages . . . and just divorced. Oh, wow, too hard, too much. Ram Dass says in *Be Here Now*, go to the desert, stretch your five senses. In my desperation, I screamed and yelled at God. And I re-read the brown pages of *Be Here Now*.

Then came *Love Everyone*. I pulled the book out of the box and doing so was like electricity; it was startling! This book was to be my experience in having my heart opened. It was nice to see the Buddhist piece in there. I can barely read two of those beautiful stories in a row and my heart opens. And in that opening, I am who I am.

One of the things that makes the spiritual adventure really grab hold of me is the depth of study one *doesn't* have to do. All you have to do is read it. It's like reading magic when I pop back into *Be Here Now*. In the brown pages, I am encouraged to move into what I Am, to realize my Self. Peace and harmony come in and fear goes away—it's a beautiful thing. This is what Baba brought to me. This is his gift.

राम

Paul Maurer

OCTOBER 25, 1986
My Dear Ram Dass,

Your book, *Journey of Awakening*, was the catalyst that finally started me meditating. Because of the subsequent positive influence of meditation on my life, that book became very special to me. When Dale Borglum, who collaborated on the book, was giving a seminar in town, I naturally had to go. A woman I didn't know named Katy sat down next to me and started talking to me like we were old friends. She later told me that she felt Maharajji very strongly as he pointed me out to her and told her she could share him with me. When we got together again, she brought me her copy of *Miracle of Love*.

After she left, I opened the book and began to read. I began to feel very strange, like something unexplainable but powerful was going to happen to me. I made it through about half a page of the first story in the book—the one where you meet Maharajji. I was overwhelmed—sobbing loudly, getting the book wet, falling to the floor, overcome with love. I barely made it through that story, through flowing eyes and many time-outs to weep and say, "Thank you, I love you," over and over again.

That night I had a "dream" of Maharajji and three other people. Maharajji set up a game where we were to run away from him in four directions on dirt roads. I traveled some distance, walking quickly. I became aware of his presence behind me. I turned around, and there he was! I started running. When I felt the need to look behind me again, there he was, almost upon me even though he was ambling along! This time he "twinkled" at me with a sly little grin.

I then found myself approaching a very dirty, dilapidated house. In the unkempt yard were two or three filthy, skinny, vicious-looking dogs, and three fat, dirty, ugly people. I was disgusted and was busy judging them all very severely. I was also scared, especially of the dogs. Just then Maharajji caught me. He backed me into this horrible scene, right into the middle of the dogs and people! I was terrified and appalled, but somehow I was more afraid of the power of Maharajji. Remember, I'd barely even heard of Maharajji before that day!

Suddenly, Maharajji looked directly into my eyes and made the motion of blowing me a kiss. Whatever he blew hit me and I became a being of love, consumed in ecstasy. The ferocious dogs came up to me sweetly and licked my hands. I looked at them and at those filthy people and I saw only love—only "us" and no "them." There was no more judgment left in me. I felt at peace. I had finally come home. I knew what my life was about.

I woke up weeping, saying over and over again, "Thank you, Maharajji, I love you, Maharajji. Thank you, Maharajji."

राम

Radha (Marisa Weppner)

In 2017 a friend brought me a Neem Karoli Baba pendant that he picked up at the spring Ram Dass retreat in Maui. Though I had been reading Ram Dass since 2001, I hadn't yet created a connection to Maharajji, so I decided to wear the pendant every day to see how it felt.

About a month later, Trevor (East Forest), who I had been friends with for a few years, stopped by. We both had recently gotten divorced. That day we were talking and he said, "You know how sometimes the universe will give you a sign and then you know that's the direction you are supposed to go in?" And the next moment he noticed my Maharajji necklace. It was like a bolt of lightning. "Maharajji," he gasped, "I just printed out a photo of him to help me. And now he's looking at me from your heart!" Before that moment we had never even talked about Ram Dass. Neither of us were looking to get into a new relationship, but Maharajji was pointing the way.

Christmas 2018, he gave me the book *Love Everyone*. I enjoyed the stories and felt like I was with Maharajji while reading the tales. Right after I'd finished the book, I had a spontaneous awakening where I literally felt I was in love with everyone, like an instant samadhi. I've never had anything like that before or since.

A few months later, Trevor said he wanted to go to Maui to record Ram Dass for his next album. I said, "I'm going with you." When Ram Dass finally wrapped the recording, Trevor was kneeling by Ram Dass's chair. He had asked Ram Dass for a name. Ram Dass was staring out at the ocean, totally tapped into his loving awareness state. Then he turned towards Trevor and said, "Krishna."

Trevor was surprised and asked, "That's it? Like Sting or Cher? Just Krishna?"

Ram Dass said, "Krishna, just Krishna." Then he turned to me and smiled, saying, "And you, you are Radha," and slapped his thigh, laughing. It was a powerful moment, a beautiful confirmation of our new relationship.

The very beginning of our connection was through Maharajji—from the pendant being there around my neck, then the book, then getting to share time together in Maui and creating the *Ram Dass x East Forest* album, and finally receiving our names together. Radha and Krishna, constant companions and the embodiment of love and devotion. It's funny how those things work. Oh, she got a book, or she got a necklace. It is so much deeper than that. Something on the surface turns out to change your life so deeply, to transform it. And Baba's doing that kind of stuff all the time.

राम

Radhika Kershaw

I'm an only child from a military family that moved every two or three years, so I was the eternal "new girl," desperately searching for somewhere to belong. When I was six, I would sit in my closet and get "quiet"—my first coping skill for a tumultuous childhood. Eventually, I learned what I was doing was actually meditation. I began to read every book I could find on Buddhism and Native American spirituality.

In high school, I discovered yoga and read *Be Here Now,* which left a lasting impact. Later, when the film *Fierce Grace* was released, I saw people I somehow recognized. How could that be? Ram Dass spoke of Maharajji, who seemed very familiar. I thought Maharajji was his exclusively. I wanted a Maharajji and began a quest to find my own.

My first trip to India made me feel at home in a way I had never known before. The noise, smells, traffic, and smoke formed a matrix I could navigate effortlessly. My deep longing for a guru returned when I came home. I searched compulsively for a living guru, but no one I met felt "right." What now? I began a Ram Dass binge, rereading all his books. I spent nearly every day for three years practicing yoga, meditating, eating a *sattvic* (pure) diet, and reading spiritual texts. I hadn't learned of the Maharajji books or bhakti . . . yet.

In 2015, I heard about the Ram Dass retreat on Maui. It was sold out, with a waiting list. Two weeks before the retreat, I called Mike Crall, who told me he had just received a cancellation an hour earlier. I booked my ticket on the spot. The first person to introduce themselves to me was Ira Rose. The first table I sat at was with Parvati Markus and Radha Baum. The retreat was a reunion of sorts. *Love Everyone* had just come out and became my divine reintroduction to Maharajji; it was all first-hand stories of those who knew him. And I had met many of them! I'm forever grateful for *Love Everyone,* my final gateway to Baba.

Afterward, I devoured every Maharajji book, and bhakti became my life. It felt as though I could almost remember the events in the books. I later told this to Ram Dass; he gazed into the ethers, patted my hand, and whispered, "soul pod."

As my relationship with Maharajji deepened, I accepted him fully as my guru, even without a body! After I learned the Hanuman Chalisa, I often sensed Baba's presence. Then one unforgettable afternoon, he revealed himself. I was going through a tough time, having one of those primal once-in-a-decade cries. I felt Maharajji put his arms around me, hold me tight, and I heard him say, "*Sub ek, sub ek*, my child." I was instantly relieved from all suffering and transported "home" once again. It was a completely visceral moment in time; I knew he was there. It was absolutely real. Years later, he showed himself to me again, that time in the form of a giant Hanuman at Ram Dass's house, but that's a whole other story.

राम

Stacey Martino Rivera

In 1995, I went to Jivamukti[22] in New York to take my first yoga class. I was there for vanity, to be strong and healthy for a play that I was doing in New York, but the *asanas* (body movements) and Krishna Das's chanting took root in my life. Shortly thereafter I moved to Los Angeles and one of my first yoga teachers was this lovely man named Ira. It was around that time that a mentor in Los Angeles handed me *Be Here Now*. It was so simple that I couldn't get it, because *I* was so complicated. Shortly thereafter I

---

22 Jivamukti Yoga, in New York City, was the iconic yoga studio where Krishna Das first began chanting in public in 1994. It closed in December 2019.

found *Miracle of Love* and proceeded to carry it around with me for many years. I kept it close, but never opened it. I guess I wasn't ready for Maharajji.

Years later my husband and I had a new baby. We were driving back East, where my family was, singing mantra the whole way. When I got there, my favorite uncle was struggling with addiction. He had introduced me to the Beatles and to mantra. I ran to the bookstore and got Krishna Das's book, *Chants of a Lifetime*, to give to him. I hadn't read it, but something called me to it.

A couple of days before I brought the book to him, I was sitting in an oak grove mourning the loss of a teacher in my artistic life, who had passed away. I literally cried out, "I'm ready. I need a teacher. Please somebody show up. I'll see you. I promise." With that my mother called down into the grove and said, "Stacey, your uncle is on the phone and he wants to talk to you right now. It's urgent."

He said, "Stacey, a whole play just came to me." He wasn't any kind of artist. "It's a play about our family and how important it is for us to know God."

My first thought was, "Okay, he's on something, and this is not good news." My second thought was, "I just asked for a teacher to show up. Is this connected?" I drove over there, singing the Chalisa but forgetting the book. He was sober; he was present. We talked about our family lineage and what spirituality meant to us. It was a beautiful healing moment, and I knew that Maharajji was somehow connected.

I read *Chants of a Lifetime* that night, all night. I thought back to all the years that Maharajji had been circling me. I fell madly, deeply, wholeheartedly in love with this person that was no longer in his body, that I knew I would never meet. I'd been raised Catholic, so gurus were far out of the realm. I said to my husband, "I am so in love with this dead Indian man. I can't explain it, but I am forever changed."

When we got back to L.A., I googled "Bhakti Los Angeles" and found a yoga teacher training class. I wrote a long note about how I'd been seized by this love, and this man named Govindas wrote back, "I've been seized by the same love. Come. Come." So I went to class, sat down, looked up at Govindas, and said, "Ira?" Years earlier, he had helped to plant the seed.

ॐ

Trevor Hall

I'm from South Carolina, from a small tourist golf-and-tennis island. I didn't know about anything Eastern, like saints, babas, or yogis. Never in a million years did I think I would be influenced by that culture. But I ended up leaving home in tenth grade to go to boarding school in Idyllwild, California, a beautiful town at the top of the mountains, east of L.A. near Palm Springs. I had been going to a prep school in South Carolina and feeling super stifled, not able to let my hair down in any way. Then all of a sudden I'm at this international arts school in Idyllwild, where kids had purple hair and you could go to class in your pajamas. It was a beautiful opening of my mind and heart.

One of the people I met there was Sam Markus, Raghu's younger brother. He was a junior and I was a sophomore. He was a rapper, making hip hop music, and a film major. We immediately took to each other. I was very inspired by Sam because he was in this beautiful space of creative energy, the opposite of what I had gone through in my prep school. He had a laptop and was recording music. He asked me to come to his dorm so we could make music all night. Let's do it!

When I walked into his room I saw only one picture on the wall, of this old man. I know this guy. Where do I know this guy from?

"Hey Sam, who is that? Is that your grandfather?" He said, no, that's an Indian saint named Maharajji, Neem Karoli Baba.

An Indian saint? What's a Baba? He said, "My father and brothers were in India in the '70s, and they met this saint." He pulled out *Miracle of Love* and opened it up and we started reading from it. And that was that. In India they say that a moment with the beloved and the river changes course. That night, that moment was it. I stayed up the whole night reading *Miracle of Love*. I'd found what I'd been searching for.

I was sixteen years old, really young, but there was no question. I fell in love with this being and it didn't matter what anybody else thought. Because Maharajji was from India, I wanted to love India. Because Maharajji loved the name of Ram, I wanted to love Ram. Because Maharajji was said to be Hanuman, I wanted to love Hanuman. My whole spiritual path was based on my love for him. I wanted to know as much as I could about anything he loved. My parents wondered what type of school they had sent their kid to.

That was the initial opening. I also had a teacher at our school named Shambo, who was a devotee of Maharajji and Sri Ramakrishna. I looked up to him because he had been to India a bunch of times. He taught me how to meditate. He was very familiar with Ram Dass and the satsang. He took me under his wing because he saw me opening to Maharajji, and gave me *By His Grace* by Dada Mukerjee. I used to skip class, go into the woods, and read Dada's book. That book and Dada's next one, *The Near and the Dear*, were the books that affected me the most. It was his way of speaking about Maharajji that made me feel like I was in this family.

After my last year of high school, I moved to L.A. because I had signed this big record deal. I was super depressed and lonely because I didn't have any friends there. That first summer Shambo called and said, "Hey, I'm coming down to Laguna Beach for the big Kali Puja." Every year in the summer for one weekend they would fly the priests in from the Dakshineswar Kali temple in India and do this huge Kali Puja. I was very taken by the community and by Kali Ma's form. I was eighteen years old at this point, and I kept going back down to Laguna to the temple because I was lonely, and they showed me love and fed me. Long story short, I lived there for about seven years. The main swami of the community, who was my first teacher, went to Allahabad every year because his guru was from Allahabad. In 2007 he invited me to go to India with him.

I'm in India, having all these emotions. I'm home and this is my place. Then we got to Allahabad. Maharajji used to come to Allahabad every winter and stayed at 4 Church Lane, Dada's house. I had been reading about it for years. These places were only in books for me and now here I was in Allahabad. I couldn't believe that I was in a place where Maharajji had been.

My last day in Allahabad, we pulled up to 4 Church Lane and I started to cry. I saw the front porch of Dada's house, his family sitting on the porch. The others opened the gate and walked in, but I said, "Just give me a second." I didn't want to show up totally a mess, but I couldn't help myself. I fell to the ground and grabbed the dirt in a frenzy and rubbed it on my forehead. Maharajji's feet had touched this dirt! I had a Ziploc bag and I filled the bag with this dirt.

Dada's niece came over and invited me to come in, come in. They were used to people coming there all the time and having experiences, but I was kind of embarrassed. In Maharajji's room at Dada's house, they keep it the exact same way as when Baba had been there. There are pictures of Maharajji all over the room. I just lost it, sobbing uncontrollably. It was a cry that came from a deep place in my body. I couldn't go out to the porch and talk to them. I was planted there at his takhat. He's my Baba and I didn't have to question that. He's real and it didn't matter if he was in a body or not.

I've been going back to India almost every year, and every time I go to Dada's house they're always like, oh, you're that crying kid.

गम

Vasu Jon Seskevich

I had grown up Methodist, interested in God but not overly religious. My mother gave me a real blessing when she said, "I'm going
to take you to this church, but you're going to have to find out on
your own what God is for you."

January 1972, in college at UMass, I read *Be Here Now*. I felt like
God was talking to me through the book. The part where Maharajji
says about Ram Dass's mother, "she is a high being . . ." cut right
through me in terms of death is not the end. I carried the book
around in my backpack all the time. I hitchhiked a lot and talked
about it to everyone. But I felt like Maharajji was Ram Dass's guru.

Ram Dass did a yearly retreat at the Rowe Conference Center
around Memorial Day. I went up to him and said, "You're my guru.
Well, as close as I'm going to get in a physical body." He invited me
to join this monthly class he did at Mirabai and Krishna Bush's in
Cambridge, which went on for like a year and a half. All this time
I'm feeling that Maharajji is Ram Dass's guru, he isn't my guru.

Then in '79 *Miracle of Love* came out. I read that book and Baba
revealed that he was my guru, too. All the voices of God that I'd
heard my whole life manifested in that book.

3
Kirtan and the Hanuman Chalisa

जै जै जै हनुमान गोसाई
कृपा करहु गुरुदेव की नाई
Jai Jai Jai Hanumana Gosa-ee
Kripa Karahu Gurudeva Kee Na-ee

Victory, Victory, Victory to You, O Hanuman,
Please Bestow your Grace on me as my Guru.
(Hanuman Chalisa, verse 37)

I first met Ram Dass in the summer of 1969 at his father's farm in New Hampshire, taken there by a guy I met at a party who asked if I wanted to go "meet a saint." I was so overwhelmed by the light emanating from Ram Dass that I moved in the next day and started to learn about this path of bhakti yoga.

One of the things Ram Dass taught us in those idyllic days was the chant *Sri Ram Jai Ram Jai Jai Ram*. Now, I'm the kind of singer who had been told in school musical productions to mouth the words, so I was naturally shy of "singing." It took a while to be convinced that God didn't really care whether I could carry a tune, and that what was in my heart would make the sounds beautiful. So I chanted. Back then we weren't doing the Hanuman Chalisa as Ram Dass hadn't learned it on his first trip to India.

When I was with Maharajji in India in 1971-72, we would sing to him, not only as a group performing *aarti* (song of praise to the guru), which K.K. Sah so lovingly taught us in the evenings at the Evelyn Hotel in Nainital, but also in individual moments. One of my most cherished memories is sitting alone with Maharajji on the porch of Dada's home after having returned from Varanasi. I sang *Hare Hare Mahadeva Shambo Kashi Vishwanatha Gange* to him . . . and he sang along with me for a line or two!

Some years after Maharajji left his body, when we were living in the New York area, Raghu and Krishna Das led weekly kirtans in our living room. I was happy to sit in the back of the room and play the *kartals* (cymbals). Things have come a long way since then, and kirtan with Krishna Das, Jai Uttal, Nina Rao, Trevor Hall, and all the other wonderful kirtan wallahs are at the forefront of bringing the bhakti experience to so many—opening hearts and letting Maharajji's love pour through.

How extraordinary that so many Westerners can sing the Hanuman Chalisa—forty verses in a language they don't speak! And what a practice it is. Need to accomplish something? To overcome an obstacle? To connect with Hanuman/Maharajji? "Sing the Chalisa," said Siddhi Ma.

If you feel called to learn the Chalisa, or to have the vibration of the names of God always floating through your home, look at Resources at the end of this book for various online entrances to the world of kirtan and the Hanuman Chalisa.

राम

Annie Levitt

My first awareness of Maharajji was in 1970 when friends took me to hear Ram Dass give a talk at the Indiana University student union in Bloomington. He was magnetic. *Be Here Now* wouldn't be published until the next year, so everything Ram Dass said that evening was completely new to me. I didn't know a darned thing about spiritual realities, but I was suffering deeply, and I wanted whatever it was that Ram Dass had.

There was no way I was going to India. My brother had died in a car accident a few months earlier, and my parents were in deep mourning. I also had no money, so I wasn't going anywhere . . . at least not geographically. The next day I scored my first hit of mescaline. *This* is what Ram Dass was pointing to! Life changed radically after that. For the next five years, I tried to recreate the magic of that first trip, to "find God." I realized that, as Ram Dass said, you could get high but you also came back down. Psychedelic experiences were fleeting; you had to do some actual practice. I settled back into "normal" life and went to nursing school.

I eventually moved into a small Vedanta ashram that opened in upstate New York, under the guidance of a charismatic and articulate Indian swami who had been in the Ramakrishna Order. The rhythm of our days included meditation, service, study, and many traditional bhakti practices, such as chanting. Eight years later, let's just say that the beautiful life of our ashram came to an end with painful disillusionment. I was sad and angry and could not even think of doing any kind of spiritual practice. After some years, however, I was drawn to attend a retreat at Insight Meditation Society in Barre, MA. No guru worship! No bhakti! It was all about awareness and meditation, none of that devotion and guru stuff.

After attending many retreats at IMS, a strange thing happened. I felt full of . . . *yikes* . . . devotion! I loved the Buddha, I wanted to hang out with him and even sing to him. *Hmm*, not the most

Buddhist of attitudes. I didn't really know what to do with all that devotion stuck inside me. I unpacked my old photos of Ramakrishna and Holy Mother and tentatively reopened my heart to them. But I was confused.

Shortly afterwards, in the international music section of our local bookstore, I found a CD called *Pilgrim Heart*, by some guy named Krishna Das. It had a photo of Ram Dass's guru, Neem Karoli Baba, on the cover. I recognized all the chants on the playlist as ones we used to sing at the ashram. I took the disc home, and from the first line I was blissed out. That Voice saturated the space in and around our home. Now I think of this as the moment when Maharajji took pity on me and threw the light switch on in an obvious way—bursting into my heart space, dissolving the dusty webs of confusion that had settled in there.

To this day, the voice of Krishna Das is a very tangible form of Maharajji for me. And since that time, Maharajji has woven a beautiful practice for me out of the threads of spiritual paths and the Beings I have loved and treasured.

राम

Bernadette Morris

By every modern measure, I was successful. I worked as a senior administrator at a well-regarded college with a comfortable income. I was physically fit, had traveled across the world many times over, and was considered a pretty woman by male suitors. I was living in New York and one day, while listening to a local radio channel, WDST in Woodstock, I heard Krishna Das chanting the *mahamantra* (*Hare Krishna Hare Ram*) It stuck in my head. I had no idea who this Krishna Das was, but I could not stop thinking about the mantra. I ordered the CD, *All One*, and played it constantly.

I am an academic, so naturally I researched Krishna Das and discovered his connection to Ram Dass, a Harvard professor who wrote many books, an acidhead in his younger days. Back in the day, I did hundreds of LSD trips, mushrooms, popped pills of every kind, and smoked pot every single day. I felt I could relate to him.

Then I had an operation on my shoulder and suffered much. The first Ram Dass book I read was *Still Here: Embracing Aging, Changing, and Dying.* The book resonated with me. Maharajji was calling. I began ordering book after book by Ram Dass. Then I ordered Krishna Das's *Flow of Grace* CD. I played Nina Rao's version of the Hanuman Chalisa and that was it, BAM! I was obsessed. I listened to nothing but the Hanuman Chalisa, every day, all day—on my ride back and forth to work, on my iPod, at home. I even played it loudly enough to hear while I was taking a shower. It was the most beautiful thing I had ever heard.

Then I sort of broke. I was having sciatica problems and then things got worse. I went from one cane to two canes, to a wheelchair, bedridden, medical center, neurosurgery, a nick on my spinal sac, a loss of feeling in my foot and leg. I was unable to work for an entire semester. My maniacal obsession with physical fitness and my appearance were gone for good. As my condition worsened, I tore out pictures of Maharajji from *Miracle of Love* and taped them up all over my bedroom walls. I wanted to see Maharajji wherever I looked.

By the time I became bedridden I was listening to the Hanuman Chalisa every day. Every morning and night I would recite the words to the Hanuman Chalisa to Krishna Das's *Flow of Grace* CD. I had the words written in an email to myself on my smartphone. (I had a lot of time on my hands.) For years now, my day cannot begin or end without doing the Chalisa. In 2013, I underwent neurosurgery and had an arduous path to recovery.

Two years later, I moved to Southern California. I chanted the Hanuman Chalisa as I drove my little car across the country.

Hanuman protected me and flew directly in front of my car, guiding me through bad weather, flash floods, and personal challenges. Maharajji accompanied me on my journey. He inspired me to bring backpacks filled with nutritious food in my car and gave me the courage to give them to homeless people in almost every state across the country. Maharajji opened up my heart. Love. . . Serve . . . Remember.

He always provides for me. My entire life has changed. Ram Dass is correct: Maharajji is the fisherman, while Krishna Das and Nina were the lures for me.

ॐ

Dana Maxey

I've studied yoga and kundalini yoga since the '60s. I started doing kirtan with Bhagavan Das in the '80s and '90s, as we all lived in the same community of Harbin Hot Springs[23]. I got a few albums of Jai's and got to know his music. He came to Puerto Vallarta in Mexico where I live part of the time. At that concert, Nubia did her beautiful dancing. When I was in California, I saw Jai play in San Rafael. They sent me an email about a summer camp at Harbin Hot Springs, my old stomping ground and spiritual home. I got to Harbin and did Jai's course for seven days.

I really didn't know anything about Neem Karoli Baba because my gurus were Anandamayi Ma and Ramana Maharshi. I just knew he was the music daddy of Krishna Das and Jai, and the whole kirtan lineage that came to America through them.

---

23 Harbin Hot Springs, in Middletown, CA, is a nonprofit, spirit-oriented retreat center.

Around day five of the course, I woke up feeling ill. It was the day our kirtan groups were going to do our performances. I moved to the back of the room, lay down, and fell asleep while the presentations were going on in front. I was in a twilight state as I could still hear the kirtan.

All these movies of India started going through my brain. I've been to Tibet and Nepal, never to India, but I knew in my heart it was India. Suddenly, I opened my eyes and I was looking right at the giant picture of Neem Karoli Baba that Jai always has on the altar. He was sitting there with that smile and his blankie, staring at me. I looked at him and thought, "You little monkey, you really sent me on quite a journey." We locked eyes and I started to cry and had this amazing emotional release.

That night I was asleep in my tent when Maharajji came to me and said in a very loud voice, "You are now finally teachable." I'm finally teachable? What does that mean? And he said, "You will know."

When I left Harbin, I headed down to Marin to see my mom. On my way, I was pulled to go to the Open Secret bookstore in San Rafael. I wondered, why am I here? My body kept walking through the bookstore, right through the back into the temple room, and there was the same picture of guruji that Jai had on his altar at the kirtan camp. I sat down and meditated and within seconds I was transported into a place of peace and bliss. I am a musician. I knew that it was time to shift into a new place with music and go into mantra.

ॐ

David Nichtern

My connection to Maharajji is through Krishna Das. I am his record producer, and I also play guitar with him, so we've had a strong musical connection for more than a dozen years. I've described him as the one person I can watch the Superbowl with and talk to about the *bardo*[24] teachings during the commercials! Of course, he is a devotee of Maharajji. I do feel like a cousin or a guest in this sangha.

When I was producing the *Kirtan Wallah* album for Krishna Das, the problem was that the songs go on for a long time. A short song might be twelve or fifteen minutes long. We call that a single! The songs accelerate in tempo as they go on, so they are not easy to cut. The problem putting music on a CD is there's a time limit of about seventy-five minutes. We had about ninety minutes of music recorded, and we were coming around to assembling it on a master. We needed it to be seventy-four minutes and thirty seconds, then you add a little bit of time between the tracks.

I tried an experiment. I decided I was going to ask Maharajji. I was being playful in my mind, so I dialed him up and talked directly to him. I said, "Maharajji, this is me, David. I'm working with your boy Krishna Das, whom I love dearly, and I want to be sure we have a good project here. The problem is we need this to come out to seventy-four minutes and thirty seconds, which will take a tremendous amount of mental work on my part, editing in Pro Tools and moving things around. I just want to handle the music part and make the best choices aesthetically for the music, and I would like you to take care of the time. Would you do that?"

I'm getting choked up thinking about this. All the musicians had come and gone, all the singers were gone, and I was in the editing suite with our engineer Jay Messina and Krishna Das. We made choices and put this song first, and a segue here, and this one after that one . . . At the end of that process, I said, "Let's see what we have." We looked at the time and it was seventy-four

---

24 The *bardo* is the state of existence between two lives on earth—what one experiences after death and before rebirth.

minutes and thirty seconds . . . to the second! That's a true story. I like the precision element to it. I've never gone back and tried to overthink it.

At the level of the *mahasiddhas* (great saints), time and space become very fluid. In Tibetan Buddhism we call these kinds of synchronicities *tendril*, auspicious coincidence. Around these powerful teachers, the tendril goes way way up.

Eric

In the early 1980s, in my twenties and studying to become a psychologist, I started listening to Ram Dass lectures on cassette recordings. When I was able to see Ram Dass live, my mind exploded with the multitude of far-out concepts, but Baba was Ram Dass's guru, not mine. I purchased a very used copy of *Miracle of Love* and something shifted; my heart opened and I started crying quite a bit. I could not pick up the book without crying. It was too powerful, and I backed away from it.

In my late twenties, I was living in Chicago and struggling mightily in graduate school. I attended a three-day workshop with Ram Dass that focused on different meditation techniques; I learned to use them not only for myself but also for my patients. It was very intellectual for the most part but very helpful. Later, I lived in Jerusalem for a year, walking around like a pseudo-holy man in the Old City, trying to study everything I could find about Jewish meditation, but all the religious rules and regulations were making me even crazier than I already was. Moving back to L.A. in my forties, I was emotionally and mentally depleted. Despite my PhD and having everything financially okay, I wasn't okay. Explorations into nearly every drug clearly made things worse.

Thankfully, I found my old friend Ram Dass's teachings again, but in a whole new light, this time through the beautiful chants of Krishna Das. I cried whenever I heard Krishna Das chanting. The beautiful combination of Genevieve's violin and the rest of the musicians and Krishna Das's voice opened a clear passage directly to Maharajji. But still, when I went to see him live for the first time, I ran out of the venue after less than twenty minutes when he started singing Hare Krishna. Having a strong Jewish background, combined with a healthy dose of skepticism in miracle stories, created a huge barrier.

It would have been impossible for anybody but Ram Dass to have gotten through to me—one neurotic intellectual Jewish psychologist talking to another—but I also needed the music because I was a Deadhead and that's what worked for me. Reading *Chants of a Lifetime* was essential.

At one point at the bottom of my path, I took the extraordinary (for me) step of flying to a retreat in Maui, where I was introduced to the Hanuman Chalisa by Nina Rao. Of course, my first response was: I am not going to learn THAT! I left that first Chalisa workshop after a few minutes, like my experience with Krishna Das, but I HAD to return. I learned that the Chalisa was one of the strongest pathways to connect to Maharajji. It became clear that this was my path and my home spiritually. I am certain it was the lack of rules and structures of an organized religion that allowed me to grow. There were only a few simple instructions: love, serve, remember, and tell the truth. This was real freedom.

In the following years, I had several one-to-one Skype sessions with Ram Dass. I decided to return to the Maui retreat, and that's when I had *the moment*—when Ram Dass introduced me to my guru. He pointed to a large picture of Baba, gave me a kiss and a mala, and said, "I LOVE YOU MORE" – the exact words my beloved grandma used to say to me. I had been thinking about her just a few moments before, while waiting for my turn with Ram Dass. I bowed to Maharajji, who is MY guru, now deeply embedded in my heart and soul.

॥म॥

Gabriela Masala

When I was a very little girl, five, six, seven years old, sometimes I'd wake up in the middle of the night and feel the undeniable presence of pure love, pure kindness, total acceptance, like an embrace. It felt male, like a godfather or a guardian grandfather. In dreams, I was sometimes shown the image of a scruffy beard and mustache and a very distinct face, but I had no idea who it was. When I was in my late teens, my sister gave me a copy of *Be Here Now*. When I opened it, for the first time I saw a picture of Maharajji. Here was the face I'd been seeing in my dreams all these years! I didn't know what to make of it. Though I was astonished, I had no context for it and just went on with my life.

When dance was my primary practice, I attended a Brazilian Dance and Music camp in California. Nubia, Jai Uttal's wife, was there with their tiny son Ezra. My daughter was a little girl as well. Our mutual dance teacher introduced us. Suddenly, I felt Maharajji so strongly.

Sometime after I took my last bow as a dancer, I had a dream that woke me up and directed me to get in my car. I ended up in the store of a Unity Church that I had never been to before. The guidance led me right to the spiritual music section and to *The Art and Science of Kirtan*, one of Jai's double CDs—the first track introduces bhakti and the rest is his beautiful music. That was my doorway into bhakti, a massive turning point for me. Maharajji brought me to Jai, brought me to the bhakti path. I fell in love with this CD.

One day I was woken up by Maharajji whispering very clearly in my ear, "You have to go to Bhakti Fest." That's where I experienced Jai's music live for the first time. I could feel Maharajji in every single cell, every little hair standing on end. Every time I hear Jai's, music, especially live, I start crying tears of grace, communion, and homecoming. It's the feeling that my deepest inner being is being washed by pure divine love with the presence of the Beloved, and the presence of this incredible, loving guide and godfather that's been with me for as long as I can remember.

I never met Maharajji; I never met Siddhi Ma. Yet every time I'm with Jai and Nubia I feel their Presence. It's a lineage of love that lives through the devotees—a quality of unconditional love that guides us to love our world and all its beings.

राम

Geetima Kala

I moved to the United States from India about fifteen years back. Growing up in India, my mother regularly chanted the puja and all that, but we were never forced to sit and meditate. When I was a typical sixteen-year-old, not listening to my parents and trying crazy stuff, my mom gave me a tiny Hanuman Chalisa booklet with Hanumanji's picture on the outside. When you opened the flap, there was Neem Karoli Baba's picture. At sixteen, I figured he was just another random guru. The very last flap had pictures of his feet. I'm like, OMG, why did they have to put *feet*?

But I got attached to the Hanuman Chalisa. It took me about six to eight months to memorize it. My parents said to do it every day and it would help me. Life gradually changed and I was able to find my profession and find peace of mind. But the relationship I had developed to the Chalisa was the most important aspect. I was so attached to the Chalisa booklet that I brought it with me everywhere.

Then I got married and we moved to the United States. My husband had a working visa, but they don't give a working visa to the spouse right away. During the year or two I was at home, not doing much, I checked out a couple of yoga schools, but . . . in India, we did yoga on concrete floors. Yoga mats? Yoga attire? That was a little too much for me. I finally found a yoga school that I liked, and the best part was the music they played. For the first time in my life, I was hearing Hindu-based spiritual music that had real *bhava* (spiritual emotion) in it. I asked, "Who are the singers?" I started listening to Krishna Das and Jai Uttal and reading about them. The name Neem Karoli Baba kept coming up. Okay, they had a guru.

Then Netflix had a documentary on Ram Dass that changed my world. I have to say that if you were introduced to Ram Dass through *Fierce Grace*, as I was, it's not the easiest introduction. He'd had a stroke and talked extremely slowly. At one point in the video he talked about going to India and meeting Baba, and they showed Kainchi Temple. Then they showed Baba's picture. It was like a thousand volts of electricity going through my body. Suddenly I realized, oh my gosh, this is the Being who has been with you since you were sixteen years old! It was a very profound experience.

Of course, I started reading all the stories on the Neem Karoli Baba Facebook page. I was finally aware of this energy that had been protecting me, helping me, guiding me. I got introduced to the Hanuman Chalisa chanting page and thought this would be a good place to feel the love that others were sharing. I'm so grateful for the people who manage these groups that provide so much of the love and support that we need. There was a young girl on the site, around sixteen years old, who was going through challenges and calling out for help. I thought I would send her the Chalisa booklet that had saved my life when I was her age. I was a little reluctant to give it up, but I sent it to her so it would bring her blessings.

I was in India in 2017 and went to Kainchi. I wanted to see that big rock where Baba used to sit and maybe hug the tree that was there. One of the stories was this tree was dying and Baba said pour Ganga water over it and it bloomed right away. I met the sweetest office person, who took my husband, my kids, my in-laws, and me into the upper ashram to see that tree. When we got back to the office, I saw Chalisa booklets on the table and he gave me one. Now I have my new Chalisa booklet with Baba's picture and Siddhi Ma's picture, with tons more prayers in it.

॥ग

Gemma DePalma

In July 2012, I didn't know anything about Maharajji or know anyone connected to him. Then one day the whole foundation of my life crumbled. My father slipped into a coma, never to reawaken. Upon his death, I learned he had led a double life—he was married to someone else, as well as to my mother, and he had another family. A nurse told me that my sister Mindy called, and I said I don't have a sister named Mindy. It turned out my father had gotten a secret divorce in Mexico from my mom and married someone else in a different state, but never told us about the divorce because he lived with us.

Everything I had known was a lie. My whole childhood, my parents' marriage, this man who raised me—how was this possible? My mother had dementia and didn't know who I was, so there was no help coming from her. On the same day I was reevaluating the truth of my life, I lost my apartment and the money I had wrapped up in that apartment. I felt dead inside, totally numb.

A friend of mine said, "I don't know how to help you, but you should come with me to see this guy sing at the old church in Sag Harbor. His name is Krishna Das." I ended up going with her and we were late, but miraculously I was in the third row. I don't remember anything he said or sang. When it was over, I felt uncomfortable, awkward, but something had shifted. I felt this little flicker, a tiny spark that I ignored because I thought anything that felt good couldn't be true. But the feeling of that night kept coming in and out.

After that, of course, I heard this type of music everywhere, but something bigger kept tapping me on the shoulder. I went by myself to my first Krishna Das retreat (my first retreat of any type at all) in Garrison, NY. I didn't know his music, but I was called to go. Nina Rao sang the Hanuman Chalisa and I just broke. I was literally shaking. I had never heard it before. I didn't know anything about it. It was mind-blowing to go from that day when my father died and I learned about his double life to now touching this space of big, big love. I didn't even know that was possible. I wasn't seeking anything; I had been running from everything. I kept doubting everything and saying, no, no, no, there's no way I could feel this good.

I had the feeling that this big space of love was from Maharajji. I don't think it had to do with the music itself; the music was the vehicle for the feeling. And then that feeling came through the stories and through the books and through meeting devotees who've been with him. It wasn't Krishna Das the person; it was everything that came through his music and stories of Maharajji.

Then I had this dream of Maharajji riding a white horse, charging through my bedroom closet. It left me with the feeling that I was going to be okay, I was going to make it through. A shining knight on a white horse was with me. That's when I started saying, *hmm*, maybe there's something here.

Later I was fortunate enough to go to Kainchi and have darshan with Siddhi Ma. When my mother died, I had several dreams about Siddhi Ma as well. With Maharajji and Siddhi Ma, my life has changed, allowing space and newness and a helping hand with all

81

the dragons that I have to slay. I know I'm under the blanket. He kept tapping me on the shoulder, saying, *you can feel this way. It's okay. You need to believe this.* And now I do.

Melissa Jaffe

I happened to have on a Hanuman pendant when I saw my ayurvedic teacher one day. He said, "Oh, you like Hanuman. You need to learn the Chalisa." I started to listen to it. I was in law school, studying for the Bar, and I listened to the Chalisa over and over again because it didn't have any words that my mind could grab onto.

One day I was all alone in my apartment and I just broke. I walked out of my room where I was studying for the Bar and listening to the Chalisa. I was crying and trembling, and I fell to the ground. It was really dramatic. Very methodically, like a lawyer, I thought, well, am I in pain? No, it wasn't pain. Ultimately, I figured out it had to be love—the biggest love I'd ever felt, beyond words. It had to be unconditional love. I looked up from the floor and there was a picture of Hanuman pulling his chest open. So that was my introduction to Maharajji, and it changed my life.

I eventually learned the Chalisa and that was my thing.

Years later I ended up getting pregnant and didn't have a lot of money as a single mom. I kept trying to register for a retreat in Maui. One day an announcement on Spotify, where I would listen to the Chalisa, said to register for the Ram Dass retreat coming up in Maui. I had just enough money and I registered at once. I didn't realize that there were only a couple of minutes before it got sold out.

When I came to Maui, I was very skeptical. I didn't know who these people were. I've met gurus before and that didn't work out. Then suddenly everyone in the room, like four hundred people, started singing the Chalisa. Everyone knew the words of the Chalisa! These had to be my people. Then Ram Dass said, "I'm the lure, you're the fish, and Maharajji is the fisherman." I felt like my whole world went from upside down to right side up. It all finally made sense.

ॐ

Nina Rao

As a young girl, we holidayed at my grandfather's house in a coastal village of South India. My grandfather was a retired engineer, and an untrained devotional singer and musician. I had my first experience of satsang at his home. My sisters, cousins, mother, aunts, and I sang with him around his harmonium. I was about nine then, and somehow those *bhajans* (devotional songs) were embedded in my mind. Then we moved to the West and my grandfather died.

In September 1996, I went to a retreat with my yoga teacher. On the schedule it said, "satsang and chanting with Krishna Das." I noticed a picture of Maharajji they had set up with a little candle, along with a photo of Taos Hanumanji. Krishna Das walked in, wearing all black back then, and Bubby was behind him wearing his construction jeans and carrying a plastic drum. I said to my friend, "This is worse than anything I could imagine. In honor of my teacher, I will come for the satsang, but I will sit in the back so I can slip out early."

Krishna Das greeted us with a few words and started singing *Sri Ram Jai Ram*. Three hours went by, and by the end of the night I was sitting right in front of him. The chanting brought back all my childhood memories of that place of well-being and feeling open and secure that came with chanting at my grandfather's house. I didn't know anybody on this retreat, but I felt like I was home.

We get complicated in our minds, so I thought it was Krishna Das. I had a huge crush on him. We got friendly and I said, "Why am I feeling these feelings toward you? I don't even know you."

He said, "It's not me."

Throughout the weekend he talked about Maharajji. I think it's important for those of us who didn't meet Maharajji in the body to hear Maharajji stories. As Krishna Das says, "Devotion is a disease. You catch it from the ones who have it." When I read the stories of all the people in *Love Everyone*, I could feel what they were feeling. Chanting is the same to me.

I needed to see Maharajji, and even though he wasn't there anymore, I wanted to go to Kainchi. Someone said that when the guru leaves the body, the ashram becomes his body. By the time I got there, it was two years after I had met Krishna Das, but I'd been singing with him consistently. Maharajji's *Ram Ram* audio recording was on Krishna Das's first CD, which was on constant repeat on my player and in my mind. Krishna Das gave me *By His Grace* to read, *The Near and the Dear*, and of course *Miracle of Love*, and I gobbled everything up.

Krishna Das said, "You go and meet Siddhi Ma." She wasn't really known at that time. I got excited because I thought I was going to find a guru (of course, she found me). Honestly, driving down those Kumaon Hills and seeing that temple, I felt I had been there a million times before, and I was coming home. I can still feel the smile on my face when I walked across the bridge. There was no doubt in my mind that I was walking into the space of Maharajji. To this day, twenty-plus years later, it feels the same... and not only in Kainchi.

My life changed, meeting Siddhi Ma then. But in the first meeting I had all these ideas in my head about how she was going to see me, and how she was going to love me, and I was going to feel my heart explode instantly, and . . . not so much. My actual impression was the same deep, intense, calm feeling I had when I was nine years old, the same presence I felt when Krishna Das was singing, the same thing I felt when I was reading Dada's book. It was pure all-encompassing *presence* for me. I had entered this world that had the shape of Maharajji, and Ma was sitting in that space; it was emanating from her and she was being held by it at the same time. We were all in it together.

There was no going back. That was it. As the days go by, I realize that Maharajji has always been here, and the feelings of presence and love and spaciousness and devotion and longing have been here forever. For me, Maharajji is that presence that connects all of us and makes us feel connected. He showed himself to me through Krishna Das and then Ram Dass, and is embodied in Siddhi Ma, but the doorway was through *Sri Ram Jai Ram.* That chant opened my eyes and my heart, and it's continued through the years.

राम

Noah Hoffeld

In 2004 I was really into Ramana Maharshi, as I still am. I was already doing practices and involved with kirtan, but I was going through quite a meltdown in terms of my relationships and my work; everything seemed to be imploding. At that time I was with the group Sri Kirtan, with Ishwari and Sruti Ram, playing cello. I was spending a lot of time in Woodstock, where they were both living. One day I ran into Sruti Ram at Mirabai Bookstore, a spiritual bookstore in Woodstock. He said, "Noah, you are a mess!" And he did something that was totally off-the-charts generous: he gave me Ram Dass's phone number and said to call him. Ram Dass got on the phone and spoke to me for a good twenty or thirty minutes and gave me some very direct practical advice about my life, as well as sharing a spiritual perspective. It was the beginning of finding my way out of that complete meltdown.

About eleven years passed as I was building up my life, starting from that seed Ram Dass had given me. I continued to do my practices and was involved with kirtan in different contexts. In early 2016 I started to experience alternating feelings of spaciousness and constriction. I wanted to talk to Ram Dass about it and to thank him in person for what he had done for me earlier, so I signed up for a personal retreat.

When I got to Ram Dass's house and into the guest cottage, I felt a force field, which was super deep and completely foreign to me. It felt like the whole property was humming. It wasn't until much later that I began to associate that feeling with Maharajji, because at the time I didn't know anything about him. I'd read several books by Ram Dass, but I was focused on his teachings on working with the mind, working with our relationships, how to be present, how to confront our neurosis, how to be a witness, working with dying folks. I never thought about Maharajji.

In my conversations with Ram Dass, he talked about his own experiences with Maharajji—how he had found unconditional love from Maharajji and how that had changed his negative feelings about himself. Maharajji's presence was creeping more and more into our conversations and into my experience of being at the house. The whole place was filled with pictures of Maharajji. I became aware that I had a relationship with him. It was a revelation to me to be in that space. I didn't know that spirituality could be super down-to-earth. That feeling of heart connectedness with this man in a blanket—a very earthy, very lovely, cozy, informal, casual sense of relatedness—was totally new to me, and incredibly needed to cut through all the formality I carried inside.

I had brought along a little collapsible practice cello and played in the cottage. We had a chanting on Sunday with Vishnu Dass for a small group of the community on Maui. On Monday we went to the beach with Ram Dass and had the swim. Ioana, my partner, showed up that day, and she and I stayed in Maui for another week after the retreat. During that time Dassi Ma texted me, saying I should come to the house on Sunday for satsang. A special guest was in town and she asked me to bring my cello. When I showed up, Krishna Das was there. He led the chanting and I got to play along. It was magical that I should be there at the same time as one of my musical heroes.

I didn't know that I was going to become a devotee of Maharajji at that point, but back in New York Nina Rao and I started playing together, and later I also started playing with Krishna Das. It took a long time for me to understand that Maharajji and Ramana could coexist side by side, but I have discovered that they can and do.

Parvati Pascale LaPoint

In January 2008, during a yoga retreat, my teacher introduced the mantra *Om Namah Shivaya*. After we had repeated it for a while, she played a chant by "this American guy with an Indian name." And there came the voice of Krishna Das. I will never forget how it touched me that first time, and every time since then. It pierced all my defenses and accessed a place within me I had never known before.

In the following months, I bought all available Krishna Das CDs and did a lot of online research about mantra, kirtan, japa, Hinduism, etc. In May, Krishna Das came to my city and I experienced kirtan live for the first time. As I was sitting in the midst of five hundred chanting people, I knew I had found a home. After the kirtan, I noticed people were lining up to talk to Krishna Das, so I did too. After I received my first of many hugs from him, I blurted out, "How can I start doing this?"

He looked at me with so much love emanating from his eyes, and said, "Just sing from the heart."

My first step was to buy a harmonium. At the time my husband had been unemployed for a while, so money was tight. A few days later, however, I was given an award at my work that included a monetary gift. After taxes, I had the exact amount left to purchase a harmonium and have it shipped to my house. It was meant to be. I started singing with people then. I learned the Hanuman Chalisa, read *Be Here Now* for the first time, and did more research. And everywhere I looked in my exploration of this bhakti universe, there was Baba. I was very much drawn to him, but I was very insecure about it. You see, I thought I was in love with Krishna Das. Was I just wanting to have the same guru as Krishna Das? Was this truly how far I would let this "crush" go?

In 2010, I attended David Newman's Kirtan College. On the last day of the retreat, David talked about the guru concept. I asked him how one could be sure about accepting a guru in their heart when that guru is no longer in the body and cannot take one on as a devotee. David asked which guru I was thinking about, and I told him it was Baba. David responded, "Well, then it's easy. Baba used to say: *When you think of me, I'll be there.*

I cried so hard and I knew then that he was with me.

Over the years, I traveled to see Krishna Das quite a bit. On many occasions he would tell the story about his devastation and feeling of abandonment after Baba left the body, and how he was told that Baba had never left him and was looking out of his eyes. I understood that this is what had happened to me: Baba looked at me through Krishna Das's eyes. I had been in love with Baba all this time. And I am eternally grateful.

राम

Sean Cain

I had learned the Hanuman Chalisa and was really itching to chant it with people. I live in Denver, so I decided to drive down to Taos for the inauguration of the new temple since they would be singing the Chalisa 108 times.

I got to the temple right around 4 a.m. and they were already chanting. It was so beautiful the way it was lit up, the sound, the sun not up yet—it was just perfect. When I first sat down in the temple, a feeling was surging through my body that felt like a combination of too much caffeine and just enough Xanax, but it took a while before I could look at the murti. I felt these blasts of energy coming toward me. There were several times that morning where the Hanuman murti seemed to be bigger or smaller than what it had been the last time I looked.

At the end of the day, I felt like I'd been through every emotion my body knew how to make. Tears of joy streamed down my face, immediately followed periods of intense depression and self-judgment. Then they wheeled Ram Dass in. I couldn't believe it: there was Ram Dass! He was beaming so much love to everyone. The place was electric. I never got to talk to him, but I have never felt such an intimate connection with another being as I felt with Ram Dass that day.

The next morning I woke up around 6 and was ready to get out of there. Then I had a thought: *Do the Chalisa.* I started singing the Chalisa and instantly rose out of the gloomy state of being. *Hmm, that was weird.* Instead of leaving, I went back to the temple and the Sundarkand singers were going full steam. Feeling very elevated, I decide to stay for the eleven Chalisas. Bliss, depression, bliss, depression—back in the whirlwind again, with the Chalisa running underneath all the drama. Then they wheeled Ram Dass in. This time I totally fell apart. I was crying so much, so grateful, feeling so loved just looking at him. Being in a group singing the Chalisa to him was so uplifting.

I couldn't believe the amount of things that had had to happen in my life for that moment to occur. That's when I started to get this feeling of being looked after, that I really hadn't made all the grave errors I'd convinced myself of. "Randomly" going to a temple in the desert didn't feel so random.

At the Maui retreat I was talking to a girl about the heart opening that we've felt so intensely through Krishna Das. She said, "It took me forever to realize that what we feel through Krishna Das . . . that's Maharajji!" The way she said it finally pierced my brain. Duh! Of course, that's Maharajji. I sobbed. There have been so many tears on this path for me, mostly of joy. I am so grateful to Maharajji. Every single second of my life had led me here, and how lucky am I?

राम

Shridhar Stephen Callahan

April 1964, when I was in 4th grade, I was hit by a truck while riding my bike. I remember the feeling of floating on the ceiling of the operating room, looking down at the medical team while they scurried around my body in their effort to save my life. There was an amazing feeling of a warm light shining on the top of my head, and what felt like the sirens described by Ulysses calling me to eternal peace. It was the most incredible feeling of peace. It wasn't until decades later that I understood this near-death experience with a bit more clarity. I was a nine-year-old Irish-Polish boy, raised Catholic, so I did know of miracles. I knew that I had lived to tell my tale, but why, dear God, why?

By 1969, I succeeded in getting myself tossed out of Our Lady of Lourdes High School and attended a public school. Free at last.

Marijuana and LSD were readily available to the hippies and, yes, I actively experimented with both frequently. *Be Here Now* was well known in the counterculture that I gladly called home. Both Tim Leary and Ram Dass changed my life in ways that I could never imagine, yet my thirst for answers remained. Why am I here? What am I supposed to do? How do I give back, contribute, repay the debt for being spared an early demise?

I tried college, marriage, the house with the white picket fence, and the 2.3 kids—and failed. I buried myself in my career and cocaine. That all came to an abrupt halt after sitting with two friends at a dinner table on Friday night . . . only to still be sitting there on Sunday morning, having smoked an ounce of freebase among the three of us. I dug even deeper into my career until one day I realized that money is not the key to happiness. *Seva* (service) became my new direction. It felt good, even if it wasn't the final answer.

Two decades later, I dated a woman who took me to my first kirtan. I was intrigued; it brought me to the place I had longed for all these years. I knew that finally I was on my path. We listened to a Krishna Das CD, and after listening to him and reading about some of our similar life experiences, I was brought to his guru, my guru, Neem Karoli Baba.

I knew why I had lived. I had survived that bike accident so many years ago to learn that we are all One and that Love is what we are.

राम

Shyama Chapin

It was the weekend after 9/11/2001. I had gone up to Harbin Hot Springs from San Francisco, where I was living, to try to chill out and relax in the pools. During a bodywork session I found myself complaining about my practice of talking to myself on my frequent long solo drives around the Central Coast of California. I used to drive alone a lot and engaged in hypothetical conversations (out loud) to keep myself awake, but this habit was starting to feel toxic. The bodyworker said, "Well, you should try chanting in the car. Get any chant recording. Chanting really helps."

I thought to myself, "Huh. I do like to sing." But my car only took cassette tapes, not CDs, so I was going to have to find a tape. When I came out of that bodywork session, I looked at the board where the events schedule was posted and saw there was a kirtan that night in the Stone Front gathering space. I don't think I knew what a kirtan was, so it must have said chanting. It was a sweet group. People were sitting around the walls, and there was a puja table with pictures of Amma and Maharajji in the middle of the room. They handed out words and we sang the Hanuman Chalisa. At the end of the kirtan, they did aarti and sang *Jaya Jagadisha Hare*. I really thought it was beautiful.

I did have *Be Here Now* somewhere on my bookshelf, but I had never noticed the picture of Maharajji that is right inside the title page. I also had been given a copy of Ram Dass and Mirabai Bush's *How Can I Help?* I liked the title, but hadn't actually read it. When I got back down to Santa Cruz, I went into Gateways Bookstore, owned by Baba Hari Dass's[25] Mount Madonna Center (another Maharajji connection that I was unaware of). At the back of Gateways they still had racks of cassettes, all recordings of the Mount Madonna choir. I had been to a concert of theirs and it wasn't quite my thing. There was only one other cassette: *Live on*

---

25 Baba Hari Dass was Ram Dass's teacher when Ram Dass spent six months in Kainchi after first meeting Maharajji. Hari Dass came to the West and inspired the founding of Mount Madonna Center for the Creative Arts and Sciences, a spiritual retreat and seminar facility. He took a vow of silence when he was 29 and remained silent until his death 66 years later in 2018 (he taught Ram Dass using a chalk board).

Earth for a Limited Time Only by Krishna Das. I thought, "It's a double; I'll get my money's worth."

I went out to the car and put it in. KD's voice was very familiar right away, and in retrospect of course I'm sure it was Maharajji that I was feeling. It was like I was looking through an album of old family photographs and seeing someone in all the pictures that I had never noticed before, but who I knew very well. Neil Young, who had been in primary rotation in my car, got bumped, and I mostly listened to that one cassette for the next seven or eight years as I drove around. It was pretty much the only thing I played. I was singing with it all the time. I loved it. It felt right. So that's how Maharajji first came and took my hand.

॥म॥

Srutih Asher Colbert

In February 2002, I was at Shivananda Ashram in the Bahamas for a teacher training. I had come from Bikram yoga and was looking for something more authentic, more classical. Every morning at the ashram, you wake up at five o'clock, bathe, and sit in silent meditation on a cement floor by 6 a.m. You meditate for thirty minutes, chant for thirty minutes, and then you have satsang or a spiritual discourse from one of the swamis. I wasn't sure what I was doing. The only other time I'd ever heard *Hare Krishna* in my life was when I saw some Hare Krishnas at the airport wearing their orange robes and banging their kartals, and my dad said, "Oh my God, let's get away from them."

Two weeks went by and then Krishna Das showed up. I had sort of heard of him. He played for five nights at my teacher training and as soon as he hit those first keys on his harmonium and we chanted *Om* together, *poof.* It was like that story Krishna Das tells

93

of how he walked into the room with Ram Dass, and from that moment on he knew that whatever he had been looking for was real and it existed. That's the same experience I had with Krishna Das. I totally connected with the chanting. I was in another world, floating above my body. I was singing, so incredibly full of love and happiness. I was crying, too. It was better than any drug I had ever done, any drink I ever had, any artificial high that I had been trying to chase. From that moment on, everything completely changed. I didn't really feel the Neem Karoli Baba connection. I'd probably transferred that onto Krishna Das.

Then I found out about the first Maui retreat at Napili Kai. I made plans to go, really because of Krishna Das. I thought, well, Ram Dass is there too. That'll be cool. When I went to the retreat and got to be with Ram Dass, again my heart exploded. I attended every retreat after that. I've been eleven times. Somewhere during those years, I did fully accept Baba as my guru. It was sort of natural, like, yes, of course.

ॐ

Steve Satterwhite

Thirty years ago, a friend gave me a tape of *Om Nama Shivayah*. Even though I had no idea what was being chanted, I listened to that tape non-stop for hours. Later she gave me a CD of Ram Dass talking about different types of yoga. When he got to bhakti yoga, I said, oh, that's what this is about. That's when the seed was planted. Then seven years ago, while I was going through a very difficult divorce, I came across a movie called *One Track Heart*[26] about Krishna Das.

---

26 *One Track Heart: The Story of Krishna Das*, directed by Jeremy Frindel (2012 documentary)

That documentary touched me and compelled me to listen to his music, which resonated deeply, as did "bhakti rap" with MC Yogi and songs by Trevor Hall.

When COVID started, I found myself feeling pretty alone and isolated, and I wondered if there was a bhakti community online. That's how I stumbled into Bhakti Yoga Shala with Govind Das and his wife Radha. They had kirtan almost every night on Instagram and the music pulled me in deeper. The next thing I knew, I had photos of Maharajji on my puja table and was reading book after book about his leelas. I even got a plaid blanket from the Taos Ashram. I was hooked.

One evening there was an online kirtan led by Astrud Castillo and her voice and music had a profound impact on me. It was as if the divine mother was calling my name. Later, I reached out to Astrud, who told me that Bhakti Yoga Shala had an online, all-day kirtan coming up for New Year's. I kept the Bhakti Yoga Shala kirtan playing all that day. A couple named Rob and Melissa came on and sang their version of the Hanuman Chalisa. Oh my God, it was so beautiful! But who was Hanuman? A monkey or a god or some sort of mythological character? What I did know is that Rob and Melissa's Hanuman Chalisa touched a vibration and spirit inside me.

The next day, I was driving and thought, I'm going to listen to Rob and Melissa's Hanuman Chalisa 108 times in a row (I actually got through about sixty of them). As I was driving out of Houston, I wondered if there was a Hanuman temple in the city. The next thing I knew I was parked in front of some vacant land with a sign that said it was the future home of the Houston Hanuman mandir! I walked on the land that was to be Hanuman's, said some prayers and drove off. That night, back at home, I was sitting at my puja table looking at Maharajji's picture. I said to him, "I want to know you. I want to serve you. Pull me deeper under your blanket." In the picture, I saw his foot was near a woman's head. I remembered one of the stories I had read that Maharajji had put his foot on a woman's head and she had a mystical experience. I said to the picture, "Just put your foot on my head like you did with that woman in the story."

A shock of energy went through my body! I don't know how long I was sitting there or where I went, but I was in bliss. After a while I crawled into bed and had vivid dreams, very similar to doing ayahuasca or psilocybin. I woke in the middle of the night, and all I could see in front of me, very clearly, was this little golden Hanuman statue. It looked like a kaleidoscope of Hanumans, going around in circles in my field of vision. It was very comforting. I bought a little golden Hanuman murti like the one in my vision from the Hanuman Maui sanctuary.

I was in this state of bliss for a couple of days, but then my energy switched to an underlying panic that lasted for months. From my research, I figured I'd had some type of *shaktipat* (transmitted spiritual energy) experience, and my system couldn't handle it. It was like I had 220 volts of electricity running through a 110-volt system. I was a nervous wreck at work and at night I couldn't sleep. I thought I was about to die or have a heart attack or something.

One day I was in my kitchen listening to the morning satsang on Bhakti Yoga Shala, and someone in the group said, "Let me ask my mom, Radha Baum, to tell the story about the time that Maharajji put his foot on her head."

I just about fell on the floor.

I figured out the person talking was Shiva Baum. I texted him and said, "Oh my God, I have got to connect with your mom." The next day I told Radha my story. We struck up a friendship, and she helped me manage the energy; she explained *shakti* (dynamic spiritual energy) and kundalini and helped me understand what was happening.

Not too long after that, I was sitting at my altar doing my homemade aarti and looking at the little Hanuman murti. I asked Hanuman, "Who are you? Reveal yourself to me." And I got an answer.

In a vision, the little black eyes on the statue popped out. Then the back of the murti opened up and it was hollow on the inside. It beckoned me to step inside the murti and put my face inside Hanuman's face, like putting on a mask. My eyes were looking out of the murti, and Hanuman was looking out through my eyes. It was if it was saying, "I'm inside of you. I'm part of you. I know everything about you, and I'm looking at your life through your eyes." Oh, wow. So, that's who Hanuman is.

Now when I look at Maharajji, I see how the divine leela is playing out. I'm an entrepreneur. On the surface, I run a tech services company, but he's using it to elevate people's lives. I have a picture of Maharajji on my desk. Every day I say to him, "Okay, I'm ready to go to work. Tell me what to do. It's your company. I'm not in control anymore." One day I picked up a book called *Sometimes Brilliant*[27] and saw how Maharajji helped to eradicate smallpox. I'm sure he's having me grow the company so that we can use our resources to work with the United Nations on their goal of eliminating hunger worldwide by 2030. I try to do exactly what he tells me to do every single day. That's all I know.

ᴴᴴ

Susan Karl

I've been on a spiritual journey throughout my adult life. Approximately eighteen years ago, I went to my first Krishna Das concert, which was local and much smaller compared to what they are now.

---

27 *Sometimes Brilliant: The Impossible Adventure of a Spiritual Seeker and Visionary Physician Who Helped Conquer the Worst Disease in History*, by Larry Brilliant (HarperOne, 2016)

I loved it! Then ten years ago, I really got into the path deeply. I heard Krishna Das chanting the Hanuman Chalisa at concerts and felt compelled to learn it, although I did not know why. In 2011, I made a commitment to chant it daily for a year. Although I didn't know much about Maharajji, I had a photo of him on my altar, but I was not consciously searching for a guru. I just felt compelled to chant, especially the Hanuman Chalisa.

One morning, after two years of chanting the Chalisa daily, I was sitting on my bed and Maharajji came to me. I didn't see him, but I heard him inside me. It was my voice, but I knew it was him. He kept saying over and over, "Be still, I am here in your heart. Be still, I'm right here in your heart." It was like a chant, very repetitive. He told me he was my guru and that he has always been here. My tears were flowing.

I have never doubted the validity of my experience. My love and devotion to Maharajji continue to deepen.

4
Photos

When words become unclear, I shall focus with photographs.
When images become inadequate, I shall be content with silence.
—ANSEL ADAMS

I first "met" Maharajji in a photo—a little black-and-white picture Ram Dass had given me the summer of '69 at his father's farm in New Hampshire. I spent the next year and a half talking to that picture. When I got to India and was sitting in front of Maharajji, one of the first things he said to me was, "You used to talk to my picture all the time. You asked many questions." It was total confirmation that he had indeed been with me before I ever touched his feet. This is how I know with such certainty that you can meet Maharajji even when he is not in a physical body.

When we were in India with Maharajji, only a few people had cameras with them—actual cameras, as there were no cell phones back then (or many landlines in India for that matter). Although Maharajji often did not allow his Indian devotees to take photos of him, the Westerners with cameras—Rameshwar Das, Balaram Das, "yellow" Krishna Das (Roy Bonney), and Mohan—were given free rein to snap away. These are the people responsible for most of the photos of Baba that grace the walls of the temples, the covers of books and CDs, phone and computer screens, and sit on the puja tables of so many homes today.

And Maharajji is still making his presence known through photos of him...

राम

Adriana Rizzolo

Sometime after I saw Ram Dass in Maui on retreat, I moved to Topanga Canyon in L.A. and went through an intense time of depression. I kept chanting because the vibration of the harmonium kept me in the world. I was awake with the owls at night, sitting in my cabin and having suicidal thoughts. There's a lot of suicide and addiction in my family. I knew that was not going to happen, but even just the thoughts were stressful. I stayed in that cabin for nine months, healing on some level from my family lineage.

I was teaching at a yoga studio and now I showed up and chanted. I began to offer kirtan once a month with two others who worked at the studio. I decided to move to that part of L.A. from Topanga. I packed up my car and went to stay with a friend. Halfway through the night I semi-woke up with the thought that my car was getting stolen, then drifted back to sleep. In the morning, my car was indeed gone, with all my belongings. A couple of days later the police found my car, and it ended up at a tow yard in Silverlake. My friend drove me there. I asked if she'd mind if I put some Krishna Das on, so *Shri Ram Jai Ram* was playing. We got to the tow yard and I kept the mantra going on my phone.

When I saw my car, there was nothing in it. Yet in this moment of having all my stuff gone, all I felt was relief. I had a person to stay with. I was being taken care of. I opened the glove compartment and a photo of Maharajji that I had gotten at the ashram in Taos fell out. As I looked at the photo, tears of relief and gratitude fell from my eyes.

I texted a photo of Maharajji's picture to my soul mom, Robin Westen. I said, "This is basically the only thing that was left in my car."

She texted back, "Never without grace."

I connected to the mystery of being held by grace and had a deep moment of feeling Maharajji.

Derek / Ganga Dass

I first got involved with Baba when I was living on Oahu and feeling really depressed after a heartbreak. A woman I knew advised me to seek out the person who was most influential in my life. To me that was Ram Dass; I wasn't at all sure about Maharajji.

Some years later at the Makawao Union Church on Maui, Krishna Das was playing. Near the middle of that evening concert, he went into the mahamantra, Hare Krishna. I was looking at the picture of Maharajji onstage and having doubts. I said to the photo, "Maharajji, I cannot go any further with this whole thing unless I know for sure that you're really with me, that you can hear what I am saying right now." I put him to the test: "If you are real, if you're really with me, you need to shut the power off in this entire place right now."

As soon as I said that, *boom!* All the power of the entire room went off—all the sound equipment, the speakers, the sound gone, and complete darkness. Then *poof!* it came right back on again. That was the most profound, immediate, unbelievable experience.

East Forest

I went through a tough patch before I had any relationship with Maharajji; he was just someone that I read about in books or heard about in talks—an entity out there who was deceased and not part of my world. I had gotten divorced and was living alone in a trailer in southern Utah, deep in the wilderness of the Grand Staircase

National Monument. It was beautiful, but I was getting into what felt like a dark night of the soul. I decided I would run every day, do my yoga, and get whatever help I could.

I heard about the *Love Everyone* book on the *Here and Now* podcast. I noticed that by reading the book I felt good; it engendered a warm feeling in me. There was a story in there where someone said, if you have a picture of Maharajji, that alone could bring business or good fortune. Well, how could it hurt? I typed "Maharajji" into Google, and the first image that came up I hit print. I stuck the image on my wall. He's looking right at you in the picture, so I would notice him looking at me when I went to bed or woke up. I felt like I was getting messages planted into my consciousness, very fierce and loving communications. Stern, like, *you should go on that run. No, you shouldn't read that.* I developed a relationship with Maharajji through that picture. I looked at this image for solace, and as a litmus test for my ideas and feelings.

Fast forward. I was sitting with my East Forest music management in a team meeting. I had this idea of recording different spiritual teachers and putting them to music. My manager suggested I focus on a record with just Ram Dass as he was a meaningful teacher to me. I had no connection to Love Serve Remember but, at the time, I was working on another record and the publicist for that album turned out to be Raghu's brother. Then I met Raghu while doing his podcast, *Mindrolling*, and I discovered we had mutual friends, like Trevor Hall and MC Yogi. I had my idea ready. Thankfully, Raghu said, "Yeah, you should do it. Here are the archives, have at it." I was completely overwhelmed by thousands of hours of Ram Dass material.

I said, "Look, I'm making an entire record about the legacy of his work. I've never met him. At a minimum, I need to look him in the eye, soul to soul."

Raghu agreed, and a few months later I went to Maui for a week to record Ram Dass. When I arrived on the first day, I'm setting up the mics and I'm quite nervous. I hit record and he looks at me for the first time. Nothing. Pure loving silence.

I'm thinking I need to ask a question. Over his shoulder on the bookshelf is a picture of Maharajji laughing. I look up at it and I get a message, just like from the photo in my trailer. Maharajji is laughing and saying, *Yeah, this is happening. And you're not on the outside. I'm not someone you just read about in books. You're on the inside. We're all on the inside of the blanket. You're part of this circle, too.*

Ram Dass was looking at me and nodding. *Do you get it? You're love, I'm love. We're souls crossing paths.* And I got it. It allowed me to let go of thinking I was just a fly on the wall who had randomly made my way into this private moment with Ram Dass. I was part of this process as much as any of us, and Maharajji was guiding the process.

राम

Hanuman Das Kane

In the summer between my junior and senior years of college, I hitchhiked around the country. I was in Massachusetts in early July 1968 and got picked up by this British couple in a typical hippie van. When I got in the back of the van, I saw a little picture on the dashboard, maybe three inches by three inches at most, of an old man in a blanket. Well, I couldn't stop looking at the picture.

I started to sob. The woman turned around and said in her British accent, "What's the matter, dear?"

I said, "Who's that a picture of?"

"That's our guru, Neem Karoli Baba."

When she said his name, I knew that was what I'd been waiting for all my life. I was crying even harder once she said his name. I clearly remember thinking my life was going to be different forever. They let me out of the van because we were going different ways. I sat on the side of the road and continued to cry tears of homecoming.

Back then there was no Internet. You couldn't research Neem Karoli Baba, and nobody I knew had heard about him, so I went on with my life.

After college I worked for a short time as an accountant, but I didn't fit in with the three-piece suit and briefcase crowd in Chicago, so I got a job doing floral designs and deliveries. I ran across a Maharajji saying—Love Everyone and Feed Everyone— and decided that my practice for a year was going to be that every single person I saw who looked into my eyes, I would say "I love you" to them. When I delivered flowers, I'd say "I love you." It made me realize that to love everybody was not going to be easy.

I was already into feeding big groups of people. In the fall of 1970, I was cooking Thanksgiving dinner for forty people at my house. The next day, while everybody was eating, I opened the box set of *Be Here Now*, which had arrived the day before. After two years of talking to him and knowing he was there, here was this book all about him. I cried for days.

And now I had lots of pictures of him.

ॐ

Julie Devi Hale, LMFT, E-RYT

I was in grad school getting my master's in psychology; in a class called Contemporary Issues of Aging we were assigned a film called *Fierce Grace*. I was in my thirties at that point, and I had forgotten about Ram Dass. I had known of him in college and then life happened. I looked him up, and there was a retreat in like two months, the first one on Maui. I had a very understanding husband at the time; I left him in charge of the three kids so I could go. And I kept going back to Maui for the next fifteen years—every retreat and every opportunity that I could in between. I was all in about love, serve, remember.

I felt shy of Maharajji because I'd heard these Ram Dass stories about how he knows everything. But I started talking to Maharajji and testing him. One day I was in a saucy mood, and I really needed some bakeware for the oven because I only had this aluminum stuff. I literally nodded at his picture, and was like, *okay?* Maybe it's just a phenomenon in L.A. that people leave good stuff out on the streets in front of their house by the trash. I'm walking my dogs and I see these two beautiful bowls of Japanese ceramic bakeware that go from oven to table . . .

When my mother was dying, Ram Dass was a tremendous support and strength for me. After she passed, I developed a closer relationship to her than I had when she was in the body, which led me to this realization: *Oh yeah, the same is true with Maharajji. I can talk to him in the same way.* I always felt his presence and his protection at the retreats. I said goodbye to Ram Dass so many times at the retreats. When he finally passed, I had immense gratitude. Thank you for hanging out in that old shoe for longer than was anywhere near comfortable. Now I talk to him over there, too.

I feel this commitment to keeping his loving awareness going. And I still talk to my favorite picture of Maharajji.

ॐ

Kavita Kat MacMillan

My association with Maharajji came through being introduced to kirtan in New York City in the '90s with Krishna Das, Bhagavan Das, and Shyamdas[28]. Twenty years later I was living in Portland, teaching yoga and sharing kirtan with my yoga community. My friend said, "I have this painting that my son's friend (Karissa Halstrom) gave me to give to Krishna Das. Maybe you could bring it to him." I opened this big beautiful painting of Maharajji. I wouldn't see Krishna Das until September when I went to Bhakti Fest, and this was the end of June, so I put it up on the wall in a prominent place.

At Bhakti Fest I sang with everybody I knew, and by Saturday I was in a very open heart space, but I could feel the place in my heart that was still closed. After dinner a friend took me into a healing meditation and told me to call in my guide. *Ping!* Maharajji showed up. Oh wow, okay. I breathed and cried and made peace with this part of my heart. I could hear Krishna Das singing.

Back in my pup tent, I rolled up the painting, went backstage, and gave it to Krishna Das. I realized I had received darshan through that image of Maharajji. When I had first unfurled it and put it on the wall, it brought Maharajji's presence into my life.

After that, I got deep into Ram Dass's teachings. I started playing music with Daniel Paul and went to Maui to do a kirtan at the Temple of Peace with him. On the day I was leaving, Dassi Ma called and said, "Hey, you guys want to come do a kirtan?" I went with Daniel and our friend Will, who plays sitar. They wheeled Ram Dass in. Next thing I know I'm singing the Chalisa right in front of Ram Dass. He's just luminous. I'm singing to him, and there's that murti of Maharajji by the window grinning at me.

---

28 Shyamdas was a Westerner who brought Indian devotional and yogic traditions to the West through more than 15 books and 6 albums of sacred chants.

I always am shy about taking photos, but I wanted a picture with Ram Dass more than anything. I asked if someone would take some photos of us. We're mooning into each other's eyes because I'm high off singing and he's high off being himself. Then we started packing up the music and the equipment. When I picked up my phone, I noticed the murti of Maharajji by the window. I snapped one more picture—of the murti.

Back at Daniel's I went to look at the photos on my phone . . . and the only picture was of the murti! Maharajji was just grinning at me.

ᜂᜀ

Leelah Das Laurie Savran

In 1972 I was married to a man who owned a very progressive and literary bookstore in Minneapolis called Savaran's Paperback. Obviously, we got the book *Be Here Now* when it first came out. I took it home and read it—a "before and after" moment in my life. At that time I was a psychic and an astrologer, so I wasn't exactly new to alternative things. In the book Ram Dass says that if you read this book, even if you never met Neem Karoli Baba in the flesh, he could still be your guru and he could still be with you in your heart.

I set the book up on the bookshelf with it open to the page with Maharajji's picture, and I started thinking, how can it be that I'd never met him? How can he be my guru? But when I looked in his eyes in the photo, I had darshan. I felt his presence and felt his energy moving into my heart and into my whole being and my soul. And to this day I feel his presence with me at all times.

ᜂᜀ

Mangala Braymiller

I was raised pretty much without religion, and in my college years I became a fervent atheist. My husband, Ganesh, started getting into Ram Dass, reading his books, listening to the podcasts. He had a little altar set up with a picture of Neem Karoli Baba on it and one of Ram Dass. I had zero interest in any of it, but I knew that it was helping him along in his life.

One night we took a low dose of LSD, so I wasn't expecting anything substantial to happen. At a certain point, however, I walked into the kitchen and hugged my husband tightly. I saw through his eyes into the vastness and black nothingness of space, then a single cell, and then the big bang; I saw the orb explode out into infinity. I soared straight through the middle of all of it, and I saw everything, everything.

After the hug, I followed him into the room with the altar. I said, "I just became one with infinity. Now what?"

Without saying a word, he pointed at the picture of Neem Karoli Baba in the center of his altar. I sat down on the pillow in front of the picture and the picture came alive, absolutely came alive. My husband left the room. I sat there alone with the small photo, and I could hear Baba speaking to me. I could feel everything he was saying—all the beauty, all the darkness, and everything in between. I was dealing with a lot of depression and suicidal ideation. He told me, "Oh, you want to turn it all off? Okay, I'll turn it off right now." And everything went black and silent, and there was nothing.

I said, "No, that's not what I want." And he turned everything back on.

I looked at him as he turned into a bright glowing white light that filled the room. I saw him transition into my father's face and angels and demons; everything was contained in that photo. We laughed and laughed. He's so funny. He'd tell me these beautiful deep truths and I'd start bawling my eyes out as I stared at his picture. I sat in front of that photo for probably five hours and didn't break my gaze. My husband would walk into the room and occasionally throw bananas at me. I'd eat a banana and laugh at the jokes, and Baba would tell me more things. We were absolutely communing and communicating.

Afterwards, I walked into the living room. I looked at my husband with the purest feeling in my heart and mind and said, "It's all right here. We don't have to look anymore. It's all right here." I'd never felt so light, never felt so happy, never felt so cleansed, so pure, so full.

The next day my husband said the different elements of my story were all like elements of stories he had read in *Love Everyone*. People who were with Baba physically in body had the same experiences I had sitting there with his photo.

I have this outpouring of gratitude because it feels like I've gotten swept up in a blanket and pulled into all the bliss that I never knew I could have. I can't say I'm an atheist anymore.

ॐ

Melanie Law

I've been a yoga teacher for about twenty-five years. Shortly after I began teaching, I started traveling to New York City with my husband. I had never spent any time on the East Coast, let alone in the big city, but I found my way to Jivamukti Yoga Center about the same time Krishna Das started offering kirtan there. I fell in love with chanting, ordered a harmonium and began sharing kirtan as part of my yoga classes back home in Colorado.

It's funny how long it took me to understand that bhakti is my path. I always thought I was just a yoga teacher who loved to sing, and I wondered who my real teacher was.

For years I followed Krishna Das around. I never did get to meet Ram Dass. Over the years, I attended a number of Jai Uttal's retreats, so between Krishna Das and Jai I always admired the photos of Maharajji.

A few winters ago, my whole family was with Jai in Costa Rica on New Year's Eve, chanting. I was gazing at Maharajji's picture up front—the one where he's holding both palms out. I had the direct feeling that he had entered the room. It was so real that I placed my hand on my son's knee and leaned over to say *the guru is here.*

That was the moment it hit me. I had tears pouring down my face. *Oh my God, of course. It's taken me twenty years to figure it out, but this is my lineage.* The transmission I was getting was so profound and beautiful. Shortly after, Maharajji's message to me was clear: Learn the Hanuman Chalisa. At the time I had no idea why he wanted me to learn it, but I followed his direction. Now the Chalisa is part of my daily practice, the anchor to my spiritual life, and my connection to Babaji's love and protection.

राम

Nicole DiSalvo Billa

I started yoga in 2001 to ease my physical pain and lose some weight. I never planned on getting into a guru thing. I certainly wasn't going to turn into one of those wacky people who have pictures of Krishna all over their house. In the very first class, the teacher played kirtan music by Krishna Das and his voice captivated me immediately. She played the same album over and over in every class. I didn't know the meaning of the words, but there was a quality of heart that was transmitted through the music. I began to experience the first inklings of safety and love I had ever encountered in my life.

Years went by before I went to a full-day workshop with Krishna Das. He talked a great deal about his guru, which wasn't very interesting to me. I was desperate for a way out of the lingering unhappiness and fear I had lived with for so long. I didn't want to hear about this dead Indian man. But there were things Krishna Das said that touched my heart, even if I couldn't understand this feeling of love and compassion that he kept talking about. And every time he talked about Maharajji, he cried. I was amazed that the memory of this love had the power to make a man cry thirty years later. Singing with him opened a door, and in the weeks following that workshop there were moments when I felt everything was okay, and more importantly, that I was okay. I wondered if I had found a guru in Krishna Das.

A few months later Krishna Das was giving a weekend workshop at an ashram near my house. At the front of the room where we sang was a picture of an Indian man with a very beautiful smile on his face. Must be his guru, I thought. He looked familiar.

In our last session with Krishna Das, I got very irritated. I was pretty sure we needed to do some singing or I would never *get it*. Krishna Das just kept telling stories about his guru and reading from the books about him. I grew more and more angry. I had been searching for so long for anything that could relieve my pain, and I was pretty sure I wasn't going to get it from hearing unbelievable miracle stories about a dead Indian man. Yet, at the same time, I could not stop staring at the guru's picture. I was hypnotized by his face. He was so beautiful.

Finally, we sang one last *Sita Ram* and the retreat was over. I sat there, utterly and completely crushed. I had come to the retreat in the hope that something would change. I had been on a spiritual quest since I was fifteen, but nothing had ever really touched my heart. And now another disappointment, another blind alley. I gave up.

Which is, of course, when I felt something give in my heart.

I was looking at Maharajji's picture and I heard a voice. I knew it was the man in the picture. I started to sob and smile. I was filled with the most incredible joy, a joy that did not deny the pain. The voice said, *You have never been alone. I have always been with you. And everything you have endured, all the suffering, has been to lead you to this moment. It was to shape you into this.*

He had been there, I now knew, when I was seventeen and lay dying on a bathroom floor, overdosing on too many drugs to count. His presence had been there when the car crashed. He had been there when my boyfriend's apartment caught on fire, and we were tripping so hard we thought it was funny. I could see how the events of my life had aligned to form a particular pattern that created me as I was. I was not a worthless failure. He had set things up so that I would become who I was. *Because he loved who I was.* That was the most important part of the feeling: I felt loved and wanted and cared for.

I knew that the presence was the man in the picture, Neem Karoli Baba. I also understood implicitly that he was the spirit and he was also a doorway to spirit. I joined the line of people saying good-bye to Krishna Das. When it was my turn he said, "Hey, why are you crying?" I told him what I had felt coming from Maharajji, and Krishna Das murmured back to me. "Of course he's here... yes, he arranged it all... yes."

There was no doubt, only faith.

ॐ

Parker

After spring semester ended, three of my close friends and I decided to take some mushrooms and MDMA to do some deep spiritual work together. Ram Dass's books and lectures serendipitously had fallen into my life several years earlier, and I had recently discovered and watched the *Love Everyone* stories on YouTube. Before the trip, I remembered a bit of Parvati's *Love Everyone* story, when she experienced a miracle on acid through Neem Karoli Baba's picture, and this led me to save a picture of Maharajji to my phone.

My intention for the journey was simple: "To be completely open, honest, and loving with myself and you guys." While waiting for the MDMA to set in, I remembered the picture on my phone. After staring into his eyes for a second or two, a place deep within me began to open, and I deeply felt light/love/energy coming through his picture and into me. A few minutes later I had an experience that I can only describe as a glimpse of awakening.

For several months afterwards I lived in an almost continuous state of immense joy. My ego is back and working as hard as ever, but I am much faster at catching it and returning to presence. The love that comes through me when I rest in presence now is something I didn't know was possible before this experience, and I know that Maharajji's grace is responsible.

राम

Sarada Strickman

It was early April, either 2003 or 2004, and I was at a kirtan at Yoga on Main in Philadelphia. There were three pictures on the wall of the studio—Anandamayi Ma, Neem Karoli Baba, and Ammaji. A week earlier I'd read that one of the ways you can receive a guru is by looking at their picture, but I didn't think too much of it.

As Bhagavan Das started to chant, Neem Karoli Baba's picture was to his right. I looked at Maharajji's picture . . . and suddenly he was sitting there on what I later realized was his takhat. He materialized wearing his traditional blanket, a small Indian man with a bald head, and he was beaming—smiling, smiling, smiling at me. The top of my head opened, and he started filling me with overflowing love. It kept pouring out of me, filling the entire Delaware Valley, the entire Northeast. It kept going and going and going. At the end of the kirtan, one of the studio managers said, "Are you going to be okay to drive home?" He did some grounding work on my ankles, and I somehow drove home, still high as a kite!

The next morning I woke up, and I could see what I now realize is "Ram" written in Sanskrit everywhere. Sometimes it was huge and I could see it in the sky. I saw it in the handle of the gas pump. In a Reese's peanut butter cup wrapper. On leaves. I literally saw Ram everywhere. The sense of love was extremely strong. At the veterinary hospital where I work, I could see Ram written in the dog's fur and in the needle and in the syringe when I was running blood work. It was everywhere.

Sunday morning I called my mother, who is a librarian and an avid reader. She asked me, "Wasn't there a book compiled about Maharajji by Ram Dass called *Miracle of Love*?" I checked it out of the library and started reading. That's when I knew with a thousand percent certainty that Maharajji was saying, *There's zero question. I'm it. I'm it.*

ॐ

Sheila Doyle

I had always considered Ram Dass to be my teacher since the early '70s and Maharajji was my teacher's guru . . . until this incident changed all that.

At one of the early spring retreats at Napili Kai in Maui, Ram Dass was speaking on the need to remove hate from our hearts and how very difficult it is to love everyone and tell the truth. One technique he used was to take a photo of the person he was having

116

trouble with and place it on his puja table as a reminder that this is a person, too, playing out his karmic predicament. I was thrilled by this suggestion, as I was having a big hate in my heart.

Just as I realized that this was what I needed to do, suddenly a white light reached out to me from Maharajji's photo. It reached into my heart and plucked out the hate. This is the best way I can describe it. The hate was completely gone. I still do not like this person and I still do not trust him, but the hate has never returned.

That was the day that I realized that Maharajji was not just Ram Dass's guru, he was also mine.

ॐ

Sonia Wilczewski

Around 1979-80, a friend had discovered the book *Be Here Now*, which he shared with me. There was the concept of guru in the book, but I didn't know who that guru was for me until many years later, around 2007, when I went to Ram Giri's house and saw this life-sized photo—Baba standing with his blanket over his shoulder. It was stunning. Who was this person? I witnessed the love between Ram Giri and this person in the photo whom he had known. His life's drive seemed to be based on the relationship he had with this person, and that was a beautiful thing.

There were other photos of Baba there, with looks that were so embracing and so filling that I learned to love the photos. I started to look for photos for myself and found there was love pouring out of these photos as well. In some he's stern, but at the same time guiding. There are many different facets in different pictures and I started to collect these photos. They are not static. When I look at them, I see changes, a shift in the underlying facial muscles, and they convey a message to me, although generally not in words.

I have photos stacked up like a deck of cards now. I take my deck and go through it until it feels like one connects. It's the right photo, the right energy that I need at that time. I stay with that photo, and that is my darshan. It's beyond words, but often it's a recalibrating of something, and that's even too logical a word. I feel like there's a tweak that shifts me toward a different course, an energetic healing.

I didn't want to know about the human person behind the photos because I thought he couldn't possibly be that good! At first I didn't want to read *Miracle of Love* or *Love Everyone* because I didn't want it affecting my own experience. I feel like he's talking to me. He's conveying cryptic things, and they do make me laugh when I figure them out. They make me feel calm and allow me to surrender more, and that is a state of grace.

I don't know how those pictures move, but they do. A lot of the images I have from 1973 are unfocused, but the eyes look right at you, and beyond. At the same time, they are completely accepting of you.

Unconditional love. There's nothing like it.

5
Temples and Ashrams

The temple bell stops but I still hear
the sound coming out of the flowers.
—Basho

When I arrived in Nainital during monsoon in 1971, I felt like I belonged on earth for the first time, even though it was pouring rain twenty-three hours a day and the walls of my room at the Evelyn Hotel were green with mold. I would be staring at those walls for six weeks as I slowly recovered from hepatitis, but I knew I was home.

When September arrived, the rains ceased and Maharajji returned to Kainchi. The walk across the bridge that spans the Kosi River into Maharajji's temple complex (officially, the Kainchi Dham Baba Neem Karoli Ashram) felt like crossing the threshold into sacred space. There were rituals to be observed, like washing our apple offerings in the fountain, shedding flip-flops, bowing before the murtis, and then making a beeline to the takhat—hearts opening wider with every step closer to Maharajji's feet.

For many, Maharajji's temple in Vrindavan (the Neeb Karori Baba Vrindavan Ashram) is home base, holding, as it does, the remembrance of his mahasamadhi cremation in the temple courtyard and the *parikrama*—the spiritual path that encircles the temples and holy spots of this ancient town—that took us down to the Jamuna River for spectacular sunsets and contemplation of the grace we were receiving from Baba.

There are temples in Rishikesh, Shimla, Neem Karoli village (in Farrukhabad), Bhumiadhar, Hanumangarh, and Delhi. Dada Mukerjee's home at 4 Church Road in Allahabad is also clearly one of Maharajji's temples, where we were always treated like family. Here in the U.S., we have a beautiful new temple for our Hanuman, the one who flew over from India. Our Hanuman murti lived in a converted milk barn in Taos that served as his temple for many years while he planted himself in the hearts of the Westerners. For many, the Hanuman Temple in Taos has proved to be spiritual home base.

Since his mahasamadhi in 1973, Maharajji's temples have become his body here on earth—physical locales that are permeated with his being. All are dedicated to Hanuman, and all hold Maharajji's essence of unconditional love.

Christy Modita Engels

Ever since high school, when I was really involved in my Methodist church, I wanted to be a minister, but they said girls couldn't do that, so I trashed all organized religion until I was in my early forties. (I did become a minister later in my fifties.)

In the '80s, my partner and I often went to Ojai on weekends. We found a spiritual bookstore where a woman was giving Tarot readings with a deck that she had made herself. During a reading she showed me a picture of an old man and said, "He is very important in your life." He looked a little like my father. And then I forgot all about it for years.

We were in that store another time and saw a flyer for a Ram Dass retreat called "Meeting of the Ways" that was going to be held in New Mexico at Lama Foundation. During that retreat Ram Dass gave us each a picture of Maharajji and said, "Take it home with you. If anybody asks you who it is, say it's your grandfather." He was, of course, the old man from the tarot deck. After we were home a short time, I could feel this playful energy in the house and knew it was Maharajji.

We kept going back to Lama every summer. One year we were driving up the hill to go to a retreat at Lama when I got this big pull to stop by the Hanuman temple in Taos. We sat down in front of Hanuman and I went into this incredible crying jag. When I read *Love Everyone*, I realized everyone has this crying jag!

Another time I was at the temple and asked if I could stay in the *dharamshala* (rest house). I was told, "Oh, that's reserved for devotees."

I blurted out, "I'm a devotee," and I had another one of those crying jags! That was the moment I knew I was Maharajji's devotee.

Mansa Devi (Allie Milroy)

I met Ram Dass in the early '70s in Vancouver, Canada. He came out in his white robes and long hair and spoke in the gym at my high school. I looked at him and it was that *boom!* kind of thing. I had grown up in a classic Anglican family. You get christened when you're a baby and then you get confirmed; you go to Sunday school and memorize a bunch of things and then you have this great pompous ceremony with the bishop. I did my churchy things, but it didn't touch my heart. And then I heard Ram Dass. *Be Here Now* became my new bible.

Many years later I learned that a friend was going to retreats, and I noticed a real change in her. One night as we were having a glass of wine, Trevor Hall was playing in the background, and she said, "Do you know who this is?"

I said, "It's Trevor Hall. I love him. My yoga teacher plays his music." I asked her to tell me about these retreats.

She said, "Oh, it's with Ram Dass."

I looked at her in surprise. "You mean my Ram Dass?"

After dinner I looked up the retreat, the little registration button was still alive and I pressed it. Whoa, this was obviously meant to happen. So I got to see Ram Dass again.

I finally made it to India in 2018. I was in Bhumiadhar at the temple on the edge of the hill. I'd heard the story of Ram Dass's first meeting Maharajji there. There's a little room with Baba's takhat and I was able to go into the room and have time alone there. When I went into the room, I didn't really know what I was supposed to be doing. I put my hands on the takhat, where there was a picture of Neem Karoli Baba. I'm thinking, okay, this is all ridiculous. What am I doing this for? What am I trying to pretend? I was resisting and resisting. I had my head down and my hands on the takhat. I could feel the energy in my arms was tight.

Suddenly, it was like a tidal wave or a big wave of the ocean came at me. I was still resisting, no, no, no, no, no. Then I heard Maharajji say, "You are okay. You are so okay." This massive wave of love came right over me. It was so unbelievable, and yeah, I burst into tears. It was the most amazing experience I have ever had.

तिय

Michael Brian Baker

As I sat on the front lawn of the Taos Ashram nineteen years ago, all I could think about was how angry I was that I got stuck at this stupid temple on my birthday and how my best friend betrayed his promise that we would head out to explore New Mexico. He was inside chanting some prayer to a monkey, so I decided I would give this meditation thing a try. I sat still and concentrated on my breath, but the blazing sun in the stillness of midday was too much to handle. My discomfort was unbearable. I spoke aloud from pure frustration and called to this "Maharajji" guy. I requested that, if he did exist, I needed just a hint of comfort so that I could experience stillness and peace.

At that moment a strong breeze appeared from nowhere, sending chills up my spine that cooled my entire being. The hair on my arms stood on end, and my mind magically stilled. I felt waves of relaxation and calm.

A short while later, I was guided to join the long line to meet Ram Dass, who had arrived unexpectedly. That day my life changed forever. Unexpectedly, unwanted, and preceded by much resistance, I received the powerful darshan of Neem Karoli Baba through

Ram Dass. I experienced an emotional purification that can only be described as miraculous.

When Ram Dass transitioned in 2019, I felt like I'd not had the chance to express authentically my gratitude for that experience. Then a friend sent me this note out of the blue: "We all experience Maharajji in our own personal way, like feeling his presence in the form of a breeze that will suddenly swirl on an otherwise windless day."

This is the way Maharajji works. He's winking at me from the subtle world of *siddhaloka*[29], reminding me that I'm still under the blanket.

ॐ

Mira Lyra Geroy

In 1986 I was living in California and wanted to go on pilgrimage. I had been shown a picture of the Taos Hanuman and decided to head to New Mexico. I was a single mom for my ten-year-old daughter, Anandi, and a devotee of Baba. While I was on this journey, I felt a connection with a being. I didn't know who this being was, but I kept feeling this being inside me, talking to me.

When I got to Taos, I was so blown away that I immediately turned around and packed up everything and in one weekend moved to Taos, found a job and a place to live. I spent the winter deep in spiritual seeking. I would get up around four a.m. to meditate. On Easter Sunday morning I heard a voice loud and clear in my head that said *walk to the temple*.

I walked and walked. They had just finished the Chalisas when I arrived. I sat in front of Hanuman and went into a deep meditation.

---

29 *Siddhaloka* is the abode of liberated perfect souls, the world of the blessed.

That's when I met Maharajji. My heart burst open and shakti shot through my body and out the top of my head. Maharajji took me on a journey and showed me a movie of my past lives and the reality of other dimensions. My heart was bursting out of my body. I merged with Maharajji, and I've never been away from him since that profound moment.

A few months later, I moved to Lama Foundation and became a resident there, doing spiritual practice all day, every day, for two years. I would come to the temple and receive darshan from Baba, but his spirit is also very strong up on Lama mountain. In fact, when the wildfire happened, he basically saved Lama from being destroyed. One devotee saw Maharajji on the mountain during that fire. There's a tiny Hanuman murti up there that was not burnt, while all around it was ash.

ॐ

Pam Lilak (Meera Puri)

A friend gave me *Be Here Now* at a time in my life when I had started down a *kriya*[30] yoga path. I did a lot of very intense sadhana in Ohio after leaving corporate America in Manhattan, and I was losing my mind because I had no support. My only saving grace was this book and listening to podcasts of Ram Dass talking about Maharajji. I had a longing to go visit Kainchi Dham.

When I got to Delhi, I first went to Baba's ashram in Vrindavan. The first sign that I saw on the wall was "Truth is the Hardest Tapasya," which hit home. We did the little parade around the

---

30 *Kriya*, Sanskrit for "action, deed, effort," refers to a practice in a yoga discipline designed to achieve a specific result.

murti and I came in front of his murti. I closed my eyes and there was a bright white light coming and going in my third eye. I opened my eyes and looked at the murti, then at the sign up on the wall that said, "The guru is not in the external world."

It wasn't until Christmas morning that I was able to get up to the mountains. We drove down the hill and there was Kainchi Dham. *Oh my God, I'm here.* Would I be disappointed? I had built this up for over five years. At the top of the steps, I could smell sweetness. Flowers. Incense. I walked in and my heart opened so much. I was crying, crying, crying, because there was so much love, a love that I'd never ever felt before.

The Devi murti accepted me as I was and, at the same time, she was saying, "It's okay, don't worry about it. This love is immense; it's everywhere, and now it's yours. It's ours. It's everyone's." I bowed down to Devi, cried, and wanted nothing but to be in this love and grace. It was freezing cold, but every morning at 6 AM I went to Kainchi for aarti. Usually it was only me and maybe one or two people from the winter staff. By the third day, every time I looked at Hanumanji, I smiled.

On June 15th I was in Kainchi Dham again for the bhandara. Thousands of people had come and the hotel didn't have room, so I slept on the floor in the hotel lobby. In the morning I sat on the steps of the ashram waiting for the gates to open. I started chanting the Hanuman Chalisa, which I had learned that year. When I started chanting, all of these people joined in. It was beautiful and I cried again.

When they opened the ashram, I went to the back, the part they only open during bhandara. I was able to go sit on the rock where Maharajji first came into this area. I sat there as long as I could and I prayed, "Maharajji, I want to stay here. It feels so good."

Then I heard, "Go home! Go home and remember me. Go home and remember me."

राम

Rick Bueschel

I've always been fascinated by India. When I had been in the Navy, I was in and out of lots of airports all over the world, and I loved the Hare Krishnas who were chanting everywhere. By the late '80s, early '90s, I was listening to tapes of Ram Dass and I signed up for his workshop at Breitenbush[31]. Back then I didn't know anything about Maharajji or Hanuman.

Ram Dass was doing *Shri Ram Jai Ram Jai Jai Ram*, and I got hooked. I decided that whatever he had, I wanted some of it. I got involved in kirtan and went to workshop after workshop. I lived about 120 miles east of Seattle in a small conservative college town, not exactly the cultural center of the universe. There were no kirtans there, so for me it was Portland, Seattle, Breitenbush, Krishna Das, and Gina Sala, a kirtan and mantra artist from Seattle who has worked with Jai Uttal and Daniel Paul.

Gina led trips to India. I went to India with her for the first time in 2012. All of us were *sadhaks*, spiritual seekers. We went to Vrindavan first and stayed right near the ISKCON temple, and I think we visited every one of the thousands of Krishna temples there. Of course, I wanted to go to Maharajji's temple. It was September 8th or 9th and Gina had us scheduled to go to the Taj Mahal on Wednesday and go to Maharajji's temple the following day.

At the Taj I had this big passport leela. I had put my passport in a zippered pocket in my cargo pants. At some point during the tour, I checked and the passport was gone. I had never unzipped the pocket.

---

31 Breitenbush Hot Springs Retreat and Conference Center, in Idanha, OR, is an off-the-grid sanctuary for workshops and personal retreats.

One of the places I looked extra hard for it was in the men's bathroom. If you can imagine it, I got down on my hands and knees in that Indian bathroom.

I was going to have to go to the embassy in Delhi and it was going to be a huge hassle. Later that night the phone rang and it was security at the Taj. They found it! I went back the next day to get the passport. That was the day we were supposed to go to Maharajji's ashram, so we postponed the temple visit for a day. At the Taj I had a good laugh with the security guards, who of course had found my passport in the men's bathroom.

Gina had a copy of *Miracle of Love*, and she opened it up right to the passport leela stories about Ram Dass.

The next day when we went to Maharajji's ashram, it was his mahasamadhi bhandara. If I hadn't lost my passport, we would have gone the day before and would have missed it. Days later things calmed down at the ashram, and I'd go at six in the morning for aarti. One day, while sitting in front of his ashes and thinking about Maharajji, words came into my mind of Maharajji saying, as clear as a bell, "I always said that if you called me, I would come to you; now you've come to me."

It was really a powerful experience.

ॐ

Susan Buck-Gordon

Sometime in the '70s, a copy of *Be Here Now* was put in my hands. A couple of years later, I went to hear Ram Dass; he was just back from India and wasn't talking about Maharajji at all. Later, my husband passed away and I read *Still Here*. I thought, I need to see Ram Dass again. I learned about the retreat on Maui and have been coming to the retreats for the last eight years. I always thought of

Ram Dass as kind of my guru, but he always said no, I'm nobody's guru. At one of the retreats Ram Dass said, "If you don't have a guru, take mine." I always thought Maharajji couldn't be my guru.

Then I went to India and was at the temple at Kainchi. That morning, a friend that I met at the first Ram Dass retreat was asking for prayers for her family. I went into Maharajji's "office" and was meditating for a long time. I put my head down on the takhat with my hands and started saying prayers to him for my friend. I heard his voice in my head saying, "Go sit with Hanuman."

I had orders now, so I went directly to the Hanuman murti. As I sat there, suddenly the murti's face changed and he turned his head towards me. He was smiling. I felt this incredible outpouring of love. We were on retreat with Ram Giri, and he told me that was darshan. I had Hanuman's darshan! That's when I knew I was connected to Maharajji.

I was in Taos for the consecration of the new temple, and the last day that I was there, I went up to the murti, and I said, "Hanuman, you're still there for me, aren't you?" Again, the smile and the outpouring of love. That was it. I knew where I belonged.

तुम

Tyler

Since my biological father had been absent throughout my life, I used every experience in life as evidence to fuel the belief that I did not matter. Then in 2013, I had a spiritual awakening of unity consciousness and chose to put my beliefs about myself off to the side so I could open to new experiences. Months prior to that awakening I had been planning my own death.

In 2016 I spent three weeks at the Lama Foundation in northern New Mexico. I had been studying consciousness and its relationship to the reality we experience, and I wanted to take some time to plant myself in a different environment so that I might grow differently. I would stay in a tent, spend thirty hours a week doing seva, and use the remaining time to connect with others, the earth, and myself more deeply—a perfect way for me to learn to let go and let God.

Once at Lama Foundation I was welcomed as if I were family; I was offered time to acclimate [Lama Foundation is at 8,300 ft.] and adjust to the new environment. A few days in and I started to feel much closer to myself and the world around me. One of my intentions was to say *yes* to things that were uncomfortable or scary for me. One day during lunch I met Will, a man around my age with long dreads, who invited me to join him going to Taos to the Hanuman Temple. I had recently read *Be Here Now* and I said yes.

At the temple we went into the main room where Hanuman lives. After we pranammed, offered our gifts, and spent some quiet time, Will suggested I go into Maharajji's office, this small room with just a takhat, a few flowers, and a picture of Baba. I pranammed, took off my malas and placed them on the takhat. Instantly my heart burst open! Tears rushed down my face, and I felt loved like never before. I realized I had come home. Every detail of my life—from begging for answers as a child about my existence, to every encounter I had with other human beings—all seemed to have led me to this moment in my life when Baba stepped in to be my father.

I had truly wanted a connection to my father. One day I picked up the phone and reached out to him. He said that he wanted to keep things the way they were. I recalled a Maharajji quote that spoke deeply to me: "The worst form of punishment is to throw someone out of your heart." I told him I loved him, and that I was open if he ever changed his mind.

I am blessed beyond belief that each day now I am reminded how much my presence does matter. When I look back on these last few years of my twenty-four years of experience on earth, not only am I blown away by the drastic difference in my day-to-day experience, but I am also overwhelmed with the love and grace gifted by my guru. I am doing my best to stay aware of the fact that I am always under his blanket.

꠪꠪

Ximena

My spiritual path started when a friend from the U.S. spent four months in Chile, where I live, and gave me a book of Eckhart Tolle. It was the first time I heard the words *ego* and *spirit* and *self* and *soul*, which I didn't understand at first. I started listening to Tolle on YouTube and began meditating. My friend returned to the U.S. and we connected through Facebook. One day he posted an article written by Ram Dass about visiting a young kid who was dying. It was the first time I heard someone talking about death in a good way, in a happy way. It was so shocking.

I kept reading about Ram Dass, and I was seeing the way Maharajji does things so perfectly. At the time I was working in an office that wasn't busy. I had to be there in front of a computer, but I was doing no work. Instead, I listened to Ram Dass talks on YouTube for six hours a day. English is not my first language, so when I heard Ram Dass talk, I had to translate. In the end I had several notebooks with notes from his talks.

I was following one of the 2015 retreats in Maui via livestream. Ram Dass was telling the story of when he first met Maharajji, about the Land Rover and thinking about his mother and the moment when Maharajji said the word *spleen*. How did Maharajji know Ram Dass was thinking about his mother? My mind brought up all these questions. Then Ram Dass led a guided meditation and said, "Imagine this being sitting in front of you and imagine a blue highway coming from his heart to your heart. Imagine this being traveling that highway to you, and he comes inside your heart and he stays inside." And that is exactly what I felt: my heart felt so big, and Maharajji was coming inside and staying there.

I ordered *Miracle of Love* and *Love Everyone*. I read the *Bhagavad Gita*. I was obsessed. I started talking to Maharajji. In the middle of all this I lost my job and had to go live with my mom. I love her, but it was hard. I found a new job. Because I was living with my mother, I saved a lot of money. One day I was listening to Ram Dass on a webcast with Ramesh, and they were talking about Hanumanji's murti in Taos. I was crying when Ram Dass said, "If you haven't seen his face (talking about this Hanuman), you have to come see it. It's worth it." I felt I had to go to Taos.

I saved enough money to live there for a year, from Hanuman Jayanti (Hanuman's birthday) in 2015 until April 2016. One day I was talking to Maharajji. I told him, "I don't think about you that much. I want to think about you more." By his grace, I became a caretaker in the Neem Karoli Baba ashram in Taos for more than two years.

6
Ram Dass

I am loving awareness.
—RAM DASS

Ram Dass often said that Maharajji is the fisherman and he is the lure—the one who can hook you into opening your heart and finding that Maharajji lives there. Ram Dass certainly was the lure for many of us who went to India to find Maharajji.

I remember falling into a profound silence the first time I saw Ram Dass in the early summer of '69, standing at the door of his father's house in New Hampshire; he was absolutely radiant, glowing with light. His brilliant blue eyes were shining with a love I had never known existed. Whatever it was Ram Dass had gotten from this mysterious being he talked about, whose name we didn't know, we wanted it from the same source. I know that those of us who came to Maharajji's feet through Ram Dass owe him a debt of gratitude that can never be repaid.

Then, for decades after Maharajji left his body, Ram Dass became the portal, the lure for countless others. They met Ram Dass through his talks and books—especially *Be Here Now* and *Miracle of Love*—through "heart-to-heart" Skype calls and YouTube videos and retreats. Some came to him for help with understanding psychedelic experiences; some to work with him on conscious death and dying; others met him through the spiritual and activist organizations he supported, like Seva or the Social Venture Network.

Many believed or wondered if Ram Dass was their guru, although he always said, "It's not me; it's Maharajji." But as time went on and he lived in the painful body that followed his massive stroke, he came to embody the "loving awareness" that was his mantra as he merged more and more deeply with Maharajji. After his passing in December 2019, Ram Dass's lectures, books, tapes, CDs, podcasts, retreats, and individual "heart-to-heart" chats still wrap new devotees lovingly in Maharajji's blanket.

जय

Dassi Ma

In 1993, after having my heart lit up by the words on a cassette tape entitled "Cultivating Compassion," two friends and I decided to drive from southern New Jersey to Washington, D.C. to see the man behind the tape. Seated on a stage designed to look like a conventional living room, Ram Dass spoke from a comfy chair in front of a photo of his guru Maharajji. As Ram Dass spoke of love, compassion, and God in terms that rang true deep inside of me, I watched his face in awe—the white man from Boston was morphing into the form of the Indian man in the blanket in the photograph! I noticed a white aura emanating from his face that made me wonder if I was high. Throughout the talk, I felt that Ram Dass was channeling Maharajji right in front of my eyes! Driving home, I felt like a giddy child—unable to fully comprehend the wonder and love I had just ingested. I had found my teacher, and from then on, all my vacation time was dedicated to Ram Dass retreats and lectures.

Some years after Ram Dass's stroke in 1997, I had a vivid dream that would change the course of my life. In the dream, I was taking care of Ram Dass. There was nothing extraordinary or supernatural about the content of the dream. To the contrary, I was helping Ram Dass with the most mundane aspects of life: giving him pills, tending to him in bed, etc. I woke up sweating with a sense of conviction that I was being called by Maharajji.

The very next day, I went into my job where I had been working as a human resources director for seventeen years, and I inquired about the possibility of an early retirement. Although my wish was not granted immediately, the seed had been planted, and I had faith that I'd end up serving Ram Dass. My life continued on, and sometime later, I ended up visiting San Anselmo where Ram Dass had formerly lived. While volunteering at the Tape Library with Marlene Roeder, Ram Dass's former assistant, she informed me that Ram Dass's caretaker was going to India, and he was in need of someone to step into the role. The next day, Glen and Marilyn Pranno invited me to join them on a trip to Maui for Ram Dass's birthday.

During that trip, after a dinner in Ram Dass's home in Haiku, he wheeled around the kitchen island and said, "So, I hear you want to be my nurse?" That adorable gesture catalyzed fifteen years of wonderful friendship, as I served as a caretaker and assistant for my teacher. During that time, he constantly reminded me that he was "the bait, but Maharajji was the fisherman." I, like so many, cultivated a relationship with Maharajji through Ram Dass.

Leading into the final moments of Ram Dass's life, my duty and spiritual work was to let go entirely. Eager for a clear pathway to the world beyond form, my teacher requested that nobody cling to his body. Ram Dass, who had been seeping deeper and deeper into Maharajji's presence over the decade and a half that I spent with him, was ready to go home. After Ram Dass's final breath, I held a picture of Maharajji over his face and said, "You're free! Go to Maharajji!"

Dr. Rick Frires (Bajrang Das)

My spiritual journey started when I was at the University of Wisconsin, Madison in the late '60s and had my first exposure to the wisdom of the East. Madison was known as the Berkeley of the Midwest in those days, with lots of riots and protest demonstrations. I was initiated into Transcendental Meditation and became a very ardent TM meditator. I found it very useful for getting me through a tumultuous time on a very turbulent campus.

I was admitted to a medical school in Mexico. Before I started my training, I happened upon a copy of *Be Here Now*. I thought, *I'm going to a foreign country, it will be challenging and I'm going to take this along.* On school breaks I would often go to the beach and find a deserted peninsula near Barra de Navidad and hang out by myself with *Be Here Now*. I'd do the intense spiritual practices that were advised in this book. Every word made so much sense to me. I really resonated with Ram Dass's story line, but I was not yet attracted to his guru, Neem Karoli Baba.

After three years I transferred to a medical school in Chicago, starting with a psychiatry rotation and clinical practice. Chicago has a free newspaper, the *Chicago Reader*, that has all the happenings in town. Wouldn't you know it, on the very first page I opened to in the first issue I picked up was this huge picture of Ram Dass with Elizabeth Kubler-Ross and Laura Huxley, advertising an upcoming local seminar on death and dying for healthcare professionals. I had never imagined Ram Dass to be a person that was actually living and accessible, so I was very, very excited because his book had meant so much to me.

Ram Dass walked out onto the stage, way before anybody else was there. He pulled up a straight-backed chair, sat cross-legged on the chair on the side of the stage, and went into a deep meditation. I thought, *Oh my god, this is so cool!* At intermission, I said to my girlfriend, "I've got to tell him how much I love him and thank him for helping me through med school. And how much *Be Here Now* means to me." There was already a big crowd of people around him, giving him flowers or handing him notes, preventing me from getting near him.

I got about twenty feet away and I was looking at him and smiling; he looked right at me. We locked eyes. Suddenly, I had no idea what was happening to me. Molecule by molecule, my body and mind completely dissolved one hundred percent and melded into the universe. "I" was gone, totally gone. I don't know if it lasted two seconds or ten minutes; it was a timeless, blissful state. Then I suddenly was back into my body, half-scared out of my mind, but also in a complete state of wonderment, disbelief, and bliss. Ram Dass was still looking at me and smiling. My hands went into namaste position and I said, "Ram Dass, I love you, thank you, I love you so much." I walked back to my seat, completely changed. I was in a blissful state that lasted for months.

Slowly but surely over ensuing years, I began to realize that Maharajji's grace was transferred to Ram Dass's heart, that Ram Dass was a vehicle for Maharajji's transmission of LOVE to us. This incredible *siddhi* that came to Ram Dass, this incredible power, the root of it was Neem Karoli Baba, Maharajji. I began to realize how incredible, loving, and powerful this guru is. And he is now my guru. Of course, he always was and always will be. We have daily conversations. I have no fear asking him for anything I seem to need because I know that he is there for me and he's got my back. Period. A hundred percent. I'm just a smitten devotee.

ॐ

Govinda

When I was growing up, my mom would play Wayne Dyer tapes and he would talk about Ram Dass, so I kind of knew who he was. Then in college I did mushrooms and read *Be Here Now*, but I wasn't taken with Maharajji. After graduate school I knew that I wanted to unplug from the intellectual world and go to an ashram . . . at least for a couple of days (laughing). I went to a retreat in Yogaville[32] in Virginia with Krishna Das and started hearing the stories about Maharajji.

When *Love Everyone* came out, I was flipping pages and there

---

32 Yogaville (Satchidananda Ashram) in Buckingham, VA, is a spiritual retreat center.

was this picture of Maharajji where his head is tilted and they're doing puja to him. I felt this tingling in my body and this electric glowing coming from him. *Whoa.* I ripped the picture out of the book and put it in a frame on a little altar that I had with a Buddha and not much else. I said, "Here, this is your space. This is for you and I honor you."

At that time I was struggling with how to be of service and how to help myself out of self-hatred. That night I was tossing and turning in bed, when all of a sudden I felt Maharajji enter the room! The hairs on my body stood up and I felt the presence of deep love. It was as though he was holding me from behind, and laughing, laughing, laughing at me, at how silly I was being. I went from complete suffering to a state of bliss and connection. That was the very first time I felt Maharajji's presence.

But I had the sense that there was something unfinished.

Several months later, I decided to take mushrooms. As I was lifting off, I started moving my body and I felt this rising energy, and it began to move me. The energy proceeded to completely take over, moving me through all these intricate spontaneous mudras and fluid movements into different positions with their own natural intelligence. I later came to understand this was kundalini energy and the movements were called *kriyas*. I know this was a psychedelic experience, but I went into a state of oneness with the universe, total bliss in every cell of my body. I was swimming in Maharajji.

After tasting that kind of love, my life really started to change. In the following six months I had these kundalini kriyas coming spontaneously, sometimes daily. I would have to stop what I was doing at work and hide in the bathroom to do these crazy backbends, and I wasn't on any drug. It was a very confusing time. Everything that was keeping me where I was in my life fell apart. The energy was clearing out every aspect of my life.

I felt very drawn to visit Ram Dass; he knew about these kinds of experiences, so I scheduled a personal retreat. Being in his presence really calmed me down. When I got the call to be a caretaker, I was ready. It's been a deepening since then. I feel like the same thing that was happening to me with the involuntary physical clearing of energy is now what I'm doing through serving Ram Dass—making room for love. It's all a continuation of what Maharajji set off. And I'm so grateful. So grateful.

ॐ

Krishna Prem (Evan Bushnell)

In fall of 2011 in Maui, Hawaii, I was interacting with *Be Here Now* for the first time at my dear friend and mentor Bodhi's house. The middle section of art and poetry spoke to me very deeply. Bodhi said, "Oh, you like that book? Do you want to meet the person who wrote it? He lives fifteen minutes down the road, let's go."

We drove to Ram Dass's house and Ram Dass was sitting in the living room by himself. I remember him looking at me and smiling. I don't know what happened in that moment, but I found it hilarious and laughed, like joyful teary-eyed laughter. Ram Dass was also laughing and we continued for some minutes in what felt strangely like a reunion. I could see it shining out of his eyes that he had found what I was seeking. It was like, where have you been? I didn't know I was even looking for you, but here you are.

I traveled back and forth from Oregon to Maui to be around Bodhi, and to show up around Ram Dass. Bodhi and Ram Dass would do events about death together. I would help out and move chairs. Sitaram Dass (Ken Sandin) was at the house as a caretaker at that time and he was getting ready to leave. I was around and available, getting the opportunity to take care of him alongside Dassi Ma.

It was interesting because I loved Ram Dass, but I wasn't looking for a guru. It was strange to see the photos of this Indian man all over the house that I was now living in. At one point I looked at Maharajji and felt him say, "I want to live in your heart."

I said, "It's open to you. You're around and I'm going to be around here, so we might as well figure this out." I was the only person living there other than Dassi Ma and Ram Dass, so it felt like I should get to know our divine roommate Maharajji.

One night I was out late and came home at 2 a.m. I was brushing my teeth and looked over at this photo of Maharajji in the bathroom. I did not understand why he looked so worried. They referred to him as the "Tiger of the Kumaon Hills." I never had seen him worried. I stopped and listened. If I had to put it into words, Maharajji said to me, "Go upstairs right now and check on Ram Dass. If he's okay, look over him like a father would a child, and if not . . ." and then the inner Maharajji music stopped.

I was freshly arrived, so I'd never been up to Ram Dass's room at night. I'd never been up to his room very much at all. I crept up the stairs and turned the corner. Ram Dass was lying on the ground. He had fallen out of his wheelchair. I said to him, "Oh my god, what do I do?"

He looked up at me and said, "You just smile."

At that point, something stopped me dead in my tracks. It felt like I had gotten hit by the most subtle, loving, and kind thunderbolt. My mind stopped but I knew what to do. I got behind him and picked him up off the ground and put him in bed. I checked his bones for breaks and said, "Would you like me to get Dassi Ma?" He said no. "Would you like me to do anything else for you?" And he said no.

I was about to walk out when he said, "How did you find me? I've been down on the ground since nine. I thought that this might be it."

I said, "Maharajji told me." And we didn't talk about it for another year and a half.

It was a profound change in my orientation toward spirit and my life. I understood through direct experience that what they say in the books is true: if you get instructions from your heart or your guru, the highest spiritual practice is to listen and to follow them. I knew then that Maharajji was my guru. I had needed that strong crack open—knowing that something had happened beyond my projection of reality and beyond my rational mind. Just to be an instrument in that, to be a string plucked in that symphony of love, was so fulfilling that it helped me deepen my service to Ram Dass.

राम

Mickey Lemle

I'm sorry I never met Maharajji in person. I have met lots of gurus, swamis, *rinpoches* (teachers of dharma), and teachers; I need to experience a person first-hand and see how I feel about them in my gut. Are they the real thing? But I do feel like I know Maharajji through Ram Dass. When I first met Ram Dass in '74, light came out of him and I think that light was Maharajji's love. He just lit up the stage. Something in Ram Dass's vibration was so powerful. Ram Dass was a conduit for Maharajji's energy, but with his own Jewish humor and flavor so that it was comprehensible to me.

When I was filming *Fierce Grace*, I went to India to film in Kainchi. I was scheduled to go on to Vrindavan and film there next, but after our filming in Kainchi, I knew I had what I needed for the film. But I wanted to go see Vrindavan anyway, even if I was not filming. Within an hour of getting to the ashram, I met Jivandath Baba, who had been Maharajji's chant master. With a translator, we had a wonderful conversation that went way into the night. He was talking about Maharajji and love. He said, "There's physical yoga, there's intellectual yoga, but they all take training and you have to really work at it. In bhakti yoga, all you have to do is open your heart and sing to God. It's the easiest form of getting close to God, and Maharajji was a real bhakti."

The next morning, we continued our conversation. Suddenly, in the middle of talking about leela, love, and Maharajji, he said, "Listen, they're going to tell you to take a right. Don't listen to them. Go straight." I thought, "That's weird," then he went on talking about life and love and beauty. Again he said, "They're going to say go right. Don't listen to them. Go straight." This happened three times in the course of the conversation. I thought, "Well, he's a nice old guy, you know." Then a car arrived to take me to Agra.

There was to be a full moon that night, and I wanted to see the Taj Mahal in the light of the full moon. As the car came into Agra, we stopped at a red light. The driver pulled down his window and asked a rickshaw driver, "Where is the Taj View Hotel?" He was told to take a right. I saw a substantial building about five blocks up that looked pretty *pukka* (very good), and I was thinking that must be the Taj View Hotel. The driver took a right and things started to get seedier and seedier. After driving several blocks, the driver asked somebody else, who told him to make a U-turn and where he had made the right turn, to go back onto the road that we had been on, and to go straight. Five blocks later there was the hotel.

I thought, the chant master predicted this, and told me three times for emphasis. If he knew this, perhaps I should listen to all that stuff he was saying about love and Maharajji. When I got back to the States, I called Ram Dass and said it felt like Maharajji's energy. He said, *absolutely*.

श्री

My way into Ram Dass was through his book with Mirabai Bush, *Compassion in Action*; it was part of an individual development plan and leadership program I was in with Bose Corporation. Then in the early 2000s I started going to Ram Dass satsang gatherings at the Open Secret bookstore in San Rafael. They had a Maharajji murti in their shrine room, which was the first time I saw a physical image of Maharajji. A few times I found myself crying and wondered, "Why am I crying?"

The last time I saw Ram Dass at Open Secret, I introduced myself and told him I was leaving a twenty-five-year career at Bose and moving to Maui. He said, "Moving to Maui? I keep telling my friends I want to move to Maui and I'm hoping one of them comes through for me! What are you going to do on Maui?" he asked.

I said, "I keep thinking I'm going to work at a grocery store."

Ram Dass said, "Maybe you'll learn how to give away food like Maharajji." From that point on I started paying more attention to the Maharajji part.

When Ram Dass came to Maui and then wound up in the hospital following the 2004 Retreat, I was asked to visit him frequently. During one visit, he said, "I've decided to stay on Maui and we're going to need a lot of help. If you would get with Sridhar and help him help me, that would be great."

I was working in Mana Foods in Paia at the time (I really did get a job at the grocery store), and I did learn how to give away food, literally giving it away until they almost fired me. I had developed a clientele that knew I was the guy to see for deeply discounted produce, so I knew at least one person that did each of the different services that Ram Dass would need. Each person I asked said, "Ram Dass? I would LOVE to help out Ram Dass!" I passed along their contact information to Sridhar.

After Ram Dass got out of the hospital, Krishna Das came to visit in December 2004. I was working in the produce department and there's Krishna Das. I had his CDs but had never been to a kirtan. I said, "Hey yo, Krishna Das. I'm a big fan of yours." He was polite and thanked me. Five minutes later, I'm down on my knees with the dustpan when Krishna Das came over and asked, "Do you know how to get to Ram Dass's house? I just flew in, and I knew I'd find somebody here to help."

I was becoming aware that something more significant was going on than I had first understood about my move to Maui.

When K.K. Sah was traveling from India for his first visit with Ram Dass in his new home, he flew to Maui with a stop in Honolulu. I agreed to escort K.K. from Honolulu to Maui and get him to Ram Dass's house. I found K.K. outside the airport terminal and introduced myself. I knew who he was from the *Fierce Grace* movie. For the next two and a half hours, he told me one Maharajji story after another, non-stop. When we got to the house, the front doors were open and Ram Dass was waiting in front of the puja table. K.K. darted into the house, crying while he dove full *dunda pranam* to Ram Dass's feet. Ram Dass was crying, I was crying. There was so much love in the room.

Maharajji's finishing touch for me was a public Robert Svoboda event I organized for the Center of Spiritual Studies. I could tell that there really wasn't a lot of synergy between Ram Dass and Robert. Every volunteer that I had lined up fell away for that night. The guy that was supposed to do sound that night bailed. And it was assumed that because I had worked at Bose, I knew everything there was to know about audio (laughing). At Bose, I had been in their consumer home entertainment division, not the pro division. I knew what a mixer was, and I could figure out how to work XLR cables, but I had never dealt with them firsthand before.

One of the things you learn in the Bose Home Hi-Fi division is that you don't want any wires showing. I set up the stage, patching together runs for the microphones and runs for the speakers. I got it all set up and ran the cables underneath the carpet on the stage so no one would see them.

When Robert and Ram Dass arrived, Ram Dass decided he wanted to sit in a different spot than the one I had set up, which required adjusting the microphone and the mic stand. There was not much room to move the cable, so I yanked and yanked. If this didn't work, I'd have to get them off the stage and lift the carpet, pull out the cables, put the carpet back down, and we had maybe a hundred people sitting in the audience. Finally, on one yank I suddenly had all this room. Well, either I had extra length I didn't think I had, or the cable had come undone. I went back to the soundboard, they started talking and nobody could hear anything. I finally got Robert's mic working through the mixer, but I couldn't manage Ram Dass's vocal. I was starting to sweat. Then out of the blue Ram Dass's mic came on. Okay, I now had full control through the mixer for both their vocals.

The night went on, everything was good as far as functionality. After everybody left, I was breaking everything down. I lifted the rug and sure enough, the cables were undone on Ram Dass's microphone. But it had worked! How had it worked without the cables connected?

We had a picture of Maharajji above the stage. I looked up and the picture was smiling at me. I started crying. There's no way that it should have worked at all. Not a chance. Yet it had. And that was it for me because it defied everything I knew.

म्

Sitaram Dass

I first read *Be Here Now* when I was twenty years old. Soon after, I was living out of my car and devoting myself to spiritual practice. This culminated in a profound and confusing experience with Christ. I spent the next year trying to connect more with Christ, but I was stuck. I couldn't find any images that I resonated with, and I didn't have a solid framework to understand that experience.

When I came across *Miracle of Love*, I fell in love. I couldn't stop reading the stories. One story really stuck out—where Ram Dass and a group of people are on a bus and meet Maharajji, who knew they were coming before they did. How could this be true? How could he know? I couldn't believe it, but at the same time I didn't think Ram Dass was lying. I really needed to meet Ram Dass, so my friends and I bought plane tickets on a whim. I learned about the heart-to-hearts Ram Dass did over Skype and sent in an email. "Hey, I'm going to be on Maui. Maybe I could do a heart-to-heart in person?" I explained my story, but I never heard a response.

The bus story is all about us thinking we're making decisions, but you know who's really doing it. I had no logical reason to think I was going to meet Ram Dass, but somehow I knew deep down it was going to work out. I sent another email and did hear a response, but it was a "maybe." Yet, I just knew. Once on Maui, I got the call from Dassi Ma, and I did get to meet Ram Dass, who was so sweet and loving. I told him the whole story, and Ram Dass said, matter of factly, "No one comes in front of me unless Maharajji sent them." I didn't know what that meant, but it felt profound.

My friend said, "Ram Dass, we're thinking about moving to Maui so we can be closer to you. If you have any work you need done around the house, we'll do it."

He said, "I've been given this big house to live in for as long as I'm alive, but we always need help. If you were here, maybe you could help with something." And that was all I needed to hear.

As I was falling asleep on the beach that night I looked out, and I could see two beings hovering off the ground. One was Jesus and one was Maharajji, and they were shape-shifting back and forth into each other. Over the next few months I shifted my focus towards the form of Maharajji because I had a real picture of him and his stories, unlike those of Jesus, were modern day.

During my time serving at Ram Dass's house, I got to meet some of the people that were on that bus and hear the story out of their own mouths. It shattered the question of whether these stories were allegory or real.

ॐ

Vishnu Dass

I was living in Santa Cruz, California, deeply involved in the Burning Man community. I was doing a lot of psychedelics when I found myself starting to experience the unity of all things. My focus changed and I started to watch documentaries about Eastern spiritual traditions. When I watched *Fierce Grace* and saw the video footage of Maharajji, my hair stood up. When the film was over, Ram Dass felt like the only person I would be able to relate to. I prayed with all of my heart after I watched *Fierce Grace*, and cried, "I'm wasting my life, I'm wasting away. Please put me in service."

A couple of weeks later I found a cookbook on the sidewalk in Santa Cruz. I had been born and raised in Arkansas, and this was a cookbook from the Junior Auxiliary of Pine Bluff, Arkansas, where my great-grandmother, Rita White, was born. I took it home and put it on the shelf. About a week later, this little gray-haired lady showed up on my front porch, looking for a room to rent in my house. My landlord had sent her there. I felt a deep resonance with her immediately. I asked, "What's your name?"

"Rita Green."

"Wow, my great-grandmother's name was Rita White! Where are you from, Rita Green?"

She said, "Well, I was born in Pine Bluff, Arkansas." That hit me.

We toured through the house and the entire time I could see that she was feeling something. She said, "I really like it here."

"Well, do you have any spiritual practices?" I was studying with a Tibetan Buddhist teacher at the time.

"No, but I have a guru. Neem Karoli Baba. I've been the temple gardener at Kainchi for thirty-three years."

I broke open at that moment.

I knew Maharajji was real the moment Rita Green showed up on my front porch. She was there for a couple of weeks, and finally I told her about what I had felt after watching *Fierce Grace*. She said, "Wow, I trained the lady that's caring for Ram Dass right now. If you want to hang out with Ram Dass, I'm a pretty good reference."

I gave away everything I owned and put a sign over my door that said, "Free Store, Donations Accepted." I had hundreds of cannabis plants I was growing in our three-car garage, and I left it all. I came to Maui with $200, two backpacks, and Ram Dass's phone number.

I met a woman, a brilliant first-generation Russian Jewish Communist atheist artist named Stephanie Farago, who lived a couple of blocks away from the hut I was renting. She had this huge art archive that she needed help putting together, so I went to work for her. I prayed, "Is this where I'm supposed to be?" I went up to her bookshelf, closed my eyes, and pulled a random book off the shelf. I opened it to a picture of Maharajji. It said, "Our Beloved Neem Karoli Baba." The book was by Swami Ramananda, a close devotee of Anandamayi Ma. I knew I was where I was supposed to be.

When she got lung cancer and sadly passed away, I was left in charge of her estate and the artist's estate. The artist, Steven

Arnold, was a surrealist black-and-white photographer, a student of Salvador Dalí, who understood the nondual nature of consciousness. Carlos Vishwanath, one of the satsang who had been in India with Maharajji, had introduced Steven Arnold to Salvador Dalí.

On Summer Solstice 2011, Ram Dass gave me a name. In the psychedelic or art communities, to be able to say *I have a guru . . .* there's this idea that you're giving up your power to something outside of yourself. It took me a while to have the bravery to say, my name is Vishnu Dass, and I have a guru who left his body in 1973 but who's just as active now as ever.

I was around Ram Dass for nearly ten years. I kind of became the household kirtan wallah. Now I am using Arnold's trust to set up a foundation for artists with AIDS, so I have found a way to serve.

ᚦᚢ

Zach Leary (Ramana)

My Dad [Timothy Leary] had a deep love for Ram Dass. They had a brotherhood and a bond that was unshakeable. But my dad didn't embrace the bhakti path or Neem Karoli Baba; he always had a bit of a tongue-in-cheek disdain for it in a way. Not so much for the practice as much as for the whole guru system because he was so anti-authoritarian.

Ram Dass was always around, especially when I was a kid. I wondered, "Why is he always smiling? He looked you in the eyes with this beam of light, and I never knew anybody else like that. I first read *Be Here Now* when I was a teenager and a Dead Head. I would go on my own exploratory journeys with psychedelics and *Be Here Now*. I knew who Neem Karoli Baba was and thought that's interesting, but I left it at that for a long time. I gravitated toward Ram Dass and listened to his talks from the Ram Dass tape library. I read every Ram Dass book, but I always felt the Maharajji connection was his thing, not mine.

My life took some zigs and zags, especially right after my dad's death. I got into substance abuse and hit a dark period in my life. As I got clean and into recovery, I developed a meditation practice, then an asana practice. One day it hit me, "I know Ram Dass." I had been to his house many times in Northern California, but I hadn't seen him in four years, since he moved to Hawaii. I felt so lucky that I could pick up the phone and go see him, which I did in 2008. I had a moment when all these different pieces of the puzzle of my life came together.

In 1981 Ram Dass had given me a hand-drawn picture that he had done of Maharajji for my parents. It says, "To Timothy and Barbara, Love, Richard." They called him Richard. Now it's the center of my altar. I'd been carrying it around with me forever. I brought it to Ram Dass during that trip in 2008, which was the first moment I went beyond Ram Dass and connected to Maharajji. I felt like I'd come home, and I was overcome with tears of joy. Tears of sadness and tears of regret, too, that I had waited so long and now Ram Dass was so much older. I could have been with him so much more. I feel like I'm the classic case of the teacher was there, but the student wasn't ready.

Now I have the deep love of a devotee, and that's the bedrock of my life. A second chapter, and I'm so grateful.

7
Retreats
and Yatras

Within you there is a stillness and sanctuary
to which you can retreat at any time and be yourself.
—HERMANN HESSE

Retreats provide an opportunity to leave the everyday world behind for a time and dedicate yourself to nourishing your spiritual development. You can absorb words of wisdom from teachers, open your heart through chanting, enter a deeper communion with yourself in meditation, and be strengthened and enriched by satsang, our family of the heart.

Throughout the decades, Ram Dass held retreats in many venues around the world, but once he moved to Maui and couldn't travel easily, all his retreats were held there—both large gatherings, like the Open Your Heart in Paradise retreats at Napili Kai in Maui that brought together over four hundred devotees at a time and became a major turning point in many lives, and personal retreats in the guest cottage at Ram Dass's home. Aching hearts felt relief, pain turned to joy, and Maharajji's presence was unmistakable.

One of the defining moments of the large Maui retreats was the "mala ceremony." The hundreds of retreatants formed a long line and one by one came up to Ram Dass to receive a hand mala, strung with a thread from Maharajji's blanket, from his hands. As *Sri Ram Jai Ram* was chanted throughout the hours the ceremony took, each person was able to look into Ram Dass's eyes and speak their heart, and then Ram Dass "introduced" them to his guru, indicating the large portrait of Maharajji—a deeply profound moment for many.

But there were also many other types of retreats (pre-pandemic)—kirtan workshops and retreats with Krishna Das, Jai Uttal, or other kirtan wallahs; immersion retreats by the Love Serve Remember Foundation centered on Ram Dass's teachings; events at the Hanuman Temple in Taos; annual bhandaras across the country; and gatherings of devotees for celebrations. Through their experiences at these retreats, many have been plugged into the living heart of the satsang. When we once again gather safely in a group, what has of necessity been a virtual connection will be real hugs again. Although Ram Dass and Maharajji may not be there in body, their loving presence will certainly be felt.

Many who have sought a deeper connection to Maharajji have at times undertaken a yatra, meaning a pilgrimage to a holy place, in which the journey itself is as important as the destination. Yatras to Maharajji's temples and the sacred places of India, as an individual or as part of a group, are a way to experience Maharajji's presence in the places he established and a way to come closer to the divine through the sacred energy of the ancient land itself and the blessings of its saints and sages.

राम

Adrian Hooper

I didn't know anything about Ram Dass or Maharajji. My husband grew up with *Be Here Now,* and a family friend of his had gone to the retreat in Maui and talked about how amazing it was. My husband asked me, "What do you think about going to this Ram Dass retreat? It's in Maui." Yes! I was picturing piña coladas, walks on the beach, sunbathing. I had injured my foot on a rogue needle in a pair of wool slippers and, in the midst of dreaming about Maui, I was offered a settlement—the exact amount of money needed to cover the cost of our flights and accommodations. Just like that, we were off to Maui.

The retreat was totally not what I expected. I had no idea about the amount of love that is generated when all the devotees are together and chanting. I was saying the words to the chants completely wrong, but I could feel the presence, the energy, the spirit of the Lord, the love. During the opening ceremony I saw Ram Dass for the first time. I had to blink my eyes a few times as I saw him glowing, blending in with the background, and pulsing and warping as if I were having a psychedelic trip (I was sober). The next day I did get to walk on the beach and a perfectly heart-shaped piece of coral washed up at my feet. I now think of this moment as my bhakti initiation.

Then there was the mala ceremony. During the ceremony, I felt a very potent force beaming from Ram Dass to me, like love from the eternal mother. Ram Dass then motioned to his right to introduce me to his guru. I knelt in front of the large portrait of Maharajji and felt an ocean of love. I was lost in tears, filled with love and peace and joy. My life was forever changed.

Andreas

Over the last few years, I was pulled to Maui through a series of gut-wrenching events and into Ram Dass's presence through an ex who was close to him. After the May retreat I remember telling Ram Dass, "I think I'm in the satsang now."

Ram Dass looked at me and said, in this very beautiful and knowing way, "Yeah, you're in Maharajji's satsang."

About three months after that retreat, I went to Garchen Rinpoche's Tibetan Buddhist center in central Arizona to dive deep into practice. Alone in a cabin, I read *Be Here Now,* which I had randomly picked up at the Taos ashram, from cover to cover for the first time, and for those three weeks I lived it. Here I was in this Tibetan Buddhist center with a powerful rinpoche holding that space . . . and I went full bhakti.

I had a photo of Maharajji I had been given at the ashram and felt very connected to him, but even in deep states of meditation I kept being disturbed by thoughts of my ex-lover; he had been my initial way into the heart and had introduced me to Maharajji. I asked Maharajji for a clear sign about him. That night I had my first and only Maharajji dream. At the end of the dream, there was a moment's close-up of Maharajji's face and he winked at me—a very mischievous and all-knowing wink-wink that still gives me goosebumps.

The next day was the end of my retreat, and I turned my phone on to integrate back into the world. Instantly it buzzed with a text saying my ex was marrying someone he had just met. *Aah!* Maharajji had given me the most black-and-white answer possible.

On my drive back to California, I went to the Hanuman temple in Taos and stayed for three weeks doing seva at the temple. Sitting in the old temple one day, I saw an ancient copy of the *Ramayana.* I remembered when I was in India about eight years earlier as a backpacker on an adventure, not as a spiritual seeker, that I had spent time in Hampi, which ended up being my favorite place in India. I had rock climbed with a friend to this temple where there were a bunch of babas, and one baba spent all day expounding on this book to me, which I now realized was the *Ramayana*. I understood nothing of what he said.

I was telling this to Hanuman Das, and he said, "You were in Hampi? That's where Hanuman was born."

I was almost in tears that the only temple I went to in India was a Hanuman temple in Hampi. I had this strong knowing then that Maharajji or Hanuman had grabbed me back then, and I have been taken care of ever since.

राम

Anjani Devi

Each time I attended the retreat in Maui I would see people loving Maharajji, and each year I thought to myself, "Awww, that's sweet." Before leaving the 2014 retreat, I bought *Miracle of Love* to see what all the hoopla was about. I read it slowly over months, a few stories at a time. Then came the random day I started wearing the pendant I had received in 2014, with Hanuman facing out and Maharajji in. When I was in a yoga class in downward dog, I looked down to see his smiling face and I smiled back, as if he were there with me. Then I started talking to Maharajji when I needed help with anything from job decisions to creamy versus crunchy peanut butter at the market.

A couple of months before the 2015 retreat, I asked Maharajji, "So, are you my guru or what? I'm either talking to you or talking to the other Gemini in my head, which is not a good sign this early in life." I needed an "aha" moment, an undeniable experience of absolute unconditional love. I needed data to please my type A/ OCD/Gemini nurse brain. If I was going to follow a dude I've never known, this needed to be in an evidence-based practice.

The morning I flew to Maui, I wrote Maharajji a letter outlining the parameters for what I needed in order to know with absolute conviction that he wanted me to follow him as a devotee. I needed him to stand with me during the mala ceremony, for Ram Dass to see him physically with me, for Ram Dass to verbalize that he saw Maharajji with me and that he was in fact my guru. In my mind this was simple and clean.

The day before the mala ceremony, when Krishna Das started singing Sri Ram, I closed my eyes in meditation and found myself in India, sitting on the sand, singing *Sri Ram Jai Ram Jai Jai Ram* for Maharajji on his takhat. When I returned, I had to remind myself where I was. The next day at the ceremony, I was able to share love and gratitude with Ram Dass and collect my mala. And then as I turned to Maharajji's picture, I did indeed see Maharajji. I physically collapsed and dissolved in tears. Although all my parameters had not been met, I fell into his darshan for the first time and fell in love with Maharajji forever.

ᐈᒼᒥᐧ

Ayden Gramm

I had pictures of several saints on the walls of my meditation room, but I didn't have a picture of Maharajji. I printed out a picture of him and put it on the windowsill. So that's where it began.

I went to the ashram in Taos, and then I went to the Maui retreat a couple of months later. In the beginning I experienced some very intense insecurity, and all this darkness assaulted me. I would have meals with people and couldn't focus on their faces. I couldn't even remember who I sat with. I felt very disconnected from my body, like my limbs weren't attached to me.

At one of the sessions, Jai Uttal told the story of Hanuman. He got to the very end where Hanuman digs his fingernails inside his chest and reveals Ram and Sita in his heart. I began to choke up. In an instant I knew who Maharajji was and who Hanuman was, and that they were one and the same. Then I was back in my body.

I remembered reading in *By His Grace* that if you kept repeating "Neem Karoli Baba, Neem Karoli Baba, Neem Karoli Baba," he would come to you. I closed my eyes and started internally saying, "Neem Karoli Baba, Neem Karoli Baba, Neem Karoli Baba." Suddenly, he was in front of me in my mind's eye! He was joyfully dancing with his arms up, bouncing back and forth from one foot to the other, really jolly. I choked up even more.

Jai began to sing the Chalisa. I kept getting higher and higher as we did several Chalisas. I realized I was connected to everyone around me. The feeling kept going that night at kirtan. By the end of the night, I didn't want to go to sleep because I didn't want the feeling to go away.

The next morning I did yoga. After the class, we were given some prasad from Kainchi. I ate the prasad and was walking back along the road to my hotel, when I remembered a dream that I had had a couple of months earlier. *I walked into this hut and there was an old man leaning against the wall, wrapped in a blanket, but I couldn't see his face or his head. He wouldn't reveal himself until I said his name. I knew his name, but I couldn't say it even though it was right on the tip of my tongue.*

As soon as I remembered this dream, I was back to the night before and how I said his name and he came to me. In that instant, I realized what he was telling me: *if you call me, I will come. I will be there for you.* My heart exploded open. I wept and wept as I walked down the street. When I got to my hotel room, I collapsed on the bed and kept sobbing. I realized he had always been there through all the hard times and all the good times. I was home.

We had the mala ceremony that day. I was so blasted open that I felt completely naked, totally seen through. When I went to get my mala, Ram Dass said, "Whoa!" And he smacked me on my head the way I knew Maharajji had done. I went up to the puja table and grabbed my heart and put it on the table and said, "It's yours. I'm yours. Take me, Maharajji." That was it for me. Bhakti is my path, and Maharajji is my guide, Maharajji and Hanuman.

प्प

Betsy Stevens and James Cox

BETSY: When I started doing yoga, I had this great yoga instructor who played Krishna Das, and there was something about Krishna Das's voice that called me, so for many years I would drive all the way up to New York by myself to chant with Krishna Das. I had come from a highly dysfunctional family, had been abused by my stepfather, and suffered from PTSD.

When I got to Maui, Ram Dass told us that Maharajji had handpicked every one of us to come to this retreat for a reason. I went for a walk on Napili Kai beach. I was saying to my boyfriend that I had never felt so loved by so many amazing people and that the satsang was my new family. I felt incredibly blessed. For some reason I looked down in that moment and saw something in the wave as it washed over my feet. There are no shells in the sand at this beach, or rocks for that matter. I scooped my hand down and picked up a red heart made of sea glass. I said, "Do you know how miraculous this is? Maharajji knows that when I was a kid I

164

used to love collecting sea glass at the beach with my aunt." I cried for days.

That's when I knew I didn't need to meet him in person; he has been with me my entire life, I just hadn't seen it before.

JAMES: I didn't know anything about Maharajji or Hanuman before going to that retreat. Betsy and I had met on Match.com literally a week after she got back from her first trip to Maui. We went on a date and she was still glowing! When April rolled around and she was going to go to Maui again, I said, "Well, you're not going without me." I had no background in yoga or chanting, but when we went, I connected to what was going on at the retreat. My spiritual beliefs for the previous thirty years had been a more gnostic interior spirituality. As Ram Dass said, "Isn't it amazing that we all got here by different paths?"

After the retreat was over—five days of bliss and learning—we're walking along the beach when Betsy had this revelation. She said, "I feel so blessed that I have this spiritual family, this satsang now." The red sea glass in the shape of a heart floated into her hand, and she was bawling. It was such a beautiful miracle. To me it powerfully illustrated Maharajji in the universe.

Ever since that day we've been collecting photos of hearts every-where we go. For me, the hearts signify Maharajji saying: *you're on the right path.* I'll be driving down the road thinking about some-thing I need to do, and I look up and see a heart. From a mindfulness standpoint and from a validation standpoint, it helps me to become more aware.

ऱ्म्

Chuck Mitchell

June 2, 1991

Dear Ram Dass and Friends,

I'm 42 years old and first came across *Be Here Now* when I was given a copy as a Valentine's gift in 1973. I kept the book with me through the years although my interest in spiritual development was slowly buried under the desires for material gain and societal pleasures. 1985 was a year of major transformation for me. I had to find a way to satisfy a raging hunger in my soul. One of the books that came my way was *The Only Dance There Is*. It answered many questions and made me realize that there was a possibility to wake up.

In the past few years I've attended your talks when you came to Austin (Texas). Last March I went to Houston for your weekend retreat. That was the experience I'd like to share with you.

For all these years I have never been able to remember Neem Karoli Baba's name. I'd read the books and discussed his teachings, but never could remember his name. Boy, has that changed. The first day of the workshop I was moved by the talks, chanting, and especially the gifts of the mala and the *aditya hridayam punyam* chant[33]. The next morning, as soon as I awakened, I reached over beside the bed, picked up the mala you had given me, and began to repeat the "aditya" mantra. Immediately I was filled with the presence of Maharajji, enfolding and absorbing me. My mind's eye could see him smiling at me. My heart was bursting open with his love for me, and mine for him. I experienced a deep peace—a peace that has not left me since then.

---

33 *Aditya hridayam punyam sarv shatru bena shenam:* All evil vanishes from life for those who keep the sun in their heart.

Maharajji is a constant component of my consciousness now. I'm not talking about some blissed-out, air-headed, aren't-I-special fantasy. This is more like a deep, cool, peaceful pool of water rising out of the depths of my being that reassures me constantly.

ॐ

Dasaratha

I was nineteen years old and on mushrooms when an artist friend gave me Ram Dass's *Be Here Now* to look at, which gave me a transmission that had a big impact on my life. It set me on a path. I read a lot of the books Ram Dass recommended, so most of my spiritual life was in books.

I got married and had kids, but something was missing. My dad died in 2015, and a series of things happened that led me into a deep depression. I'd come home from work and be on the couch drinking and watching TV. I'd reached a point where I didn't want to live anymore, and I didn't want my kids to see their father like this. One day my wife and I were listening to Duncan Trussell's podcast. Duncan was talking about the Ram Dass retreat in Maui and my wife, who was never interested in all the Ram Dass stuff, said, "Why don't you go to one of those retreats?" I'm like, are you serious? Do you want to go with me? She said, "NOOOOO, but maybe you should go."

Lama Surya Das, Duncan, and Trevor Hall were going to be there. I love Trevor Hall's music. All right, I'm going. I was really intimidated because I was a complete introvert, and I didn't know what to expect. I thought it was going to be a bunch of LA yoga ladies, you know? I had read *The Near and the Dear*, *By His Grace*, and *Love Everyone*. I wanted to see if what I had read was real. Do these people really love each other? Is that possible? The biggest loves in my life were my wife and kids. If I could learn to love everybody like that, what would life be like?

At the retreat, I could feel the love coming off Ram Dass. Then it became clear to me, oh, this isn't about Ram Dass, it's about Maharajji. That clicked. Then came the mala ceremony. I got in line behind Trevor and Emory, and Duncan was behind me with his girlfriend. As I waited in line, I was thinking about all the spiritual writings I'd read that always said the master will appear when the student is ready. I was feeling sorry for myself, thinking, this is great for Raghu and for Krishna Das and Ram Dass. They've had Maharajji. How come I'm in this all alone?

Ram Dass was explaining how the malas had a thread of Maharajji's blanket. Right as I was wondering where's my guru, Ram Dass said, "And then I'm going to introduce you to Maharajji," and he motioned towards the picture. As soon as Ram Dass said, I'm going to introduce you to Maharajji, it was like he said, you are never alone. All of a sudden I got overwhelmed with emotion and started bawling. I didn't understand what was happening. It was the biggest cry I've ever had. Trevor turned around and held me and tried to console me. Duncan had his hand on my shoulder. It took me about half the line, but then I got composed. When I got up to Ram Dass, the crying started all over again, snot and all. I kneeled down in front of him, and he stroked the back of my hand to console me. And my life's been completely different since that day.

When I got home from the retreat, all the relationships in my life transformed. The baggage I had with my mom was gone, and I could tell her I loved her. My brother is a born-again Christian; we didn't talk for a year because he thought Ram Dass was dragging me and my family to hell. But he's seen such a huge change in me the last four years that he's come to respect Ram Dass, to whatever degree he can. My wife has been supportive, even if we're not on the same page. She saw the healing in me. She's helped me with the Ram Dass Fellowship I put together in Orlando. Now she has a Maharajji pendant she wears all the time. I brought my kids to a retreat in Ojai, and they loved it. When they met everybody and experienced the environment, they said, "You make so much more sense to us now!"

I did a personal retreat with Ram Dass at his house in Maui. I talked about my family and he told me, "You've done something I've never been able to do. You have made family and satsang one." I asked him for a name, and he said, "I'm going to ask Maharajji." Ram Dass meditated for a few minutes, opened his eyes and said, "Dasaratha, the father of Ram."

ॐ

"Swami" Dave

In middle school in West Seattle, we started experimenting with psychedelics. We were too young for Vietnam and no one was watching the store. Why not have some fun? But I was the odd ball, in that I was always the God seeker. Later I read Yogananda's *Autobiography of a Yogi*, then I got hold of *Be Here Now* and was knocked out by it. There was something about Maharajji . . .

My mom was Catholic, and my dad wasn't, so I was loosely raised with CCD classes[34], but the approach was fear-based for me. As a young adult, when I would to go to church, I'd always run into somebody who thought my faith wasn't quite right because I had this weird Hindu/Buddhist stuff going on. They would tell me, dude, that's dangerous. You're not on the right path. I quit going to church.

---

34 Confraternity of Christian Doctrine, the religious education arm of the Catholic church.

My wife said, well, why don't you seek out other people that are like you? But when I went to many spiritual places, they almost seemed competitive, like who's meditating the best or who's got the most spirituality. The Maui retreat is the only thing I do in a group. It's so loving and welcoming. I talk to people there who have done the most intense spiritual practices around the world, and they often say that there's nothing quite like this retreat; you get to swim in an ocean of love with people from completely different backgrounds, religious affiliations, cultural and ethnic differences.

A couple of years ago I was the top bidder on a photograph of Maharajji in the retreat silent auction. Mike Crall came up to me and said, "You know Dave, that's the picture of Maharajji that was on Ram Dass's puja table for twenty-five years." Wow! I am always talking to Maharajji in that picture. If I quiet myself down, I can get in alignment with what I perceive to be Maharajji's energy. Getting tuned in with Maharajji freed me to have a relationship with Christ. When I meditate, I'll think about Jesus and about Maharajji. I'm so appreciative that they were willing to take form on the earth for us.

Debbie Wallis

I had a beautiful marriage of twenty-eight years, then my husband died unexpectedly of a heart attack in his sleep. I couldn't make sense of it. After Craig passed, I was angry with God. That was when my true awakening began and I started my spiritual journey. I would sit for many hours in meditation and receive downloads of direction on how to handle things, and even a long "external" auditory message in his voice. Throughout my life I've experienced many strange phenomena and have had two full apparitions from deceased spirits. I wanted to understand if the things I was experiencing were, in fact, real. I came upon Ram Dass's teachings. And in December 2019, with a lot of apprehension about traveling on my own, I attended one of his retreats in Maui.

On one of the first days of the retreat, Krishna Das was talking; it appeared he went inside himself, as though searching for what he wanted to say next. Suddenly a thought of my husband popped into my head. Just then, Krishna Das opened his eyes, looked in my direction, and said, "It's okay to live." I thought I was going to explode right there. As soon as I could leave the pavilion, I went straight back to my room and broke down in hysterical tears. I was obviously harboring some survivor's guilt that left me unable to move forward without Craig. Instantaneously, my physical heart, which had been hurting since he had left the physical world, no longer was in pain. That release of energy was the grace of a higher being, for sure.

The last day of the retreat I was very sad and was in a "poor me" mood as I ate alone. I went to the pavilion for Krishna Das's final kirtan and looked for the people I had been hanging with but couldn't find them, so I grabbed my shawl and went to sit in one of the chairs down by the beach, trying to understand my emotions. It was a gorgeous night, the waves slapped on the shoreline and the moon was full.

I had made an American Indian drum earlier that summer as part of my healing process. There was a whole Native ritual around birthing your drum. I was to follow up by doing a private ceremony when the right time presented itself. I had taken a little deer hide piece of the drum to Hawaii with the full intention that I was going to release my husband and the pain I had been carrying for those three years. I called out to Maharajji, "Please help me to release all of this sadness in my heart."

I had just spoken to Maharajji when I heard a drum beating. The sound was close to me. I remembered Ram Dass's statement about how Maharajji would show up in drag. The drumming was getting closer and closer; I saw another retreat attendee beating his native drum to the right of me. What were the odds of that?

I went to him and asked, "I wonder if you'd do me a favor? Would you walk behind me as I step into the ocean and drum?" He agreed without asking any questions. I walked down to the water, he a few feet behind me drumming away as the waves washed over my feet, over my ankles, and then over my thighs. After saying a few words to my husband, I pushed the deer hide piece into the sand under the water. Then I washed my arms and my face and thanked the gentleman. He hugged me and that was that. I never saw him again.

When I wrote in my journal that night, on the top of the page was a verse written by Alan Cohen: "The spirit of love arranges all meetings in divine order for the highest good of all concerned." It was a tremendous healing for me.

Duncan Kerr

The last year has been an incredible unfolding for me. I got introduced to Jack Kornfield and sat with him at Spirit Rock. I have a dear friend, Andrew, who came to this retreat in Maui last year. Every time we got together he would tell me I should come to this retreat.

About a month before the fall retreat, he said, "You're coming, right?" I gave in and said okay. It was all sold out and he "magicked" a ticket. I thought, I've got to do a little bit of background. I had a copy of *Be Here Now* but had never read the book before. I listened to a few old lectures while I was driving, and I started to do some chanting in the car.

I came to the retreat, and it unfolded in a beautiful way with all these wonderful teachers and Ram Dass's presence. On day three of the retreat, I was sitting with my dear friend Danielle during a very intense morning session. At the end, we both looked at each other and said, okay, we need to get in the ocean. We swam out and were floating with our hearts up to the sky and this question manifested: *Why am I here?* What came to me was that I've got this deep need to be seen.

That night in the dining room we sat at a table next to the teachers' table. We were having our food when Ram Dass and entourage came in. I was sitting with my back to the wall and I looked at Ram Dass as he was going past me. He turned, sat up straight in his wheelchair, and looked right at me. I felt this incredible energy, this deep, beautiful, powerful, gentle, fragile glow, which I had glimpsed in the sessions. Now it was so profound. It was like a delicate leaf or a flower right in my heart, fluttering in the wind, vibrating. I had to close my eyes for a moment. When I opened my eyes again, Ram Dass was still looking at me. Then he passed by and was gone.

Time stopped. I was fully aware, I could hear and see everything, but I couldn't move. I realized my wish had been granted. I'd been *seen* for the first time with complete unconditional love. I knew that was Maharajji coming through.

ॐ

Ellen Keiser

August 16, 1994
Dear Monkey Types,

In the summer of 1986, I went to Lama for a Ram Dass retreat, a much-needed time of peace to sort out the chaos that was my life at that time. I was in a deep depression, unsure of where to go next, but Lama seemed like a safe haven. During the week I was there, I was walking near the dome one day looking down, as depressed people do. On the ground I saw a tiny silver reflecting heart. I picked it up and put it in my pocket. When I got home from Lama, I put the little heart in my jewelry box and left it there. It seemed special.

About six months later, I was cleaning my house and I found the little heart on the coffee table in the living room. I stuffed it into my pocket and went on with my cleaning. As I vacuumed the stairs, I found it again, thinking it had fallen out of my pocket. I put it back in my pocket again. When my cleaning expedition brought me upstairs, I went to put the heart back in my jewelry box, and I found that the original one was already there. I now had three reflecting hearts.

Months later I read *Miracle of Love* for the first time and understood that those hearts were a gift from Maharajji. "Cleanse the mirror of your heart and you will see God." The three hearts became a symbol of Maharajji's love for me, and as such they began to take on very great importance in my life. I bought a special handmade pouch to keep them in and carried them around with me, and generally made them into something holy. That was when I knew they had to go.

I lost one down a crack in the floorboards of an old house I was living in, and suddenly the other two seemed incomplete. I decided to keep one, but I had to let go of the other one. I didn't want to rely on them as a reminder of Maharajji's power to do miracles or of his love for me. When I went back to Lama a few years later, I brought one of the little hearts into the Ganesh space behind the kitchen. I said a prayer and left it on the puja table there. I don't know if anyone ever found it or if it vanished by the same method it had first appeared. But I do know that it was Maharajji's love that turned the one into three.

Hanuman Das Porter (Honolulu)

I started to practice yoga in 1976. At the time I was averse to anything religious, yet I did not equate yoga with either religion or spirituality. My teacher introduced me to the Eight Limbs of Yoga, Ram Dass and *Be Here Now*, the kirtan of Bhagavan Das, and Hanuman, the monkey god. I loved all of them immediately, though I had no interest whatsoever in the little old Indian man in the blanket.

My first retreat on Maui in 2002 began to awaken my latent spirituality, then I attended the 2009 Open Your Heart in Paradise retreat, and the nightly kirtan with Krishna Das was transformational, as was the 2010 retreat with Sharon Salzberg and *metta* (loving-kindness) meditation. I did feel my heart opening gradually at each retreat (that's why I kept coming back), but I still felt I was missing something. During the 2011 Maui retreat, my intention was to reach out to Maharajji, asking in earnest to come to know him in my heart, to experience the love they all talked about.

Krishna Das commented that Maharajji "radiated love like the sun . . . and all we wanted to do was sunbathe." I lay back, gazed at Maharajji, and sang to him. I felt the love growing stronger with each chant. Moments after the final chant ended, the armor enclosing my heart shattered, and a terrifying, loud, screeching sound emerged from the depths of my heart—a deeply wounded little boy crying out in agony. I could hardly believe my ears! It sounded like nothing I have ever heard, and certainly never from my own body. I covered my face with my arms and wailed on and on as waves of emotional release came again and again. I felt so embarrassed, yet at the same time I felt supported, safe, and loved as my heart opened in paradise in such a big dramatic way!

On Sunday during the mala ceremony, I accepted my mala joyously and bowed to Maharajji's photo. I peered at Maharajji's photo and thanked him for his grace in opening my heart, even though I had little faith. It looked like he was talking to me. I noticed the blanket on the table looked much like those I've seen in his photos, so I reached to touch a piece of his blanket. I cried and cried some more until I felt someone come from behind to hold me and give me a comforting hug. I composed myself a bit and then realized no one was there!

For decades I had kept Maharajji at bay, but when I finally decided I wanted to know him in my heart, he answered my prayers. Now I know Ram Dass, Krishna Das, and the rest have been speaking the truth: one can come to know and experience firsthand Neem Karoli Baba even though he left his body more than forty-five years ago. Maharajji shines his Grace upon me and to me it is not simply faith; my experiences with Maharajji have been quite real!

ॐ

Jai Hanuman

I grew up in Ukraine in a Jewish, atheistic family. When I was a teenager, my family immigrated to the States right before the collapse of the Soviet Union. When I was about twenty, I started martial arts training, and a few years later I began a meditation practice to complement that training. This was my gateway into spirituality. In 2013 I did a training with a shaman, and during one session she took us on an inner journey to find a human guide. There was no hard objective, like finding the guru; it was more to find a mentor.

About a month before I started the training, I had watched *Fierce Grace* and felt a kinship with Ram Dass. Being a musician, I was also attracted to Krishna Das's kirtan, especially the Hanuman Chalisa. There was a video of Krishna Das singing the Chalisa to a cascade of Maharajji's pictures, and I found myself drawn to Maharajji, but it was just a movie and a video clip; I didn't really give him much more thought. But as soon as the ceremony with the shaman started and I closed my eyes, I saw Maharajji. *Okay, that must be because I just watched this movie.* I went through an intense visionary journey for hours; at the end, a lotus flower bloomed and there was Maharajji sitting in it. He was laughing, his eyes twinkled. "It's still me, silly," he said. It was such a powerful and unequivocal experience that the next day I bought a ticket to come to my first ever retreat in Maui.

Given my cultural background, the concept of guru and bhakti was extremely alien and negative. At the retreat, Ram Dass talked about having the same feelings when he first met Maharajji, until he got blown open. I had a lot of resistance, but I was also inspired by Ram Dass—the sweetness of his energy and his willingness to share himself, wheelchair-bound—and he had a powerful impact on me. And even though I really enjoyed Krishna Das's kirtan, I wasn't feeling the bhakti thing.

Then came the mala ceremony. I was meditating and observing when all of a sudden I started seeing white light. It first materialized around Ram Dass, and then the whole space started filling with this light. My ears started to ring. I looked around the pavilion and wondered, "Is this really happening? Is anybody else seeing this?" Nobody else seemed to see what I was seeing.

The white light started building and building inside me. My chest hurt badly. *Oh my God, I think I'm having a heart attack.* Something like a cork popped inside me and I cried like a baby for the next two hours. That was it. That was my initiation into bhakti. A few years later I did a personal retreat with Ram Dass. It was the honor of my life to receive my yogi name from him. Since then, my relationship with Maharajji has been building; I am always connected to his presence and guidance.

राम

I had a spiritual experience during my freshman year of high school. There were about a thousand people at a Christian retreat talking about giving yourself to Jesus. When they said to stand up and accept Jesus, I felt pulled up and the waterworks started, which lasted for two or three hours. At thirteen years old, I didn't really understand what was happening, but it lit a spiritual fire in me.

When I got to college, my dad got really sick, and I watched him suffer for almost three years. It put me in the dark night of the soul. I joined a Christian fraternity in college, but it was spiritually unfulfilling because at that point I wasn't buying into religion. The only thing that helped was the knowledge of my prior experience, knowing that there was more than what I saw with my eyes.

For school, I was living in Knoxville, Tennessee, but when my dad passed away in 2015, I moved home for six months. I really needed to reconnect with my family after Dad died. The night I went back home I did mushrooms, which gave me a spiritual feeling that I hadn't felt in a while. I told my cousin, Corey, as I knew he'd experimented with psychedelics, and he gave me *Be Here Now*. I read half of the book that night and finished the rest in the morning. The spiritual fire was really burning now!

When I returned to Knoxville, Corey's job wasn't working out and he came to stay in my spare room. The night he moved in we decided to do some LSD. I heard high-pitched humming noises and felt like I was the entire universe, an experience of bliss and union. I thought I was "the man in the blanket." All I wanted to do was give love to anyone who was near me at that moment.

I came to the Maui retreat because I wanted to meet Ram Dass. On the first morning of the retreat, they were talking about surrender to the guru. Going back to the Christian camp experience, I thought I had tried to surrender to God then. *Maharajji, I don't know who you are, and I don't know anything about gurus, but I feel it. They call it*

Maharajji, I call it God. It doesn't matter. I surrendered to the will of the universe.

At the mala ceremony, I was looking at a picture of my dad on my phone. His leg was in a brace and his shoulder was messed up, but he had so much joy in his face in the picture, even though he looked like death. I showed that picture to Ram Dass and said, "My dad passed away last year . . ." Tears. Unable to speak. Ram Dass took the phone and looked at the picture of my dad and meditated on it for a long time. Ram Dass looked up and said, "Well, we both still love you."

It was like Hanuman ripping his heart wide open. I was holding Ram Dass's hand and I loved everyone in this moment! It was so powerful. Maharajji was obviously present. But there was another person that I sensed, and I think my father's presence was there. Throughout the whole rest of the day, I was crying. I understood unbearable love!

राम

Katja

I went to Maui to see Ram Dass, as he had been so influential in my spiritual journey. I knew that he had a guru, but for me it was all about Ram Dass. The first morning of the retreat I heard people talking about Maharajji, but he was not in my consciousness. That first morning we did an exercise where we had to stare into somebody's eyes. After about five minutes, suddenly I felt like I could see right through her eyes into her soul. Then I got this expansive feeling like I was looking into the universe . . . and she became Maharajji, although at the time I didn't recognize him. Not like it was a ghost or I saw some apparition—she became him, as if I could reach out and take his hand!

179

I'm a rational person, trained in science. I'm in the medical field and very conventional. I'm not someone who normally has visions. I have a very strong Christian background and I thought, *Well, if I were going to see anyone, it should be the Virgin Mary, it should be Mary Magdalene, it should be Jesus. There's no reason why Maharajji would come to me. I'm not a devotee.* I was looking in his eyes and I was a bit taken aback, but I felt bliss. I felt peace. The interesting thing was my attention kept going to his left side, to a pattern that I couldn't make out. It was like a checkerboard of different colors. I kept thinking, *Why would the background be important if I'm looking at him?* Okay, whatever. When it was over, I recognized who it was as I had seen photos of him. Wow, it was amazing that I saw Maharajji on day one of the retreat!

The next day I was looking up at Maharajji's picture. He was so present for me now. I suddenly saw his blanket. That's what the pattern had been—his blanket! I had a very strong connection to the concept of a security blanket. It represented a compassionate embrace for me, as well as protection and warmth. Now I knew why I thought that pattern was so important.

A few days later we were having kirtan with Krishna Das. I've always been a bit self-conscious, but I was so captivated that I got up and danced. And suddenly I had this surrender moment where I allowed it all to be. I let the blocks fall away and allowed the music to move me. We were in this vortex of ecstasy, and I felt like I was Maharajji. He was me. I was everyone in the room and we were all one. I loved every single person in that room, and I didn't even know who all these hundreds of people were. In that moment I felt like I had when I looked into Maharajji's eyes that first morning.

Then I felt his presence in the entire room and Maharajji spoke to me. He either said, "Your heart is mine now" or "I have your heart." Not that somebody possessed my heart or I had given it away, but because I had been willing to relinquish blocks inside myself, my heart was now part of the grand consciousness. I felt his presence coming towards me as he spoke those words.

Since that connection with him, I feel him very present, as if he is part of me, giving me insight into my higher consciousness. He's embracing, compassionate. I feel like I am very loved. It's all quite amazing.

ॐ

Kelly Rego

In 2014 I already considered myself a devotee of Maharajji just from listening to the Ram Dass podcasts. I read *Miracle of Love,* and my own relationship developed through that book. I saved pictures of Maharajji, who looked to me like my grandpa. In listening to the podcasts, I found out that Raghu Markus lived in Asheville. When my friend and I were on a road trip and passed through Asheville, we wanted to meet Raghu because we wanted to meet someone who had actually met Maharajji. When we took a walk together, I told Raghu that I'd done marketing in the past, and that is how I started working for the Love Serve Remember Foundation.

I started coming to the retreats on Maui. At my third or fourth retreat, in a meditation in the morning I had a feeling of real grief come over me about my dad, who would have really enjoyed being there with adults who were devoted to God because he was very Catholic. We could have shared this level of devotion.

The next to last night of the retreat, some people were hanging out in my room. Everyone had left the balcony except this guy named Jonathan. I was telling him about the meditation and my grief. Suddenly, his breathing changed and got much slower. He said, "Your dad has something to say to you." His voice got very deep; the sound had this authority that had not been there before.

He said, "From the moment of your first breath to the moment of your last breath, I will always be with you. I'm so proud of you."

Mind you, I had never met my dad or heard him speak. My father died when I was eight months old, so that's been a theme in my life—I've always wanted him to say something directly to me. I had this feeling in my chest, and right at that moment Jonathan said, "You can feel this in your chest because it's the truth." Then Jonathan bent over, and when he sat up it was all over.

I stayed out on the balcony for hours. I had gotten the one thing I'd always wanted in my life, which I thought was impossible. I really didn't think I was ever going to have a direct word from my father. I felt like my devotion and focus on my inner world and chanting had brought me to this place where I could receive the biggest gift I could ever ask for. I've always had to believe that there's a father figure that loves me; I had just never met him. From my dad to Maharajji is not that different a relationship in terms of feeling their love without having the physical confirmation.

That was the first time I met Jonathan. Six months later we met again at the December retreat, something sparked, and now we're married. I figured my dad gave him his blessing.

Lisa Ball-McIsaac

When I was 17, I was homeless, living on a beach in Florida, and addicted to drugs and alcohol. I wanted to die, but I was too chicken shit to kill myself. My family are addicts, in and out of 12-step recovery, so I knew plenty about addiction growing up, and I didn't want it for myself, but I was so lost.

One night I looked up at the sky and saw this bright, bright star, and I knew in my heart I had to follow it. I walked towards the end of the pier. Suddenly, the sky opened up, and I saw my stepdad's face there in the sky. He had passed years before, and now he was smiling and so happy. I felt such love. I was at the edge of the pier having this intense experience of love, and all the answers to everything in the universe came pouring in. I knew everything automatically. Everything made sense. A wind blew and I knew why. When I came back from the pier and tried to tell people what had happened, they thought I was insane.

At that moment I knew that I couldn't keep using drugs. I started a 12-step program. Stopping use was easy for me because I knew I was not going to be who my soul incarnated to be if I was using. Recovery is a spiritual program. You live by spiritual principles.

I found Ram Dass over eighteen years ago through *Be Here Now*. About ten years later, I started listening to his lectures every day and reading his books. His message resonated with me. I always thought it was weird that my greatest teacher's path was that of the guru because I never really resonated with that. I didn't get it until I finally made it to the Open Your Heart in Paradise retreat in May 2019. I met Ram Dass and said hello; we were looking into each other's eyes and I broke into two! Just broke! I went to my hotel room and cried harder than I have ever, ever cried.

I asked my husband why I was broken in half. He said, "Well, you were in the presence of the greatest love, and that's Maharajji, who is being transmitted through Ram Dass." Now I love Maharajji so much. It's been a weird thing for me to accept and admit that. I always thought a guru was good for you if you had that need, but it's not about need at all. I always thought it was kind of a crutch, but it's not. It's like he's always, always been there.

I had wondered how I was ever going to have an experience again like the moment of enlightenment on the pier, which had simply been given to me. Afterwards, I had gotten into a very deep depression because I was mad at God. How could you show me the answers to the universe and not give it to me again? I didn't know how to get it or what it was. Then I came to the retreat and felt that love—the same as the experience on the beach. That was it. I had come home.

Lonny Travis

My story starts in 1990 as I was leaving a thirty-day drug rehab program. I had fallen into the world of cocaine at the age of twenty-two after life didn't turn out quite the way I thought it should. Imagine that. I was introduced to the 12 steps of AA, and I saw the prize in *Step 12*: "Having had a spiritual awakening as the result of these steps . . ." The "spiritual awakening" caught my eye. I joined an AA group in Wichita where I met Terry O, who gave me some meditation cassette tapes to listen to. From the very first word of the cassette labeled "Ram Dass," I knew I had found truth.

Terry had over twenty years of sobriety by the time our paths crossed. One night he shared his awakening with me. While going through withdrawal, he kept surrendering all his pain to God, and suddenly he was surrounded in white light that embraced him with unconditional love. He never drank alcohol again. After hearing about Terry's awakening, I was bound and determined to have one myself, so I spent hours in meditation and prayer, saying, *I surrender, I surrender*. I look back with a smile because I was in no way surrendering anything.

I listened to Ram Dass over and over for hours. I got to the point where I was hardly sleeping at all. One morning I arrived at work without remembering driving there. I felt so free, so unattached. I could see God's grace working in every soul's life. I walked up to my boss and told her I quit. I worked at the largest aircraft company in the U.S., a very desirable job in Wichita, but I walked right out the door that morning and drove to my mom's house, where I was living.

I pulled into the driveway in total bliss and awe, six months sober from any alcohol or drugs. I walked up to our front door and stuck my house key into the lock. At the very instant when my key went into the lock, I felt the keys get pulled out of my hand and through the door—right through the door!—and I'm standing there locked out of my house, bewildered. If there was anything left of my rational mind, it was gone now. I looked up at the overcast sky and felt this huge, totally loving vibration. I fell to my knees with my forehead to the ground and cried like I'd never cried before.

Coming out of that experience was when the real work began. My boss hadn't followed through with me quitting. She let me take a thirty-day leave from work so I could put my life back together, and I am very grateful to still have the same job today.

By the end of 2016, I had read about everything I could get my hands on about Maharajji. I had listened to hundreds of Ram Dass YouTube videos. I started having dreams about Maharajji. I was getting a performance bonus at work, which covered the cost of a trip to Maui for the 2017 retreat. All I really wanted to do was to thank Ram Dass personally for all the service he had done. Although Terry had passed away, I silently asked him to join me on this trip to Maui.

I had never experienced kirtan or satsang, and I didn't know a soul there, but I wanted to get as close as I could to the front. I sat on the floor and stared at the huge picture of Maharajji on the wall. Ram Dass came out on stage right in front of me, and I could feel the love emanating out of his being—the same love that I felt flowing through everyone there. Ram Dass said, "You are here because Maharajji wanted you here." Those were powerful words to my soul.

Once the talk ended, a short line formed of folks wanting to talk to Ram Dass. I was finally going to meet Ram Dass! My eyes started to well up with tears as I got close to him. I took a knee in front of his wheelchair so I could see him eye to eye. I tried to speak, but I started crying and crying, and my head fell to his lap. He reached his left hand around my head and hugged me till I regained composure. I lifted my head and said, "Thank you so much, Ram Dass, for all your work and love. You saved my life through your teachings."

He looked me in the eye with a big smile on his face and said, "Not me, it was Maharajji, it was God." He told me to spread Maharajji's love, and repeated it again, "Spread Maharajji's love, yes." It felt like the teacher had released me to his guru. In that very instant I felt so connected to Maharajji and all the people there at the retreat. As I walked away from him, I realized I hadn't cried that hard since the day I had the keys pulled out of my hand.

One evening while Krishna Das was chanting, I closed my eyes and got lost in the chant. Then like a ball of light, it hit me that I was sitting with my legs crossed, eyes closed, in Maui, listening to Ram Dass, surrounded by beautiful souls. Tears running down my face, I sat full of gratitude and love for the gift and mystery of our lives. I had silently asked Maharajji if he was the one who pulled those keys out of my hand back in 1990. The tears were the result of his answer.

Michelle Mott

I'd been listening to and chanting with Krishna Das and had heard about Maharajji through him. I'd also listened to some of Ram Dass's talks, but then a friend told me about *Fierce Grace*. I'd been living with chronic pain for about twenty years and Ram Dass really spoke to me in that movie. When I got an email about the 2010 Open Your Heart in Paradise retreat, I knew I had to be there.

I may have seen a photo of Maharajji and heard a few stories about him, but I had no real expectations about him at the retreat, nor did I have any preparation for what I was walking into. When I entered the pavilion in Maui, I saw the huge photo of Maharajji and immediately began weeping. I felt like I had come Home. Each day of the retreat brought a deeper level of marinating in his love. I wept that entire week and could feel my heart literally exploding with love, so much so that I broke out in blisters on the front and back of my heart chakra.

I now have photos of Baba everywhere and practice bhakti yoga. I try to keep as close a relationship with him as I can, which is interesting since I never met him in the body, but I know that he and his love are ever present in my heart. As a result, I'm able not only to love others, but also to love myself

At one retreat, I was experiencing intense pain from the traveling, so during my morning beach meditation I said to Maharajji, "I really need help. I feel like I'm not truly living or loving in this life because the pain keeps me restricted."

At that very moment, it started raining. My ego's first response was to get frustrated and run to shelter, but I decided to sit there. And then it hit me. Krishna Das had shared a story about how grace is raining down on us all the time, and all we have to do is open our hands to receive it. The message went straight to my heart. I started laughing and crying, then I held my hands out wide open. I knew that my pain was grace.

Ram Dass said that his stroke was grace, and in that moment, I realized that pain is what had put me on the path to meditation, Buddhism, and bhakti yoga, which ultimately led me to Maharajji. The pain was a pure loving gift that brought me to him. This realization completely shifted my relationship with pain. When pain arises, it brings me closer to Baba, and for that I'm eternally grateful.

॥५॥

Renu Chaudhary

I'm Indian. My parents are both from Northern India, Punjab and Chandigarh area. I was born in Sacramento and grew up in the San Francisco area. My mom followed Vedanta, and I went to classes with her, so I had a great foundation in the Vedas and mantras. My dad would go to the temple maybe once a year. We didn't really connect with our Indian culture that much. Then my parents, who had an arranged marriage, got divorced when I was ten. When I was eighteen, I was out of there as soon as I could get a car, and I took a hiatus from spiritual stuff for twenty years.

In 2017 a friend who I met playing soccer several years previously was going to go to this retreat in Maui. I loved Hawaii. I figured I would go with him just to hang out. I had heard the name Ram Dass but didn't know anything or anyone else. The night before we were to go on the retreat, my friend said he couldn't go. I was plunged into social anxiety—I'm going to be all alone; I'm not going to know anyone; nobody's going to eat lunch with me. But I was committed to going, so I went.

For the first welcome meal, I was by myself. I saw this older gentleman and was about to be brave and go up to him when I realized it was K.K. Sah and he was part of the retreat. Oh, I'm sorry. I felt tremendously out of place. I sat in the corner looking down at my plate and had this tremendous wall around me. Then this lady said, "Can I sit with you?" My heart lifted. This lady and I went to the first kirtan together. I didn't know what to expect because I had never been touched by mantras. Well, I was here. I would give it a shot. I could go to the beach tomorrow.

We had chosen a spot towards the back. As I was sitting there, Ram Dass passed by and I started to understand the gravity of my fortune. Krishna Das sang *Sri Ram Jai Ram* for a while, then he went into the Hare Krishna waltz. Twenty minutes later, my anxiety and nervousness had lifted. I have no doubt that Maharajji opened my heart through Krishna Das's music and his presence. And that's how I met Maharajji. Later when I heard about how Krishna Das met Maharajji through Ram Dass, it made sense to me. It happened to me through Krishna Das.

I completely dove into the retreat. The next morning was Sharon Salzberg and her loving-kindness practice. I put that into action and my whole life changed. When I came back from the retreat, I found it very easy to meditate. Again, I assumed that was Maharajji's grace. He got me hooked and things naturally started to fall away in my life as I adopted chanting with Krishna Das and practicing Sharon's lovingkindness meditation daily.

I had been asking for a real meeting with Maharajji, in a dream if nothing else. Finally, I got one. I dreamt I was at a retreat and there were hundreds of people there. I was sitting at a table with Krishna Das. Ram Dass came in and he was walking, very tall and straight up. He looked at me and I could tell it wasn't him, it was Maharajji. He looked right at me; I had the feeling that I was with Maharajji. His presence was there, and it gave me so much peace and so much strength.

I didn't miss a single retreat in Maui after that first one.

उप

Sharon Sita Roll

I had been doing asana with my mother since I was a young child but had no idea about the depths of yoga. In 2000, a dear friend of mine lost her son to heart disease, and I thought yoga would be good for these children, so I went to Omega to do a yoga teacher training. During the in-depth intensive training, every time I closed my eyes all I could see was an elephant and a cat. Well, the elephant was obviously Ganesh, but this cat guy kept coming to me. In the Omega Bookstore I saw a picture of Hanuman. Not a cat, it was a monkey! Darshan blessings were preparing me for what was to come.

The following week Ram Dass was coming to Omega. People were excited. They suggested I buy Ram Dass's book; he'd sign it and give me a hug. Hey, I like hugs. It was my wedding anniversary, and I was apart from my husband, so I figured I'd get Ram Dass to sign it, and I'd give my husband the book as a gift.

During the last training of that day, my kundalini released, although this is a word I did not know at the time. Waves of energy shot through me and I was gone. Words can't describe the experience of flying through past lives and the universe and oneness. Tears were streaming out of my eyes as I emerged, I floated rather than walked.

My friend came up to me and she had this beautiful rainbow halo around her. We walked to the lake where I saw this guy in a wheelchair, who emanated the biggest rainbow of all. That evening, he was in the main hall over at the puja table. I was an atheist at that time. I closed my eyes and asked my ancestors if I was supposed to be with this man, Ram Dass. The next thing I knew, I was kneeling next to his wheelchair. I told Ram Dass about my kundalini releasing and he clapped his hands happily. I looked in his eyes and shot into oneness again. He signed the book and hugged me. I sat down next to the puja table in a state of awe. I looked up and saw the picture of Neem Karoli Baba. My heart flew open. I loved everybody in the room. I loved the air between us. I loved everything. I got up and started dancing.

My whole life changed. Atheist then, big dopey bhakti now. I never did teach children with heart issues. My path turned out quite different because I lost my health, but the blessings still abound. I literally was in bed for two years and continue to be challenged. I have very bad vertigo, as if I'm on a boat all the time. Baba and Ram Dass's love and teachings have helped me. The room was swirling as I was sitting in kirtan the day Ram Dass named me Sita. I began chanting with all my heart while gazing into Neem Karoli Baba's eyes. I found myself centered in his eyes! Any time the vertigo gets too bad, I know I am centered in his grace. There I find balance; there I find home.

ᵏᵘ

Tracy Sutton

I'm a therapist and do palliative work. I'd been reading Ram Dass's work for a couple of decades, but I knew nothing about Maharajji. Then I came to the retreat in Maui. The second night in the kirtan I looked up at the picture of Maharajji and the picture spoke; I thought I was going nuts. Professionally, I was a little concerned, but it was a very loving message. He said, "Why do you create all of these levels of suffering for yourself?" I really was creating suffering for myself because of an interaction I'd had that morning that had hit me right in the core of my personal "stuff." I had been vacillating between bliss and dark thoughts, back and forth, back and forth. Then the picture spoke and giggled.

Later Ram Dass was doing his "I am loving awareness" meditation. His speech wasn't metered. It wasn't regular timing. From where I was sitting in the back of the pavilion, there were about ten of us that could see and hear a bird. Every time Ram Dass finished saying, "I am loving awareness," this bird would whistle a tune. The first time it happened, I thought it was interesting. After about the fourth or fifth time, the bunch of us sitting back there started giggling. At some point Ram Dass said, "I am loving awareness," and the bird flew off, and Ram Dass was finished. It honestly felt like a visitation from Babaji, being present with us all. It was just so beautiful that it brought me to tears of joy.

8

Cry for Help

God is the best listener.
You don't need to shout, nor cry out loud,
because he hears even the very silent prayer
of a sincere heart.
—ANONYMOUS

There are times when the world falls apart, the ground crumbles beneath you, and all you can do is cry out, *please help me!* A loved one is in danger or dying, your relationship is broken, your addiction is overwhelming you, your child is sick and you don't know what to do. The cry that emerges from that place of desperation reaches Maharajji, you are heard, and the healing can begin.

Sometimes you don't even need to ask.

When I was in India with Maharajji, I was smoking beedis, these awful little cigarettes made from betel leaves wrapped around a small amount of low-grade tobacco flake. I knew I should quit, and it was really bothering me that I hadn't been able to, but the social aspects of smoking were appealing. One day as I entered the ashram, Maharajji said, quite bluntly, "I caught you red-handed. Stop smoking beedis! I am the CID[35] of the heart." He called me over to sit in front of him, put his feet in my lap, and held my hand. I gave away my pack of beedis. After lunch, Maharajji called me up to congratulate me on not smoking beedis anymore. Instant reinforcement!

He knows your heart, and his help is always available.

ॐ

---

35 The CID in India is the equivalent of the CIA in the U.S.

Chris Janeczko

I had been a follower of Ram Dass for quite a long time but never really felt any relationship with Neem Karoli Baba. About twenty years ago my child went through an episode, one of many, where she was so depressed that she was suicidal. I'd already lost a close family member to suicide right around the time she was born, so I knew the signs all too well. On this night my child had again disappeared. I couldn't get her to answer her phone, she wasn't home, and her friends didn't know where she was. I had convinced myself that she had harmed herself and I was frantic with worry. After exhausting all possibilities of finding her, I sat down on my meditation cushion, lit a candle, and faced the photograph of Maharajji. I asked him to please help.

I was crying so hard that, at first, I didn't realize there was an additional noise in the room. I opened my eyes and saw that the candle flame had turned into a blue seated Maharajji and that the noise I was hearing was a high-pitched sort of chatter. Although I couldn't understand the noise, somehow it was telling me that everything was alright, that my daughter was fine, and that he had the situation under control. This flame and talking lasted for only about five minutes, but at the end of it I felt a sense of total peace and relaxation. I could go to sleep and no longer worry. I slept right there, in front of the candle and picture. When I woke up I had a message from my child, who was out of harm's way after a very bad time.

Many years later I saw a video of Maharajji with sound. The sound I heard that night matched what I heard on the video. Maharajji has been in my heart ever since.

Gobind (Gary Smith)

I was living in a bubble in a small town in Ohio, trying to find my way through life in the early '70s, when I read *Be Here Now* and began my spiritual journey. Somehow Baba slowly drew me in until the '80s, when I realized that he was my guru. I didn't have anybody to support me as far as spiritual things went, so I pretty much floundered around on my own for a lot of years.

In 1998, I was at the ashram in Taos when I found out that my wife had cancer. She died on September 11, 2000, the anniversary of the day Maharajji left the body. I was a fireman, so 9/11 is always one of *those* days for me. My son was eight years old when his mom died. Ten years later he got involved with opioids.

I was finally able to go to India in 2013. My son was out of rehab and seemed to be doing well. I really didn't know the extent of his problem. Then my mom passed away right before I went. When I finally left, everything seemed fine. I was in India for about three months. I met Shri Siddhi Ma and had darshan with her several times. I went to aarti every morning and night. Then I went to Rishikesh and Vrindavan, where I prayed to Baba to please help my family.

When I got back everything fell apart. My son was once again in rehab. Unless you have a family member with an opioid problem, it's hard to describe what you go through. I didn't understand why all this was happening on my return from a wonderful trip to India. Not only was my son having a problem with his health and being an addict, but the police were now involved because of what he had to do to support his habit. I mean, we're talking about a dozen felonies, and I'm thinking, how is he going to get out of this? He owed a bunch of money, which I worked out with a detective, who said, "As long as he tells me the truth, I'm going to help him."

I remembered that Neem Karoli Baba always said to tell the truth. I said to my son, "Look, you've got to tell the truth, no matter what."

He told the detective everything. He even got to know Neem Karoli Baba at that point because I started giving him some books. His faith really grew.

He's been clean now for six years and everything somehow got taken care of. Not only that, but Maharajji repaired the damage done to the family. Nobody had wanted to have anything to do with my son and dealing with the legal system is scary. When I was going through all this, I got a letter from a Neem Karoli Baba devotee, who wrote at a time when I really needed somebody to talk to, which lifted me up. I'm forever grateful for how it all worked out.

राम

Lee Mirabai Harrington

Beginning in spring 2017, I had many moments of fear and depression because Western doctors had told me I was losing the ability to walk (from spine and bone disorders) and that the only thing that could "save my legs" would be fusion surgery, but my spine was too weak for surgery. Catch-22. I was on crutches in the fall and not able to drive well. I simply didn't have the gumption to drive three hours to Western Massachusetts for Maharajji's mahasamadhi bhandara, even if my destination was such a beautiful one. I called my friend Adam, whining that I was too depressed to go to the gathering. "My right leg isn't working very well. It's not safe for me to drive."

"Just come, madam," Adam said, speaking in the Indian accent he often used to make a spiritual point. "Come. Get in your car and drive."

Sometimes we need simple advice, right? I got in my car and drove, but within twenty minutes I realized it was going to be very painful to drive the entire way. I pulled over at a rest area off the New York

Thruway to think things through. I said, "Maharajji, if you want me to come to this bhandara, I am going to need some support."

Within seconds a car pulled into the parking space right next to mine and out stepped four beloved Ram *bhaktas* (beloveds) that I knew from New York: Rhoney, Martin, Vayu Das, and Keshav. They were a lively bunch, laughing about how crowded it was for all four of them to be crammed into a small car. You need to understand the size of this rest area—and the scope of the New York State Thruway—to understand that this was not just a random occurrence. We exchanged hugs and laughed at the "coincidence" of running into each other, and realized we were all headed to the same place.

When I explained my driving predicament and told them that I had just asked Maharajji for some support, it was decided that Keshav would drive my minivan, and we would convoy together on the trips to and from Conway. This little episode helped me realize that miracles are simply recognizing that whatever we need in the moment can and will be delivered, with grace. Ever since then, I've referred to Maharajji as my "Practical Guide" and "The Great Organizer."

It was a wonderful gathering. Singing, laughing, connecting, seeing old friends, making new ones. I was riding high on the delight that Maharajji had sent me friends when I needed them, and I felt so grateful to be there among people who were so full of love. After lunch we sang more chalisas. Everyone was dancing, clapping, stamping their feet. I was at the back sitting in a chair, my crutches leaning against the barn wall. I was suddenly struck with the deepest sorrow. It was an old self-pity, and I started to quietly cry, thinking, *I am all alone. There is no one to take care of me if I wind up in a wheelchair.* Meanwhile, the inner Maharajji was saying, *None of this is true.*

But I don't know if I am going to be able to walk tomorrow, I cried.

No one knows, he said. Very firmly. That wisdom was like a thunderclap. It brought me out of my mind-trap of pity and back into the room: dozens of people sitting around the musicians, playing kartals, shakers, or simply singing and swaying. Women were twirling around me on the barn floor, their skirts whirling with the sound of tiny bells. A fat toddler clapped her hands happily out of time. *None of them know if they are going to be able to walk tomorrow*, Maharajji said.

Even though everything I've ever read, studied, or practiced in any spiritual tradition has carried the message to *live in the moment*, I'd never really grasped its meaning until Maharajji phrased it like that. His picture hung in the center of the barn. I looked at his warm smile and those eternal eyes. I stopped crying, hoisted myself up on my crutches, and danced.

ॐ

Madhurai Sumhara

I had been in Kerala in India for a yoga teacher training. When I came back, I was planning to move out West, but I came down with a mysterious illness. I had tests done, including for parasites, but the doctors couldn't find anything wrong. Every morning I woke up with my body shaking, vomiting, and diarrhea. Every single morning. After a few hours it would all go away and I would be fine. It was very weird. It became clear to me that it was something spiritual and the answer was to throw myself more fully into my practices.

I put everything in my car and drove West, following Spirit. At one point I was driving through New Mexico. I had never heard of Neem Karoli Baba, but a friend told me about the temple in Taos and said they did aarti there. I thought, oh, that would be nice. When I got to the Hanuman Temple, I had been sick for almost two months and was getting very weak. I had been doing everything I could for my spiritual cleansing, all the ceremonies I could do on my own, all the energy work that I knew how to do. I realized this was beyond me. I really needed help or I felt like I would die.

I woke up in my car outside the Hanuman Temple, and it was one of the worst mornings. I was so sick. I remember lying there, praying, please let me die now, or send me an angel and a medicine man to heal me because I can't do this on my own.

When the doors of the temple opened for aarti, I went into the back room, the office with the takhat. I looked at Maharajji's picture and fell down in full pranam. I was praying and praying and crying and crying for an angel and a medicine man to save me or to just let it be over. Just then a young man walked in and scooped me right up in a hug. I cried and cried and cried. I didn't tell him what was going on, but I did say that I was going to travel North through Wyoming. He said, "You're going to Wyoming? That's so funny because I've been here at the ashram serving Maharajji for six months, but tomorrow I leave to go to Wyoming to see my mentor, a Lakota medicine man."

I had gotten my angel and my medicine man.

We spent two days at the temple before we left, and I could feel the grace of it from that moment on. I could feel Maharajji's presence as I was being pulled to him. A couple of days later we went to Wyoming. He brought me to Frank, a Lakota medicine man, who did powerful ceremonies and energy work with me, and healed me in a day.

Ever since, it's been an endless thank you to Maharajji for saving my life.

॥म्॥

Rama Chandra Das (Rob Lundsgaard)

Less than a week before going to India to lead a retreat, I got out of bed in the middle of the night, but when I stood up I nearly fell over because of a sudden onset of dizziness. I grabbed the wall to keep myself upright. It wasn't just a momentary thing, though; it lasted thirty to forty seconds. *Whoa, that was strange.* Later that morning, it happened again, less intense this time, but still there.

The next afternoon, I went to a yoga class. Halfway through the class, we were on our backs, and the teacher had us turn onto our left side. The moment I turned, the dizziness rushed back in, so strong that I was spinning wildly on the inside. The teacher came over and instantly diagnosed the problem, "Vertigo?" I nodded, and he helped me to find a good position; the dizziness faded away.

When we arrived in India a couple days later, I was feeling dizzy, but couldn't tell if it was the travel or the vertigo. Our room at the guesthouse in Vrindavan wasn't ready yet, so we rested in a temporary room and fell fast asleep. Two hours later, the phone rang. I leapt out of bed with a scream! My heart was racing as I picked up the phone to learn our room was ready. A wave of nausea and dizziness overwhelmed me, more powerful than any previous episodes. I moaned and held my head, lost in an abyss of dizziness. I clutched at the wall as we walked to our new room. Eventually, the internal motion subsided and I fell back asleep. For the rest of the day, we slept, ate, and slept again until I finally felt good enough to venture out.

We walked the parikrama the next morning, and I felt okay during most of it, lost in the beauty of the Vrindavan sunrise. We stopped at Maharajji's ashram. Everything was fine until I attempted to pranam at Baba's mahasamadhi. As my forehead touched the ground, a wave of vertigo rushed in, and I sat up immediately. Here I was in Vrindavan, and I couldn't even pranam! I began praying to

Baba, "Please help me Baba, I'm freaking out right now. I need this vertigo to go away." But it got progressively worse. Our retreat was getting closer, and I was feeling overwhelmed by the idea of leading the group with this new disability. Over and over, I prayed to Baba, "Please help me Baba, I'm scared and I need you to help me!"

On our final day in Vrindavan, I got out of bed around 5 a.m. with tears streaming down my face. The dizziness had gotten so bad that I hadn't slept all night. Melissa grabbed her phone and began searching "vertigo" and the "Epley maneuver," which my mother had mentioned. This led to a series of YouTube videos by Dr. Johns, who specialized in vertigo treatment. One of the causes of this sort of vertigo is related to special crystals in your central ear that help the body balance itself, but occasionally they can get dislodged and move into the outer canals. There are three different canals in each ear the crystals can go into, so the variables are significant. I was overwhelmed with all the different tests to diagnose it correctly, but after a couple of tests, we determined the crystals were in the horizontal canal of the right ear. We kept researching and found a potential cure: a series of simple movements. It seemed like a long shot, but I was desperate! I did the recommended exercise while my wife Melissa timed me. When it was done, I felt different. I sat there, marveling at the feeling I was having. How could a simple movement have solved this whole issue?

I lay back on my back and turned to the side. No dizziness. Oh, my Ram! Was it possible? I stood up quickly, no dizziness! Unbelievable! I was cured, just like that; in fact, I felt more stable and secure than I had in over a week!

I was so happy, but I kept waiting for the vertigo to come back. To test it further, I decided to try a child's pose on the bed. Nervously, I came to my hands and knees, closed my eyes, and lowered my head to the mattress. Relief washed over me as no dizziness appeared, and I began to cry. I immediately thought of Baba and knew that his hand had been guiding us that morning as we poured through the literally hundreds of possible videos, leading us to Dr. Johns. "I must go to Baba's ashram to say thank you."

As soon as I had that thought, there was a knock on the door. It was still only about 7 a.m., so Melissa and I looked at each other in surprise. I opened the door to see a short man in his sixties. When he saw me, he began to apologize. "I'm so sorry, Prahbu, I am at the wrong door. So sorry."

I smiled at the sweet devotee, "No problem. No need to apologize."

"Thank you, Prabhu, have a blessed day," he said as he began to turn away.

"What's your name?" I blurted out.

He turned back and smiled, "Guru Kripa, my name is Guru Kripa."

I was flabbergasted. "Your name is Guru Kripa? You mean, the grace of the guru?"

He smiled even wider, "Yes, Guru's Grace. That's my name." Then he simply walked away.

He had arrived at the moment I thought of my gratitude to Baba. It was crystal-clear—it was the guru's grace that cured me.

The vertigo has not returned, and Guru Kripa is still with me.

ॐ

Stever Dallmann (Ramabhakta)

I was always a nerdy, spiritual kid. I grew up in a family of alcoholics and I'd be running off to church by myself. When I was three or four years old, my family would hear me talking in my room with my "friend," who came out of my wall and talked to me at night. He sat there in his blanket and said he loved me.

When I was fifteen years old, I found the Integral Yoga Institute. I got a mantra and started on my spiritual path in a more formal sense.

I got hold of Ram Dass's book, *Be Here Now,* and experimented with a few mushrooms. Then I found cocaine and alcohol, so in the '80s I had no spiritual path that I was aware of. I tried for a couple of years to get clean and sober, but I was really struggling.

One day I was in a park in San Francisco near a big beautiful cypress tree, praying, "I give up. God, you've got to do something. You've got to help me." And the tree started glowing with light. I get choked up even today when I tell this story. There was a bearded face in the tree that said, *I love you and I'm with you always.* From that moment on, something changed. I felt that love and it gave me the strength I needed to find my way into recovery.

I started meditating and doing practices and synchronicities kept happening. I re-read the Ram Dass books. My heart opened and I saw that Maharajji had been with me the whole time. One day Maharajji just said, *Here I am*, and I realized, *oh, that was the guy in the tree.*

जय

Susan Mangel

When I was in college in the mid-'70s, I met a guy who probably mentioned Ram Dass and gave me a copy of the ISKCON version of the *Bhagavad Gita*, which I hid in my closet because I thought my father would get upset. But it wasn't until 2006 that I was looking for a spiritual retreat. It kept coming back to the Ram Dass retreat being the thing that I was meant to go to, so I came to a small retreat held at Hale Akua in October of 2006.

I listened to Ram Dass and learned about Maharajji, and it changed my life. My relationship with my parents wasn't bad, but I never thought about unconditional love in the way that Ram Dass introduced it. It took me some time to feel completely comfortable with Maharajji. A couple years after meeting Ram Dass, I was volunteering and helping with the bookstore over in Haiku when my heart cracked open and I was sobbing.

When my mom got ill, she was about Ram Dass's age. She had met him in 2012 when I brought her to Maui, and she never stopped talking about it. I really needed to tap in and ask Maharajji for his help when she went into the hospital with kidney failure. I was worried and said to Maharajji, "What can I do to help her? Please help us."

I was in the emergency room for six hours while they were trying to get her a room. I stepped out for a minute to get a drink. When I came back through the doors, there was an orderly who was taking her out of the ER and to a room. I could see immediately something was very wrong. The orderly didn't realize that she was having a stroke. I thought she was dying. She couldn't speak. I screamed for the doctors; they were able to do a procedure that completely reversed the paralysis, reversed her inability to speak and recognize things. I felt like even though the stroke happened, there was a lot of grace.

About seven months later, she started to decline, with a lot of suffering. I would meet with Maharajji in the evenings; I'd be lying in bed, crying to him: "What do I do? I need guidance." I was begging him, "Please, she's suffering. She's not speaking, not eating. I don't want to see her suffer anymore. Please take her under your blanket." The next day it was kind of miraculous that my brother, sister in-law, my sister, and I were all there in the room, and within two hours she passed away.

I had been heard.

Val Chaney

I came to the retreat in Maui because I love Ram Dass. I understood that what Ram Dass was transmitting was Maharajji, but he wasn't in the forefront for me. I saw him as maybe the same thing as Christ, which was the narrative I grew up with; I was able to access "It" through Jesus. I had the same kind of upbringing Pete Holmes, my husband, did—very fundamental Christian. We had pictures of Maharajji in our house because of Pete. I would look at the pictures, but I wasn't really interested in engaging in a relationship with him. I didn't know how I felt about it all. When I saw that big picture of Maharajji at the retreat, I got it, but I wondered: am I just trading Jesus for Maharajji? I called him "Maharaj-Jesus."

When we came to the retreat, our daughter was eight months old. When she was four months old, she had had a bad UTI with a high fever, and we had to go to the emergency room. She had to get a catheter put in multiple times, and I worried that it was traumatic for her. It was traumatic for us, too, the hardest thing I've ever gone through. When we came to the retreat in May, she was acting exactly how she had when she had the UTI—with the exact same symptoms. I fell apart. I knew, the way you know when you're a mother, what was happening. I was rocking her, and she was doing this heavy breathing that she had only ever done from the pain of the UTI.

Pete was out swimming in the ocean, so I was alone with her trying to get her to sleep. Her body was so tense; she was doing that breathing and I couldn't get her to relax. I was crying. It suddenly occurred to me to ask Maharajji to intervene. I was very specific. I remember saying, "All right, Maharajji, this isn't a test. You don't have to prove yourself. That's not what this is. But here I am. I'm here at this retreat and you're on my mind. And so, if you could help us out with this, that would be great. But it's not a test." That's a big Christian thing: don't test God. But it's also that I didn't want it to be like, this is your chance to prove yourself and then I'll be in your camp.

As soon as I said those words to Maharajji, instantly her whole body relaxed, and she gave this deep exhale. And I knew, just like I had known that it was a UTI, I knew in that moment it was gone. And it was. There was no sign of it after that. I came out of the room and saw Pete in the ocean, and we had a beautiful swim. I was crying and I told Pete what had happened. It felt like we were swimming in love.

9
Dreams

Trust in dreams,
for in them is hidden the gate to eternity.
—Khalil Gibran

To sleep, perchance to dream... and in that dream to have darshan of Maharajji. Darshan is more than simply the "sight" of a holy person; it is the experience of being in the presence of the sacred, of knowing you are truly and deeply loved, a spiritual understanding of previously unrecognized truth. If it happens in a so-called "dream," you feel that what you are experiencing is more real than any dream, possibly more real than anything you have ever felt.

Sometimes the dream can be frightening because of its intrinsic power, or confusing. Perhaps you don't know who the person in the dream is. It may be Maharajji's way of introducing himself to your awareness. Or perhaps his way of enticing you into his presence. Or validation of your connection to him. Or simply a blessing.

It is easy enough to ignore the dreams that are nothing more than run-off from your daily life, but a darshan dream is impossible to ignore. It may be a long and complex dream, or a fleeting moment of looking into Maharajji's eyes and feeling his love, but the power of these nighttime flights into that which is beyond your waking awareness can be life-changing.

Bo Lozoff

From: Prison Ashram Project
September 1986

Dear Krishna Das,

Hey there! I've never really mentioned how and why Maharajji and the big monkey came to rest in our lives. The story goes back many years…

From the time I was about five or six until I was about nine or ten, I had a recurring dream. I would wake up in the middle of the night terrified that I was paralyzed—couldn't move, couldn't scream, nothing. Yet as I would lay there and eventually calm down, I hoped I could have the dream again. It was terror, but a sort of terror that made me want to experience it again and again. Here's the dream:

I found myself alone, walking through a magical sort of forest, with huge trees like I had never seen in any woods in this part of the world. I always felt a little spooked but entranced, and I would walk along this winding forest path and then see a man standing right there in front of me as I came around a turn. He was scary, but more like a magician or sorcerer than a villain. I would look up to his face, into his eyes. When I gazed straight into his eyes, I woke up terrified time after time.

I couldn't handle those eyes. Yet for years, having that scary dream was my favorite adventure.

I mostly forgot all about the dreams as I grew up, until Sita, my wife, picked up *Be Here Now*, and the photo of Maharajji stirred a flicker of recognition. But it still didn't hit me until his first Mahasamadhi in 1974. I had spent it with Ram Dass and Anjani in New Hampshire, and Ram Dass gave me a prized photo of Maharajji to take home with me. The reason it was prized to me was that you could see one of his eyes clearly, staring straight ahead. That *really* stirred some vague recognition. About a week later, while doing a gazing meditation on that photo, all the dreams came flooding back clearly, and I realized that Maharajji had been my sorcerer in the magical forest all those years!

This is the first time I've ever really told that whole story.

Love, Bo

ॐ

Claire Libin

In 1994 I broke my kneecap and had to take a break from my Ashtanga yoga practice at Jivamukti. At the time I was working in the theater and had Monday nights off. Krishna Das had started doing kirtan on Monday nights at Jivamukti with a few people, so I went. While singing to Ram, I suddenly felt like I was a part of everything. Afterward, I said to Krishna Das that I didn't understand what had happened, but I felt so blissful and happy. He casually replied, "That's Maharajji." I was captivated.

Soon I was having vivid dreams of Maharajji.

In one dream, *I was watching a rerun of a 1970's TV show when I saw Maharajji in one scene, with writing across his shaved head from one side to the other.* The darshan was so strong I fell to the ground in full pranam. Years later, I saw a photo of Maharajji with Ram written in paste across his head and knew that was what I had seen in my dream.

In another dream, *Maharajji was in the apartment directly across the street from the apartment I grew up in in NYC. Many people were pranamming to him. I went closer and pranammed. Maharajji put his hand on my head. I looked straight into his eyes, and he gazed into mine for quite some time.* I knew he was my guru from that moment on.

In a Christmas morning dream, *Maharajji came into a very large room filled with people. I went right up to him and kissed him on his head. He seemed a bit surprised but looked at me and smiled. Then he sat next to me, and I felt so happy. We were all singing, and he kept smiling.*

The charming and charismatic Maharajji came in dreams at the beginning of his courtship of me. As the years passed, I felt Maharajji was so much more than the form I loved in my dreams. To me now, he is the embodiment of bliss and pure love in my heart and being, and in the universe. I aspire to feel his presence continually, and I would treasure more wonderful darshan dreams.

राम

Don St. Clair (Nataraj)

I'm a latter-day Neem Karoli Baba devotee and kirtan guitar wallah. Like many, I was introduced to Maharajji by *Be Here Now* when I was a twenty-one-year-old yogi in 1981. I had a few magical connections to the lineage and Hanuman, but in 1984 in Boulder, CO, something truly miraculous happened.

I was in between houses, sleeping in the upstairs storeroom of a crystal shop. Downstairs, directly below the room I was in and pointing up at me, was a store display of two giant three-foot tall crystals. Each of the two nights I was there I had a powerful dream. In the first, I *dreamt of a woman, obviously Indian, who came up to me, hands upraised like a hieroglyphic. She simply said to me: "I serve Vayu."* I had no idea what that meant or who Vayu was.

The next night, I had the most profound dream in which I met my guru. The entire dream was just one moment long and consisted of *a glimpse of an older grey-haired man, obviously a guru, whose image I did not remember at all, and in the flash of a moment he transformed into a young Indian boy with the most beautiful loving eyes. I also heard one spoken word—something like "D'aari."*

A week later, I went Sufi dancing in Boulder and bumped into my now dear friend, Benjy Wertheimer, the big-hearted kirtan musician. I told Benjy about my dreams and he said, "Well, Vayu was the ancient Vedic wind god who was the father of Hanuman, and some say Neem Karoli Baba was an incarnation of Hanuman. And Neem Karoli Baba has an elder devotee by the name of Tiwari."

With that, the room *spun* around me. I may have collapsed to the floor. In the center of the swirl of my tunnel vision, I saw Maharajji's face looking right at me with an unmistakable look of *Acha, got ya*! It was his undeniable darshan. He revealed his eternal presence, unfettered by mere life and death; it ripped crystal tears from my soul.

I recently watched Krishna Das's movie (*One Track Heart*) in which he talks about Mr. Tiwari in America, and that Tiwari had visited that very same crystal shop the year before I was there! We are woven into Maharajji's miraculous blanket of love!

राम

Emily Lakshmi Merrill

I got into Ram Dass through his podcast. I was at a low point in my life, and Ram Dass became my way through, but there was still this lingering feeling that I was missing out on Maharajji. Slowly, as I immersed myself into Ram Dass's teachings more and more, I had this beautiful realization that Maharajji *is* my guru.

I finally got to Maharajji's temples in India. I felt like I was falling in love with him more and more every day. One day Sharada (Angie Stopperan) was telling me her Maharajji story, and how he was showing her things that had happened in her life in the past. I

215

was crying as I listened to her story. I had dropped into this space with her where he felt so present.

All of a sudden, I had this vision of Maharajji showing me all the times that he had been there for me in my childhood when I was suffering, before I even knew who Ram Dass or Maharajji were. In the vision, he showed me a moment when I was lying on my bedroom floor with my head down on the ground, crying and screaming that I was so done with life. I was seeing from the perspective of standing in the corner of the room looking back at myself on the floor. I saw Maharajji walk in the door of my room; he reached down and held my hand. I saw a few other times during my childhood when I was really down, when I was five, six years old. Maharajji was in my bedroom in those moments, as if he had chosen me, and was there throughout my whole life. He waited until I was twenty-two years old to wake me up to him, but he had been there the entire time.

I've been able to relax into my life and let it flow. Recently, I've had his darshan in my dreams. As soon as Maharajji's there, I'll sit down with him and make eye contact. It feels so real. It's that moment of pure surrender when he looks into your eyes, knowing that he knows everything about you. He's seen it all since childhood, even past lives.

The message I often take away from my dreams is: *How can I serve you and how can I spread more love?*

राम

Ganesh Das Braymiller

When psychedelics and podcasts found their way into my mental diet, it was Duncan Trussell who guided me to the *Here & Now* podcast with Ram Dass, which soon permeated every aspect of my daily existence. Around this time, my wife Mangala received a job opportunity in Asheville, NC, but was only given three days to decide. I had never been there, but clear as day I heard the host of *Here & Now* echoing in my head, "Raghu Markus, from Asheville, North Carolina..." On a whim, I reached out to Raghu. He said if we made the jump to Asheville, we should meet for satsang.

We landed at a small cabin tucked away in the Appalachian Mountains. My transfer hadn't gone through yet, Mangala was busy with her new job, the car broke down upon arriving, and our stuff was in storage—so I found myself stranded for weeks in this new place with only one book, *Miracle of Love*. In this space between my old and new lives, I began to feel what I later learned was bhava – devotional essence. Upon getting my car back, I reached out to Raghu.

The night before our first meeting, I dreamed *I was on a dusty red street surrounded by people. I turned left, and there was Maharajji, shining brighter than the sun, dressed in all white. I threw myself to the ground due to the sheer intensity of the brightness.* I instantly awoke with more shakti than I've ever felt in my life.

Welcomed like old family to the Asheville satsang, we soon found ourselves on a guided Ram Dass-themed yatra through India. One night, as I was leading a Chalisa, I flubbed the last note. The next day at Hanumangarh—one of Maharajji's Himalayan ashrams—I was still quietly upset with myself for being so sloppy, when a friend motioned me up to Maharajji's takhat and pointed. Enclosed in glass, there was a page from Maharajji's notebook with the mantra *Ram Ram* written down the whole page. I noticed that the handwriting was messy. I broke down crying. I had been absolved. Maharajji had let me know that it's okay to be a "sloppy bhakti."

A year later, my grandfather died. He had listened every day to a video of Mangala and I singing the Hanuman Chalisa and said to the family, "Do you know what it feels like when your heart smiles?" Since meeting Maharajji, I do.

Govind Das

I was at the Bodhi Tree, a spiritual bookstore in Los Angeles. I was teaching yoga at the time, and somebody came up to me and said, "Did you hear that Ram Dass just had a stroke?" I didn't even know who Ram Dass was. A couple of years later I was seeing an ayurvedic doctor, who had kirtan playing in his office. The music struck such a deep chord in my heart; I could hear that it was music as prayer. Wanting to combine yoga and kirtan, I went to New York for a teacher training from Yogi Hari from the Sivananda tradition because he had kirtan as a main part of it.

After the teacher training, a friend gave me a Ram Dass tape. Ram Dass was talking about Maharajji, bhakti yoga, and this path of the heart. I knew this was the path that I was to follow, even though I didn't quite understand it. Then I went to a class at the Jivamukti Yoga Studio and heard kirtan being played like I hadn't heard before. After class I went to the teacher and asked, "Who is this? Where do I get this music?"

"Oh, this is Krishna Das. He does kirtan here every Monday night. He just released his first album, and we also have a Bhagavan Das tape you might like." Both cassettes had a picture of Neem Karoli Baba, so literally within 24 hours, I was hit from three different angles: Ram Dass, Bhagavan Das, and Krishna Das.

When I was back in California, Krishna Das came to do kirtan at Border's Bookstore on the Third Street Promenade in Santa Monica. This was the first time that Krishna Das had come to California to chant publicly. He was signing audiotapes of his album and then he was going to chant. I was the first person there, and the first person I met was Shiva Baum[36], the second was Raghu.

---

36 See Shiva Baum's story, p. 269.

The stories that Krishna Das told that night were the most real thing I had ever felt in my heart. Yes, this was a path that I was supposed to follow.

Sometime later I had a dream. *I was with Maharajji. He was sitting in a chair, and I was sitting at his feet, crying and crying. He was giggling and laughing and playing with me. I kept crying more and more. I was crying from joy because I had finally found my way back home. And Maharajji was home.* When I woke up, real tears were flowing from my eyes. I felt my life changing. In some way I had been initiated into bhakti, into this path of guru kripa, and to Maharajji as my guru.

Krishna Das had a kirtan in Santa Monica a few weeks later, and Raghu was there. I told them about this dream, and Raghu said, "Neem Karoli Baba is not living in a body anymore, but this is how he often gives darshan. He visits people, whether in dreams or in meditation. This is very special, a very great gift. I would recommend, if it feels right for you, to put a picture of him on your altar or where you meditate."

Twenty years later, that picture is still there.

राम

Greg Woods

September 18, 1990
Ram Dass,

A few nights ago, I dreamed of Maharajji. *I was in a large room or hall filled with individuals in Indian dress. Maharajji had a white cloth wrapped around him and was followed by one or two men. As he moved through the crowd, I approached him and pranammed. He looked at me and either said, "What do you want?" or I just knew his intention.*

I said, "I love you," but it came out garbled, like a record played at a slow speed. He curled his lip, cocked his head to the right and said, "What?" His face was so close and clear that I could see the stubble of his moustache. It was wonderful but frustrating. I repeated, again with difficulty, "I love you."

He said, "Oh, you love me? Then what do you have for me?"

My mind was in a state of confusion as I followed him to the platform at the end of the hall. He turned around and stretched out his hand toward me. He was opening and closing his hand as if to say, "Come on, let's have it!" I frantically began feeling my pants pockets for something. My wallet was gone and I felt oddly relieved. In my right back pocket were my comb and handkerchief; in my right front pocket were my keys; in the left front pocket I had a crucifix, a rosary, two pictures of Rajinder Singh, and a picture of you I cut out of a listing from the Hanuman Tape Library.

Well, I gave him my comb and handkerchief. It seemed ridiculous to me, even in the dream, but I couldn't give him my keys or my security stash! (I carry the pictures in my wallet and the crucifix and rosary in my pocket in the waking state). *He took my offering, looked at it, and appeared to find it interesting. Then he stretched forth his hand as if to say, "Let's have it!" I gave him my keys. As he was holding them up in the light from a window, I wondered if he might let me have them back long enough to have copies made! He was jangling the keys in the light and giving me a strange smile.*

My first thought upon waking was *my God, Maharajji, you can have it all!* I couldn't believe I gave him my comb instead of myself. Maybe, at some level I don't want to let go, but I think I do! What do you make of this?

राम

Jai Ram Lentine

I grew up conservative Catholic, then became an angry atheist type, devouring religious books but questioning everything. In graduate school I plunged into the world of public health, which led me to connect with T. Steve Jones[37]. He was on the board of Seva with Ram Dass and Mirabai Bush. By that time I had a family with young kids, but still felt like there was a hole, an emptiness in my life. I worked with Steve Jones on HIV prevention for drug users. He talked to me about smallpox eradication and Dr. Larry Brilliant and told me Ram Dass had married him and his wife, but he never said anything about Maharajji.

Around 2012, after a few years of doing hatha yoga, I had this powerful dream the day before my thirty-ninth birthday that really shifted things for me. *A large dark man was seated to my right at a bar reading something. A small monkey man was sitting on the bar in front of him, in front of what he was reading. His master said, "Go away now." The thing kissed his fingers. I felt warm and safe next to his master, like a father, and I too kissed his fingers.* Later, I realized that that small monkey man was Hanuman. It was so weird, so out of context, but I guess it was a prelude for what was to come.

About a year later, my whole life fell apart, and I lost my family through a messy divorce. I was devastated. I was getting the Love Serve Remember stories on my Facebook feed; in these posts Ram Dass keeps saying, ".... and then my guru looked at me with unconditional love." I felt so jealous. Okay, universe, if you have unconditional love, I want some! I kind of shook my fist at the universe . . . give it to me!

Within a few weeks I started to have this feeling inside of warmth. It grew into a sense of unconditional love for myself, and then when

---

37 Dr. T. Stephen Jones, public health researcher, part of the WHO smallpox eradication team, and one of the founding members of Seva Foundation.

I looked around at everyone, I had unconditional love for everyone else as well! It grew and peaked and then faded away over about six weeks. But I had had the taste of something I had not even known existed, and I knew it was connected to Ram Dass. At this point I still was not understanding that this was Maharajji, but I thought I've got to go thank Ram Dass for this incredible gift.

I saw that there was a retreat in Maui and went there in the spring of 2015 to say thank you. At the retreat, Ram Dass introduced us to Maharajji through the mala ceremony. I started to connect the pieces: the dream and Hanuman, the unconditional love, kirtan, and Maharajji. I've been back about every six months. The healing that I've had over the years from being with Ram Dass opened my heart. I found forgiveness, and the experience of unconditional love is extraordinary.

॥श्री॥

Kate Rabinowitz

I grew up in Cambridge, Massachusetts, two blocks away from David[38] and Mary McClelland's house. My mom worked with Mary, and I used to go to these big parties there. I was nine or ten years old, hanging out with all these hippies. I knew Ram Dass as Richard Alpert. We moved to Seattle, but I ended up back east when I went to college. One summer I stayed at the McClelland's house, and they had *Miracle of Love*. I read every single page. After college I went to India, but the India of *Miracle of Love* was not the India that I touched upon.

---

38 David McClelland was chair of the Department of Psychology and Social Relations at Harvard University, who helped Ram Dass (then Richard Alpert) get his position at Harvard as a psychology professor.

Years went by and I was introduced to Rameshwar Das by our mutual friend Rose, who knew him from Seva board meetings. When we were dating, we went to a bhandara in Taos. The Hanuman Chalisas and aarti felt familiar, but I didn't quite know what I was doing there. When I married Ramesh and we had our kids, it felt like I had married into the satsang.

Then we went to Kainchi. I was thinking, what are we doing in this temple? We were mostly sitting around waiting for darshan of Siddhi Ma. I was doing my yoga practice. Siddhi Ma knew I was restless, so she would give me work to do. When it came time to leave I was thinking, okay, we're finally going to *do* something, not just sit around a temple. But then I got very sick. It felt like knives moving through me, and I could hardly breathe, so we were stuck in Kainchi. I was seriously afraid! Siddhi Ma came to our room and gave me a homeopathic remedy.

That night I had a dream that was not a dream.

I was walking up a hill. I had a bicycle and all my stuff was loaded on the bike. Ramesh was walking next to me. I kept wanting Ramesh to carry my bags, to carry my stuff, but he said I had to carry my own. It was heavy, so I had to keep letting go of bags. I was worried that we weren't going to get any food when we got to the top of the mountain, so I was trying to scrounge food the whole way up. We stopped at a Chinese restaurant and I got all the soy sauce packets and little crackers; I had a real scarcity thing going on. We got to the top of this hill, and I looked through this field and saw Maharajji. He was talking at a podium, and there were a lot of people around. He looked over at me so sharply it felt like he was looking right into me. He said, "I've been waiting for you." I walked over to where he was and I was totally bathed in this love. It was this timeless, incredible, never want it to end, the most ecstatic . . . and then I wasn't even there anymore.

I woke up from that dream and told Ramesh that Maharajji had been with me all night and I didn't want it to end. Ramesh told

Ma, and then all the Mas and everyone came running "Oh, darshan, darshan!" I had to tell them the dream again and again.

Years later, when our daughter Anna was killed[39], I lost faith in everything I was doing—the Hanuman Chalisa, praying, chanting, making prasad and feeding people, teaching my children about compassion and being good. Nothing mattered. Friends in India would say Maharajji does everything. So if Maharajji does everything, did he kill Anna? Whether it's Maharajji or the laws of the universe, things happen despite my best plans, and everything now for me is because of Anna, because of her life and her death.

Being at the Maui retreat with people who are also involved in the mystery helped me feel more about what Maharajji's love is. During the mala ceremony, there are images of Maharajji and Hanuman behind Ram Dass, and way at the top of the tent, there's this light coming through from the sky, and that's Anna. There's a light that's way beyond even Anna. The only thing that seems real to me is that light, or what sparkles in the dewdrop on the leaf. I don't know how I'm being guided. But I do know that I don't know, and that I'm very open to it being different in a good way, in a way like that love I first read about in *Miracle of Love* and felt in my dream.

ॐ

Krishna (Shawn Gray)

I was in a bad place in my life and didn't really know what to do, so I started meditating and studying Buddhism. It helped a little but didn't really fill the void. Around this time, I ordered *Be Here Now*. When I opened it, I thought, what is this? I put it on my shelf and

---

39 Anna Mirabai Lytton was 14 years old and about to graduate 8th grade when she was hit by an SUV while riding her bicycle.

didn't crack it open again until two years later. I did keep listening to Ram Dass podcasts, but I wasn't interested in Maharajji.

During this time I began seeing the numbers 911 everywhere. I would see it on the clock, license plates, other unusual places. I saw it enough to start freaking me out, but I didn't tell anyone. Then one day the house alarm started going off. It scared me to death, as I had never heard it before. I went to disarm it and it was 9:11 a.m. My heart almost leapt out of my chest.

This continued for another year. I kept seeing 911 and couldn't figure out what it was about. Then I went to bed one night and looked across the room and saw a huge face. It was Maharajji's face, and at the same time I heard a loud metallic-like sound, like someone hitting a fifty-five-gallon drum. Chills ran down my body, and I stayed perfectly still and slowly the image faded.

That night I had a dream that was in HD quality. I could see every little detail. *I was in a stone room with large windows and white light coming in. Across the room was a figure with a sheet draped over his head. When he started walking towards me, the sheet pressed into his face, and I could tell it was Maharajji.*

The next day I woke up and immediately started reading about Maharajji. I knew nothing about him. The first thing I saw was he died on September 11th—9/11. This flooded me with emotion and love, and I broke down crying. Since then I have been studying and praying. Before all this I was leading a horrible life. I ended up telling my wife the truth about things I had done in the past, which I probably would have never done without Maharajji's help. We have since split up, but I feel such relief from telling the truth. I know there will be something more for me by following my heart and staying in truth.

॥ म ॥

Barry, my husband, was part of the Sufi community here in Kansas City. Nineteen years ago we went on a trip to the East coast. Barry had just bought Krishna Das's CD *Pilgrim Heart*, which we listened to as we traveled.

In Pennsylvania, we were staying at a friend's cabin, and Barry took the girls out to give me time for a nap. I put on the CD and fell asleep. Then I had a dream: *I'm sitting cross-legged next to a pond. I'm enveloped in music and, although I don't see anyone, we're singing kirtan. I feel so much love, so much bliss. Then out of the middle of the pond rises the head of some bald man with ears that are sticking out. He looks at me as I'm singing and smiles. His hand rises up, like from the bottom of the pond, and he's holding this sea-weedy mud. He glides over to me. I turn my hand over and he places all that gunk and muck in my hand. I cover it with my other hand and start to rub it back and forth. I feel the kirtan throughout my whole body. It was the first time I'd ever felt unconditional love. I'm rubbing and rubbing and rubbing. At some point the music stops, and I look down at my hand and I'm holding a pearl.*

I told Barry about the dream and wondered what it could mean. Who could the man in the pond be?

Next we visited my friend Jeannie in Vermont. After the kids were all in bed, we went upstairs to talk. She had a little altar in her room, and she reached underneath and brought out *Miracle of Love*. I looked at the cover and said, "Hey, that's the guy I had a dream about!" She handed me the book and said, "I guess this is for you."

When Australia was on fire, the news was so upsetting to me: the political situation, koala bears getting burned up, all the pain. I turned to my picture of Maharajji and cried out, "Why is this happening? What is going on?" It was a heartfelt cry about all the suffering. Then that night I had a dream: *I was in a room, putting on my coat, getting ready to leave. I had just spent time with Maharajji, but*

I didn't recognize him. I thought he was a friend. I'm zipping up my coat and I turn to him. You know how his ears stick out a little bit, right? He starts to pull his ear and I see a thin line appearing on his neck. He pulls, and his head is coming off his body. Then the scene shifts and there's a man who's lying on the takhat where Maharajji was. The man is crying, crying, crying. He looks up at me and says, "He chose to spend time with you. And then he gave you his head." I look down at my hands and I'm holding Maharajji's head. So that's the second time I dreamed about Maharajji's head, the "godhead."

I don't talk about Maharajji much, but I have pictures of him everywhere in my house. In January, a Sufi friend handed me a green cloth. When I unwrapped it, it was filled with ashes. She said, "These are Maharajji's ashes." Her old boyfriend had been at Maharajji's cremation. She had them for years and years, and she suddenly felt to give them to me.

जय

Lynne Jackier

I've read many books about Buddhism and have been doing various meditation practices on and off for decades. I learned about Krishna Das from watching the movie *Fierce Grace* in 2009 while I was searching for ways to be present for my mother, who was at the end of a long illness. I started listening to CDs of chanting and went to my first kirtan retreat in the fall of that year. That was the first time I heard about Maharajji. I was raised to be skeptical and the following dreams were unexpected and startlingly vivid.

October 29, 2010

Krishna Das was leading kirtan somewhere nearby. I went into the place, which looked like my regular yoga studio with hardwood floors and big windows. Only about fifteen people were there.

Krishna Das was sitting on the floor in front of two windows. Maharajji was with him, which surprised me because I knew that Maharajji had died many years ago. I saw that some people were lying down, so I did too, and we began to meditate. I was filled with a lightness and joy that I knew came from Maharajji. It filled my senses, a blinding light the color of sunshine filled my entire field of vision (even though my eyes were closed), and I bubbled over with a delighted laugh. I sat up, amazed, and Krishna Das caught my eye and said, "I knew you would get it." When I woke up I felt much lighter, depression gone, and pain in my lower back much better.

February 1, 2016

I was at a very big kirtan; thousands were there. I saw Krishna Das with Maharajji in the distance. There were rumors that a young man and young woman who were devotees of another guru had been "stolen" by Maharajji. Suddenly, I bumped into Krishna Das and, as often happens in real life, I felt awkward and said dumb things. I think I mentioned this "scandal." Krishna Das chatted with me a bit until we came to Maharajji's blanket in an alcove off the main room. The Dalai Lama was on the blanket, playing with toy dinosaurs like a small boy. I sat down on the blanket and picked up a dinosaur to play too. I was still feeling self-conscious about my interaction with Krishna Das. I looked up at him, said goodbye, and turned back to the Dalai Lama. Suddenly, I felt Krishna Das was back, but it was Maharajji, who blew softly in my hair and kissed my head over and over like a parent with a very small child. My discomfort about my interaction with Krishna Das left.

August 12, 2018

This dream came as my husband and I were sleeping on a mat on the floor next to my father's bed in our home. My father had dementia and we cared for him during the last year of his life. It was very intense and overwhelming. I was so grateful for this dream.

I am driving down Main Street in the town where I grew up. Out the window I see a group of people in Indian dress walking down the sidewalk. One person is pushing a wheelchair. In the wheelchair is Neem Karoli Baba! Later, I'm at a Krishna Das retreat getting some tea and Krishna Das walks up to get some too. I tell Krishna Das that I saw Maharajji. With great embarrassment, I had thought at the time, "I should tell Krishna Das that he's here!" and then realized that, of course, he is here because Krishna Das is here. Later, Krishna Das gives me a hand-written note inviting me to come back at 2:30 a.m. to have Maharajji's darshan. In the dream the note was very clear and I could read the words. I went back home and told my husband about the invitation, but I was unable to go because I had to stay on the mat overnight with my dad.

Now I realize that the invitation to have Maharajji's darshan at 2:30 a.m. was an invitation to see my service to my father as that darshan. Maharajji was in a wheelchair at the beginning of the dream just as my father was in his last few months.

ॐ

Maria-Radha Maese

In 2009, I saw the movie *Fierce Grace*. I didn't know who Ram Dass was, but I did think he was very courageous. Shortly after that I was taking a meditation class, and the teacher asked us to call someone in, but before I had a chance to call anyone, Ram Dass came in. Later I had a dream. *From behind a tree out came Maharajji; he was very small and childlike. I knew who he was from watching the movie, but I didn't know anything about him. Maharajji was standing there smiling and I just stared at him. Ram Dass was sitting in his wheelchair. I put my head on his lap; he stroked my hair and I woke up.* So that was my very first experience with Maharajji. He came out from behind a tree and smiled. I had that dream a few times.

After that Maharajji started coming regularly in my dreams, but I still couldn't accept him. I grew up Roman Catholic, and this was very hard for me to accept. I called him the crazy man of my dreams; he wouldn't leave me alone.

In one dream we were walking through a street bazaar, with vendors on both sides. We were looking at people who were all dressed so beautifully. I said, "Baba, who's that?"

He said, "That's me."

I said, "That's not you."

"Yes, and that's me. And that's me." He was laughing and laughing. I couldn't get a straight answer out of him.

There was an old man sitting on the floor with this mangy-looking dog next to him. The man was doing malas, and the dog was sitting there staring at his owner with so much love. I said to Baba, "And who's that man?"

He said, "That's me."

"Who is that dog? Is that you too?" I was being snotty with him.

"No, that's you."

I woke up, and my first thought was that Maharajji had called me a mangy dog! Why was he insulting me? I didn't understand. Now, of course, I know that the man was him, and the dog was me looking at him with love. For almost two years, the dreams were very frequent and confused me to no end. I was always getting angry with him. I would try to talk to him in a dream and he would laugh at me.

Then came the dream that changed my life.

My car was parked on top of a cliff that overlooked the city, and Maharajji and I were sitting on lawn chairs in front of the car. The moon was shining brightly and the lights of the city below twinkled with activity. "Heart as Wide as the World," my favorite Krishna Das song, was playing on the radio. I started singing along. Baba listened and swayed his head back and forth, enjoying the music. He got up from the chair, and we stood together, leaning on the front of the car looking out over the cliff. I put my arm through his arm as I would my father and we looked over the city.

Then Maharajji touched my heart and a web of light came out of me, straight from my heart, hands, eyes, mouth. It spread out and seemed to connect everything. We looked out at what seemed to be the entire world stretched out on a flat infinite plane. It was breathtakingly beautiful. The web began to change and the strands spread out until it became like a sheet of liquid light.

Then Baba looked to me and said, "Sing." I slowly chanted Sri Ram Jai Ram, Jai Jai Ram. *As I sang, the sheet of light began to vibrate. It was pulsating. It moved through everything, but it never separated. I stopped singing for a second to ask Maharajji what he was trying to show me, but as soon as I stopped singing, the vibration and movement stopped. I looked over at him and his eyes were closed. He looked so peaceful, I couldn't disturb him. I went back to singing and the vibration started again.*

The sheet of light began to open vertically, like an accordion lying on its side. It grew until everyone and everything was submerged in it. When I realized that we were also submerged in this infinite sheet of liquid light, I felt like I was being smothered, and I gasped and stopped singing; just like that it was all gone. I asked Maharajji what it was and he said, "You are needed. You had to see so you can understand it is important."

I know he was showing me that I am not alone, that all living things are all connected. It changed my life. It took away that feeling of being alone and made me understand that the energy I give off affects others and that we really are all one. I did love Maharajji very much and I accepted him in my life.

I don't dream of him that often anymore. Now I cherish it every time he comes. I see that every dream has a message. I no longer rack my brain to try and figure it out. The last dream I had: *Maharajji brought Ram Dass along and he wasn't in a wheelchair. Ram Dass was sitting on a rock and he let me put my head on his lap. He was stroking my hair and I woke up feeling so peaceful and so happy. I knew he was with Maharajji.*

तम्

Mary Jo Belongea

In 1976, a friend gave me the book *Be Here Now*. I was ecstatic from reading it, so I bought all of Ram Dass's books and tapes and had the strange feeling that I might work with him someday.

I signed up for a meditation course and asked the man at the center, "Do you know how I can find Ram Dass? I want to go to one of his lectures." He told me to call the Seva Foundation. Judy Gallagher, the office manager, gave me the information I was looking for and then I asked about the Seva Foundation. Judy told me about Seva's work to cure and alleviate blindness in India and Nepal. When she said that, my heart knew this was the place where I was supposed to volunteer! Right away they needed help on follow-up after a talk that had been held the previous night.

Shortly after that, Ram Dass was named chairman of the board of Seva and they said, "Mary Jo, since you know so much about his work, would you like to handle his correspondence while he's on tour?" *Absolutely!*

Ram Dass told me, "Just listen to your heart." That was my instruction. A lot of the letters were from people telling Ram Dass these beautiful stories about Maharajji. I wished Maharajji was my guru, but I thought of him as Ram Dass's guru.

One time the whole Seva staff came to my house when Ram Dass was in town and he talked with the staff. That night I had my first dream of Maharajji. *I was walking toward a door. Ram Dass opened the door and invited me in. Ram Dass was radiating when I came in. When he opened the door, the room was filled with radiant light. It was so unbelievably beautiful—the love and radiance and this heightened feeling in my heart. It was pure love. Maharajji was sitting up on a platform. All the people that I knew from Seva were there. A lot of the board members were devotees of Maharajji and they were all sitting before him. I sat with them. It felt like an initiation of some sort, like I had been invited into this room with Maharajji.*

The second dream I had was when my youngest son, Ryan, was seven; we found ourselves in India in this dream. *We were in front of a big wooden gate. I knew that I had to knock on the gate, so I did. Girija Brilliant*[40] *came to the gate. We were friends and she let me inside. She asked why I was there. I said, "We came to see Maharajji."*

She said, "Let me ask if I can take you to him." When she came back, she said that he would see us. Ryan and I pranammed to him, and then we were kneeling before him. He said, "Why are you here?"

"We came to see you, Maharajji." And he hit us both on the head.

I lost consciousness, so I don't know what happened after that. But I read in books that he often hit people on the head. I learned later that when you go to Kainchi, you're supposed to knock on a gate. And when I got to India, I recognized the temple at Kainchi as the one I'd seen in the dream.

My ex didn't like any of this "guru stuff," while I was very drawn to it. In my third dream, *I was sitting next to Maharajji on what I would call a large coffee table (a takhat). He and his blanket were wrapped around me. I was totally wrapped in his blanket. It was powerfully loving and sweet. I felt completely safe and enfolded by his unconditional love and grace.* After that I started to go through the divorce. I felt like that darshan dream was grace to help me get through it.

---

40 Girija Brilliant has an MPH and Ph.D. in social epidemiology and lots of experience in global health. She was in India with Maharajji along with her husband, Dr. Larry Brilliant, and participated in the WHO vaccination program to eradicate smallpox. She is one of the founders of Seva Foundation.

The last significant dream happened nine years ago. My son Ryan was not doing well and I was at a loss as to how to help him. I was praying to Maharajji regularly. One afternoon I had darshan in a lucid dream. *Ram Dass took me to Maharajji, who was sitting on a platform. I sat in front of Maharajji, who looked at me deeply for what felt like an hour. It was so powerful, so penetrating. It felt like I was being filled in some beautiful way. Then he kissed me on the forehead.* Two weeks after that beautiful dream, Ryan died.

These dreams have helped so much, knowing that I was loved and supported. I felt with Maharajji that there's a transmission of some sort that I can't describe. I've been through great losses in my life, but I feel like I had the strength to get through them because of my connection to Maharajji. He's always present. I went back to school and became a psychotherapist. Maharajji guides me regularly in my work with people.

ॐ

Paul Lloyd Thomas

Like for so many others, Maharajji's initial "hook and bait" for me was Ram Dass and *Be Here Now.* I had already been into meditation and mysticism for many years. I even completed my B.A. at Naropa University[41] but somehow had evaded Ram Dass there. In 2015 *Be Here Now* made its debut into my hands and heart. I soon discovered the treasure trove of Ram Dass lectures and developed an insatiable appetite for them. I went from, "*Hmm,* sounds like Ram Dass's guru

---

41 Naropa University, in Boulder, CO, blends Eastern philosophy and Western scholarship.

was an interesting guy," to "*Hmm*, what kind of frame should I get for my favorite Maharajji photo?"

At that point, Neem Karoli Baba had his foot in the door, but I didn't give him the keys to the house until the early morning of December 7, 2015. I awoke from the most extraordinary dream that didn't feel like a dream.

I was following Maharajji down the dirt road I live off. He was plodding along while gleefully talking with a large group of devotees, who surrounded him like a flock of baby ducks following their mother. I was with my mother and Krishna Das, hanging back a bit behind the group, just watching with excitement.

It was dawn. I sat in a green pastural field with great mountains on the horizon. Scattered across the peaks, stars still shimmered and glistened from the night. A warm ethereal feeling pervaded my being. Other people were sitting nearby. Some distance away, Maharajji sat on his takhat with devotees around him. I thought excitedly, "Wow, that's Maharajji over there!" But I was a first-timer and was quite content in my "sweet spot," observing the scene. "I don't want to impose myself on Maharajji or anyone," I thought. After some time, Maharajji pointed and waved at me. Startled, I hesitated, uncertain as to what to do. A few moments later, he was right in front of me sitting in the grass, wrapped in a dark brown blanket with the morning light radiating behind him.

I became like a deer in headlights, mesmerized in a perpetual "wow-gasm" from head to toe, a state of rapturous astonishment. It was everything I had been reading about him. He was as present as the mountains yet vast as the cosmos, exuding an aura of penetrating wisdom, humor, and compassion. There was no music, yet I heard a great soundless sound—a shining divinity roaring like a waterfall—as if Maharajji was at the center of a huge thundering gong or trumpet.

I now sat across from Baba on the side of a dirt road. One or two Indian devotees stood beside him. At one point Baba leaned over and with

a serious tone said to one of the devotees, "Until he opens his heart . . ."
As if he meant, "I can't work with this (me) until...," or "such and such
won't happen until..." His words hung in the air with great weight.
Anxiously, I protested, "I'm trying, Maharajji, but when I open my
heart, I get prickled by the closed hearts of others." I pictured bumping
into spiky sea urchins. Maharajji said, "Give that to me."

We were back on the hillside, but now Maharajji sat a bit farther
away, lying on his side and resting his head on his hand. I gazed up at
his twinkling eyes. Returning the gaze, he said, "King Solomon will
shine light upon you when he finds you." Then suddenly his skin turned
Krishna blue, and his hair and beard grew long, almost like dreadlocks. It
was blue Hanuman! Or Hanuman, Krishna, and Shiva in one. A wide
grin spread across his face. He gave me a funny, reassuring, cosmic wink
that said, "Pretty far out, huh?!" I laughed and sat in stupefied awe.
Maharajji shape-shifted back into his human body, and like something
out of Star Trek, he "beamed up" in a quick flash and was gone!

I was swaying in a daze. Out of nowhere, my college friend Becca
came over and said, "He spent time with you today. I never talked to
him!"

I responded, "That's his teaching too, Becca . . . that's his teaching too."

I was writing in my journal over and over again, "King Solomon
will shine light upon you when he finds you."

I jolted up in bed, still half in the dream. 5:44 a.m. The dream
energy poured through into my waking state. Maharajji reverberated
in my bones. In blissful bewilderment, I went to the window, half
expecting to see Maharajji walking across the field. The stars glowed
with such empyrean majesty and mystery. Returning to my bed, I
grabbed my journal and began to write.

ॐ

Ramananda John E. Welshons

In the summer of 1971, I heard a tape of a lecture Ram Dass had given in 1969. In those days he was referring to Neem Karoli Baba just as "Maharajji." The sweetness with which Ram Dass spoke about him captivated me. I had been studying Eastern teachers—primarily Meher Baba, Ramakrishna, and Yogananda—so it was very interesting to hear Ram Dass's stories about Maharajji. I especially liked the fact that many of them were funny. That delighted me—Maharajji's ability to see the cosmic humor in everything.

In May of 1973, I met Ram Dass. Some friends and I brought him to the University of South Florida. The day he arrived we went out to lunch at the local vegetarian restaurant. I was sitting across the table from Ram Dass. I glanced over at him. Our eyes met, and suddenly we had this incredibly powerful connection. It felt like the whole universe had fallen away. All I could see were Ram Dass's eyes surrounded by light. Then Ram Dass spoke: "I love you more than you could ever love yourself"—a quote from Meher Baba. We shared a few moments of silence. Ram Dass said, "You and I are not we, but one"— another quote from Meher Baba. I was floating in this incredibly blissful space, the likes of which I'd never experienced before. That was nearly fifty years ago and it's still one of the most powerful moments of my life.

In 1979, Ram Dass and I started working together. I noticed that he never seemed to be lonely. I had just gone through a very painful breakup. I sat down in front of my puja where I had a beautiful photo of Maharajji. I looked into his eyes and said, "Maharajji, can you help me to not feel lonely?" I don't know what he did, but I haven't felt one moment of loneliness since then. I began to feel Maharajji's presence everywhere—with me, in me, and around me . . . all the time.

So I experienced Maharajji taking away my loneliness and allow-ing me to be held in the arms of love. I had been connected with

Meher Baba since 1969. I never got to meet Maharajji, nor did I get to meet Meher Baba, but Meher Baba was very stern about the notion that if you were going to be a devotee of his, you really shouldn't hang out with other teachers. One night before I went to bed, I sat in meditation and prayed, "Meher Baba, it feels really good to be with Ram Dass and to feel the essence of Maharajji in my heart. I just want to know if it's okay with you."

That night I had an incredibly vivid dream. *I saw Meher Baba sitting on a chair, almost like a throne—not regal but very, very powerful. He was smiling and holding up his right hand in a mudra with index finger and thumb touching, his sign for "perfect." As he was sitting there, he suddenly turned into Maharajji. Then Maharajji was looking at me and smiling and holding his hand in the same mudra as Meher Baba. Maharajji then turned back into Meher Baba, then back into Maharajji. Far out. Then the chair separated into two chairs. Now Maharajji and Meher Baba were sitting side-by-side, both smiling. Suddenly, Ram Dass appeared, sitting on the floor in front of them in the lotus position. Maharajji and Meher Baba were both patting Ram Dass on the head, as if they were saying, "Very good. Very good. We love Ram Dass."*

It was such a powerful answer to a very sincere and deep prayer. From then on, I never had any question in my mind or in my heart about the appropriateness of being with and working with Ram Dass or holding Maharajji in my heart. At various times in my life I have felt closer to Maharajji and other times closer to Meher Baba, but it doesn't matter because they're both . . . really . . . pure unconditional Love.

Sub Ek, all One.

हरी

Ram Tom (Thomas Tompkins)

Baba left the body before my parents were even married. I had a lot of bad addictions, but I am now clean for six years thanks to too many people to name, but the most important of all is Baba's grace.

I met Krishna Das in Albany, NY, and he invited my friend and me to his retreat in Garrison, NY. During a workshop, I had a feeling come over me of Neem Karoli Baba. And that night I had a dream of Baba and Dada sitting in the exact place I was at during the workshop. It was a very strange but overwhelming experience for me. Since then I have been so connected to Baba's unconditional love.

I have had a lot of real darshan with Baba through dreams. The most powerful one was when my best friend's grandmother, Mema, was in the process of leaving the body. She was the most loving person I'd known. I had a dream one night: *I was driving through India with Baba in the passenger seat and Mema in the back seat. She was a very small woman and even smaller in the dream. Baba was yelling orders at me and didn't stop talking. "Turn right, no to the left, keep going straight. What are you doing? Go faster, turn left." And in between he kept looking back at Mema and saying, "Come on Ma, it's okay. It's okay, Ma, we are going to get there. Don't worry, Ma, don't worry. Trust me, Ma, we will get there. Don't be afraid."* That morning I woke up to a phone call that Mema had left her body. I truly believe Baba was telling her it's okay, just come with him.

ॐ

Randall Reel

I grew up in Orange County and L.A.—a white Republican. My dad's an engineer. My mom is a teacher with no religion. How did I end up worshipping a big concrete orange monkey in the mountains of the Himalayas?

I was on a job in New York with a friend. We were talking about psychic abilities and how rare that was, and how people don't seem to talk about them or exercise them. He said, "You've got to read this book, *Be Here Now*." The whole time I was reading it, I felt like I was getting a warm hug; when the book was over the hug ended, so I read every single Ram Dass book to continue the hug.

One day I'm sitting on my bed with *Be Here Now* open to a picture of Maharajji. I was looking at him and it dawned on me: "It's you! You're the warm hug! You're doing this and you're doing it through Ram Dass." My life had changed and I never even met Ram Dass.

Three days later I got a call from a friend who said, "That guy you like, Ram Dass, is going to be lecturing in Pasadena. Would you like to go?" I had a dream the night before the lecture of this man with a gray beard. I had to get through him to get to Ram Dass. Turned out that was the guy taking my ticket at Pasadena in March of 1996.

Then I met Maharajji in a dream. *There was a crowd and we were bustling about. We were somewhere in India, and there was a dirt floor in the room. I was trying to get to Maharajji, when suddenly he was right in front of me. He looked at me and grabbed my right hand and held my ring finger, right where the ring goes. My whole body started to fill up with this radiant light energy. I filled up with it and was blissed out of my gourd.* I woke up feeling that way.

When I told Krishna Das about that dream, he very sternly said, "Those aren't dreams. That's Maharajji. That's as Maharajji as it gets!"

राम

Rita Ryan

A friend I used to meditate with gave me a Krishna Das CD. He went on and on about how Krishna Das went to India and met this guru and became Krishna Das. The music didn't resonate with me (too much like Catholic Mass organ music) and turned me off (of course, I love him now). Then he showed me the cover of the CD—Krishna Das is standing above Maharajji, who's sitting on the ground. I said, "Why did he put a homeless person on the cover of his CD?"

My friend said, "That's not a homeless person. That's Krishna Das's guru."

I lived in L.A., and every time I saw a homeless person after that, every one of them turned into Krishna Das's guru. I thought I was losing my mind. Then I thought, *maybe this guy's got some juice, maybe he really is a saint.* Having been raised Catholic, I was familiar with saints and mystical encounters. Okay, he was reaching out to me through homeless people, so I was giving money, buying them lunch, doing all kinds of things to be of service to homeless people.

I've always been devoted to Mother Mary and have a very strong bond with her. I pray the rosary, my major takeaway from Catholicism. Soon I had this beautiful lucid dream: *A little boy took my hand. It was somewhere far away, like India, where I've never been. We were walking by dying people, and he took me into a room that looked like a little dark temple, a refuge from suffering. The Divine Mother was standing there, illuminated, and the little boy ran up to her and hugged her. I walked up to her and was immediately in bliss.*

She said only three words to me, "Love my son." She put her hand out and pointed to Christ and Maharajji, sitting across the room right next to each other. I hadn't noticed them before. Maharajji was sitting there with Christ, and he rolled over and laughed and was shaking his finger. Christ was stiffly sitting there like a statue, as in my childhood home.

I grew up in an Irish Catholic family, went to Catholic school and convent high school, but I never got the "Jesus juice" like everybody else did. When Maharajji was laughing in the dream, I realized then that I couldn't have opened myself to him without Mother Mary's permission. When she said, "Love my son," that was it. I was caught hook, line, and sinker.

Two weeks later my life literally fell apart. I had to go through a painful court trial that lasted three years; I lost many friends and was even betrayed by family members, but Mother Mary had brought Maharajji to me in the nick of time. I had Maharajji by my side every time I walked into court, and I had to walk into court sixty times with my children, never knowing if I would be allowed to walk out with them. I would look at the California seal behind the judge's head and so many times I would see Maharajji there. Miraculously, the truth started coming out, and justice prevailed.

Ever since then, I've felt so protected by him and can handle anything I go through. I always have him with me. I'm still connected to homeless people, and my children are very connected to homeless people. So that's how he got me. And it's been beautiful ever since.

Robert Skutelsky

Dear Krishna Das:

In June of 1972, after immersion in *Be Here Now*, Ram Dass, Hilda, etc., I decided to make the mandatory journey to the East. I was all of twenty-two years old and had just graduated from college. I took the $2,000 or so that I had saved from driving a cab around New York City the previous three years. The woman that I lived with at the time and I took off for India. We flew to Zurich, Switzerland, to begin our overland journey.

One evening we were staying in a small cottage in the Swiss Alps and, as was my custom at the time, I read myself to sleep from *Autobiography of a Yogi*. I was using a picture of Maharajji as a bookmark. When I felt myself falling asleep, I placed the picture of Maharajji in the book in the place that I had stopped.

That night I had very intense, realistic dreams of being in Maharajji's presence, a presence in which I felt total love and acceptance. The next morning when I reached for the book, I noticed that Maharajji's picture was missing. I looked inside every page of the book, on the floor, under the pillows, under the bed, in between the mattress and the box spring. There was no picture. As far as I could tell, it had simply disappeared.

We spent about four months in South India and in January of 1973, headed north to Vrindavan to see Maharajji. He was not there, and no one that we spoke to seemed to know where he was. Feeling totally exhausted and just about broke, we returned to the U.S. without his physical darshan. As it turned out, the dream experience was the most powerful experience of Maharajji I ever had.

राम

Sat-ji (Jim Bergstrom)

I was attending Kalamazoo college in Michigan and was no stranger to yoga, Indian metaphysics, Zen, and all branches of philosophy. I found Western philosophy to be stuck mainly in the left brain. At age thirteen I had discovered Eastern thought through *Zen Combat*[42], a small book on martial arts and Eastern philosophies.

---

42 *Zen Combat: A Complete Guide to the Original Arts of Attack and Defense*, by Jay Gluck (Ballantine, 1961).

I was studying judo and deeply immersed in *Black Belt* magazine, learning about men like O-Sensei Morihei Uyeshiba and ancient Shaolin Temple teachers that stressed the spiritual side, not merely the physical aspects of those arts.

Then came *Be Here Now*. It was a much deeper introduction to the world of yogis, sadhus, gurus, and true saints. I was fascinated by the story of Neem Karoli Baba. It seemed perfectly real to me because I had somehow already accepted that there were beings on this planet who had such pure love and intention, beings who had gone beyond mere yogic study to become living examples of the Path. Jesus was one of those rare beings. Leave out questionable details like the virgin birth and Jesus was still so much more than a master teacher.

I honestly didn't expect that I would be given Maharajji's grace simply by reading about him in *Be Here Now* and wanting to believe that there are beings on planet Earth like him, like Jesus, that were One with all beings in a state of pure love. I wasn't looking for a guru by any means. I wanted knowledge and guidance for changing my life, for improving my journey.

Of course, when the time is right . . .

My first darshan was about a year-and-a-half before Neem Karoli Baba's mahasamadhi. It took place in a "dream." Many others have followed over the years.

February 4, 1972: *Hari Dass Baba led me up a mountain path to the top. Maharajji was standing there and spoke to me. Rainbow colors came from his mouth instead of words and floated in the air. The air and sky were golden and bright. Maharajji looked deep into my eyes and said one sentence, something to do with "two halves" and "blue and orange." I was so happy to be with him, like coming home after a long, long journey.*

I know that he is still alive in a way that I do not fully understand. Is he once again in another earthly incarnation, homing in on all his devotees' vibes across the continents? Or is it his oneness with the

Universe that allows his presence to be timeless? Could it merely be that devotion brings him near?

These are all questions that I don't need to resolve.

ूप

Timothy Profeta

My wife Taylor and I were in between houses and staying with my in-laws for about six weeks. We put most of our belongings into storage, but I pulled out two books to read—the *Odyssey* by Homer and *Be Here Now* by Ram Dass. I started reading *Be Here Now* in January 2021. A few weeks later we learned Taylor was pregnant. Her sister found out she was pregnant at about the same time, a little bit farther ahead. Both sisters were having baby girls, but her sister had complications with extra amniotic fluid, and her daughter had a blockage in her intestines. She was about thirty-two weeks pregnant when she felt no movement and lost her child. I heard a Ram Dass talk on Be Here Now Network about how some souls have so little work to do that they'll leave when they are a fetus. She lost the baby in July. After the funeral, my wife was eight months pregnant.

I went to bed one night and dreamed *I was in an auditorium watching a debate over a divorce. In my dream I thought, okay, I don't want to be here for this. I'm walking up the aisle of this big auditorium and I see Maharajji sitting there in his blanket. Someone, who I now understand to be Dada, was next to him. I felt totally understood. I felt totally known. I felt as if my whole being was exposed. And I started weeping in my dream.*

He motioned to me to touch the top of his head. I touched the top of his head, and he was caressing me, and I was weeping. He said, "Isn't it all such a dance—the living and the killing?" As he said that,

I felt him touching my head, and my consciousness snapped into the most spacious awareness I've ever been in. I was aware of the subtlest forms of beings—one was unmistakably my niece who had left us, and the other was unmistakably my daughter, who was about to be born. I understood in that moment that there was a coming and going, passing in and out of that space. And then I woke up. Before all this, I was a terrified agnostic. Now, this dream is one of the dearest and realest experiences of my life.

A month later, my wife Taylor went into labor on September 7th, her great-grandmother's birthday. The labor went on and on through that day and the next, with rounds of Pitocin and multiple epidurals. They kept monitoring the baby's heart rate, which would drop into an unsafe zone during strong contractions. I was terrified. What if our baby didn't make it to this world?

I asked the doctor if I had time to go for a walk, and I went down to the hospital chapel to try to meditate. I prayed to Maharajji, "Please give me any sign that it's going to be okay." I felt a bit more calm and went back up to the room. The epidural was giving Taylor the chance to catch a little sleep. As I sat, I guiltily opened my cell phone and *very guiltily* went on Instagram. The first picture I saw was of Maharajji with a caption that said, "Don't worry about anything. I've got everything under control." I closed my phone, feeling okay but still nervous. Taylor spent three and a half hours pushing, but our daughter's head was stuck. Our baby girl was delivered by C-section on September 8th.

A month after she was born, I had another Maharajji dream, so clear it felt like high definition. *I was in India in a very humble room with a takhat. I was holding Eleanor, my daughter, and I understood I was to put her down on the takhat. She was a month old and couldn't roll over, so it felt all right. She was moving around very far from the edge. But I'm thinking, as a new dad, "I should be holding her, guarding her." As I'm thinking that, Maharajji comes into the room, and I know he's coming to see her. He looks at me and yells, "What are you doing?*

Come hold her for me." I hold her and he looks at her; he's playing with *her cheeks and he keeps cooing, welcome, welcome little one, in the most playful way.*

I experienced the space of the infinite love of God all around me and within myself. And I understood Maharajji's unconditional love.

10

Many Roads Home

Where thou art,
that is home.
—EMILY DICKINSON

How many ways can Maharajji communicate with you? It's endless. You may connect to his presence by wrapping yourself in a special shawl or by looking to buy a chair. You may have been born into it, married into it, or awakened to his love through a dog's wet kisses. He may have shown up in your life when you thought you were on a totally different path.

Or it may be a combination of many factors—meeting the right person at the right time, a book followed by a kirtan followed by a retreat all culminating in one defining moment of recognition. Or it may creep up on you, a slow dawning of awareness that yes, you are being held, guided, protected, and loved.

Paths are many, but they all eventually lead you home.

Andrew Allen

In 2003, while studying bodywork at Harbin Hot Springs, I met a Neem Karoli Baba devotee by the name of Mahavir (Bob Homsy) who led regular kirtans in his home; my wife and I regularly attended these events for a few years. He always had photos of Maharajji around, but I didn't think much about him at the time. Around 2008 Mahavir retired and moved away. I was feeling that something in my life was missing without the regular kirtans/satsang gatherings. Then we attended a live kirtan that Jai was offering at Open Secret Bookstore. Jai had some flyers for an upcoming workshop at Esalen in the spring of 2010. What could be better that Jai leading a kirtan workshop at Esalen?

During the workshop, Jai was telling stories about Maharajji. I would find myself sitting up a little straighter and being a bit more interested and focused. Towards the end of the workshop, Jai told the story about Maharajji's passing, where he said the words *Jai Jagdeesh Hare* and left his body, and I had a very profound physical experience. I felt a rush of energy up my spine and my eyes immediately began flooding with water. I was embarrassed and turned away so that no one could see me being so emotional. I profoundly felt Maharajji's presence in my body and immediately knew that my search for a guru was over. That feeling of him being with me has never left since that day.

ﬀﬄ

Ankit

From the age of twenty-four onwards, I've been trying to figure myself out. I attracted a number of toxic partners, which started to awaken me. Subconsciously, I put out a call for a mentor or a healer, and my spiritual coach showed up. While working with him, he showed me a picture of Neem Karoli Baba. I look nothing like Neem Karoli Baba, but I saw myself in that picture. And from that day on, things started to change.

I was born in Delhi, and I know some of the Indian myths and the history, but I'm not spiritual. I could always feel people's energy, so I played with the occult a little and read Osho and did meditation, but I would deny God. My coach suggested I read *Miracle of Love*. Before I finished reading that book, I knew Maharajji was Hanuman! When I was a kid, I'd bury myself in Indian comic books about the gods, and I loved Hanuman.

Then a short while ago, I felt something pour into me. I can't explain the quality of the energy other than it felt a lot like coming home. I saw that everything was love and I started to have these awakenings. I kept reading *Miracle of Love* because it filled me with so much love. Then I read *Love Everyone*. I could feel the amount of love that poured through that book! By the end of that book, I said to Maharajji, "Hey, I want to understand what's happening to me better and to know you better. Who should I talk to?" And he directed me to different people that were written about in *Love Everyone*, like Daniel Goleman, as I had met his son briefly in college. I asked Baba, what message do you have for them? He threw seven apples at Dan as prasad. I got no response from Dan, but Maharajji is very, very proud of him.

While cruising around Facebook, I found Radha Baum's Go-FundMe page. The pull was immediate. Maharajji was insistent that I send her a specific amount because she needed help and I was to give it to her. It was a lot of money to give to someone I didn't know. He just kept at it and the pull was impossible to resist. I sent a message to Parvati, the contact on Radha's Go-FundMe page, to make sure it was still ongoing. I sent the funds and wondered what the significance of the number was. It was making me feel crazy.

Then I spoke with Radha, who told me, "You aren't going crazy. It's a very significant number. I haven't been able to work since I broke my neck in a car accident, but I found a doctor who has a treatment, and he recommended that I get a brace that costs exactly the amount of money you sent. This is Maharajji. This is what he does. And this is the proof of what happened to you, which is so extraordinary."

Throughout this process, I've learned to step into a very intuitive space for myself. I go with whatever comes up now. I'm just a tech sales guy in the Bay area who was trying to break a cycle of attachment to the wrong women and genuinely trying to be comfortable in my own skin. Instead, I've been catapulted into one crazy spiritual change after another. Now when my heart beats, I hear *Ram Ram Ram* in my head. I'm not a big fan of mantras or anything like that, but it's happening to me. Maharajji helped me deeply reconnect with my father before he died. If we weren't in lockdown, Maharajji has instructed me to go to Taos, to his temple there. Then, when we can travel again, I need to go to Kainchi.

He never left.

राम

Annapurna Alisa Sydell

When I was a little girl, my mother was addicted to heroin, so I lived with another family where there was a lot of violence. I was hit and called names, which was humiliating and horrible, but I would feel protected by a blanket that would descend between me and the violence. Even though the person hitting me often had bruise marks on their arms, I never had a mark on me.

As a young girl I often felt the presence of God. I even thought about becoming a rabbi. When I was twelve years old, I had an experience where I wandered outside late at night and that same kind of protective presence came to me. I continued to feel that presence, even as a teenager running away from home and joining the Children of God in Hawaii, one of those notorious cults on the FBI list, where nothing bad ever happened to me. Even as a teenager living on the streets, and after I was done running away and entered back into the foster care system, I always had this mysterious protection.

When I was finishing my doctorate in clinical psychology and working in an AIDS hospice, Maharajji made his presence known again. At the Bodhi Tree Bookstore in Los Angeles, they had pictures of many teachers and saints all around the top of the walls. One night I looked up and saw the picture of Maharajji. I was standing in front of all these books filed under Ram Dass. I picked up *Miracle of Love* and saw the picture of Maharajji. I immediately recognized the blanket that had protected me as a child. There was no doubt at all. From that moment on, I knew I was on the journey of bhakti yoga and guru kripa.

ॐ

Duncan Trussell

Nearly everyone at my liberal arts college had a copy of *Be Here Now*. It seemed like there was one in every dorm, along with a *Baraka* DVD, tarot cards, and a poorly-hidden bong. I borrowed a copy from my friend and flipped through the book. I came to a picture of Maharajji, and my first thought was, "I know that guy." He didn't look at all like any of my uncles, but somehow my brain spit out, "This guy's in my family. He reminds me of Uncle Jimmy." Which was weird because my Uncle Jimmy, a Southern lawyer, didn't look at all like a baba in a blanket.

After college I moved to Los Angeles and started doing stand-up comedy and pitching TV shows. I ended up getting a pilot presentation deal from Comedy Central. One of my lame ideas for the show was that I would take a lot of mushrooms and film myself trying to play baseball. In retrospect, I realize how insanely dumb this idea was. I hadn't thought through the reality of what it would feel like to be extremely high on mushrooms on top of all the pressure of trying to make a funny show. Also, it was shadowed by the reality that my mom recently had been diagnosed with breast cancer. Not exactly a perfect set and setting for a mushroom trip.

I stepped outside when the mushrooms were kicking in and closed my eyes. And then I saw Maharajji; he was laughing and smiling and beaming at me. Not talking, but what came through was: "It's going to be fine; no matter what, you're going to be fine." He didn't mean my show was going to be fine (he was right about that as Comedy Central hated it!) or even that my mom was going to be fine; he meant, "These are little things, nothing compared to what there is."

A year before my mom died, I found myself in a terrible depression and a rotten break up. Nothing was working out. I had read somewhere that if you ever find yourself in a horrible space, you should offer to help. I reached out to the Love Serve Remember Foundation because I thought I should do some service for a spiritual group. I emailed Raghu and said, "I know how to do podcasts; maybe I can help you with podcasts." I ended by asking Raghu to be on my podcast.

I was completely prepared to be disappointed by Raghu. I pictured someone in an embarrassing spiritual costume—too many beads and a fashion cane with a crystal and feathers on top. Even if he didn't look like a Lord of the Rings character, he would probably steal something from my house. I was very cynical in those days.

Instead of anything my paranoia had conjured up, Raghu presented himself in a button-up shirt and jeans. Not a crystal in sight.

We did our first podcast, and it was like we were picking up a conversation we had been having forever. He told me stories of Maharajji and hanging out with Ram Dass. The hour we had scheduled for the podcast went by in a flash, and he left. I went into my bathroom and was staring at myself in the mirror, high as a kite, thinking, "Oh man, that was so rude of me to get that stoned around a podcast guest!" I was completely blasted. Then I realized I hadn't gotten high! It was just something about meeting that energy for the first time. Just the stories alone were enough to shift my consciousness in a radical way.

Sometime later, I was sitting on the floor of my kitchen, and my girlfriend had just adopted this sick old cat with AIDS. I wish I could say I had that kind of compassion. I had tried to dissuade her from getting attached to a dying cat who, upon getting comfortable at our rental, had taken to clawing up the walls. I'm sitting on the floor of the kitchen, and my two dogs come and sit around me, and then that cat, who had not really been that social, also came up. All these animals were sitting around me, and I realized, God, I love these animals! I really love them! And I love them no matter what they do. I don't care that the cat has AIDS or that the poodles' bark can shatter glass. I just love them no matter what. I unconditionally love these cats and dogs.

Ooh, is that what Maharajji felt all the time about everybody? Is that who he was? And THAT was the most I've ever felt him, because in that moment it was the same as, "Oh my god, he's right here." This is the thing they keep talking about: nuclear-level love. It was like that love I was feeling for these animals suddenly was getting transferred to me from Maharajji. And that was the most amazing feeling.

It's such a cliché thing to say, but you can't underestimate the power of love. And you can't underestimate what happens when people come together under the umbrella of love. I feel so lucky that this group of people, my satsang, exist at all. I don't honestly know where I'd be if I hadn't come into contact with Maharajji. Thankfully, as Dada puts it, "Once he catches hold of you, he doesn't let go."

ॐ

Gagan Jared and Jyoti Levy

GAGAN: I was a "good Jewish boy," a high holy days Jew. I grew up reciting these prayers in Hebrew to Adonai or God, not really knowing what the words meant. In high school, I got into mushrooms and LSD, and someone gave me *Be Here Now*. When I read it, Maharajji didn't catch my eye so much; it was more the psychedelics and Ram Dass because he also grew up as a nice Jewish boy. I was always searching, taking threshold doses of psychedelics to try to break through. I came to the same conclusion that Ram Dass did: the high didn't last. I'd go up, I'd come down, harvesting what I could.

When I got to college, I got into Buddhism and philosophy and the *jnana* (knowledge) yoga path. After college I came back into Judaism more. Around this time I was introduced to Raghu. When we started talking, he and I immediately fell in love.

Then Raghu took Jyoti and me to Taos. We sat in the temple and Raghu started singing the Hanuman Chalisa, which I didn't know then. I was looking at this beautiful statue of Hanuman that didn't hold much significance to me, although I knew it was significant to Raghu. But when he started singing and playing the harmonium, I was gone, like I was on a psychedelic trip! I had no idea of time and space. I had listened to almost all of Ram Dass's talks, but I hadn't fully connected with the devotional Hindu side.

After being at the temple in Taos, I started understanding more and more that Maharajji was the source of so much that I loved about Ram Dass, and so much that I was drawn to. *Miracle of Love* really pulled me in, and Maharajji became a focal point. I noticed that when I thought of spirit or god or whatever you want to call this higher power, it was faceless before Maharajji came into my life.

Maharajji's teachings—love everyone, feed everyone—these are things that I've always been drawn to. Faith without the miracles is a hard surrender, especially for me, who grew up questioning everything with a very skeptical mind. But I believe the people that I love have had authentic experiences, and if they tell me something, then it's worth exploring. Now I have my own experiences or feelings of what's real for me. I don't need the miracles.

JYOTI: I started off Catholic. Spirituality was something I was always looking for in church and in books. When Jared (Gagan) met Raghu, I was already familiar with *Be Here Now*; I knew who Ram Dass was, but I was just along for the ride. We went to Hawaii and met the satsang; we had our first lunch in Maui sitting with Ram Dass and Krishna Das. Then we got to go to Kainchi. The entire week we were there at the ashram we had a lot of time with Siddhi Ma, who blessed us with Hindi names: Gagan ("limitless sky") and Jyoti ("the flame"), but I was still not a devotee.

When we were in India, Gagan could eat all the food, but Raghu and I had sensitive stomachs so we would be in our rooms with peanut butter and crackers. I said to Raghu, "You guys were so lucky because you got to be here with Maharajji, and you were basically slapped in the face into spirituality. He was here telling you your past and your future and doing these amazing blessings in front of your eyes. You got this huge blessing to be with him in the body."

That night I was writing in my journal, reflecting on everything that had gotten me to India. Here I was from a middle-class, first generation, very dysfunctional family full of addicts and chaos. There were no steps I could have taken to get to India, but I was there. I had the blessings of Ram Dass and Krishna Das, and the way Raghu took us completely under his wing and became like a spiritual papa for us. Nina taught us the chalisa. And it hit me that it was all grace, all Maharajji's grace.

From that moment everything changed for me because I realized I had blessing after blessing after blessing.

ॐ

Julianna Raye

I come from a background of having done a lot of very rigorous mindfulness and Zen retreats with Shinzen Young and Sasaki Roshi. I came across *Be Here Now* on my parents' bookshelf, and I'd read pieces of it when I would go home. Ram Dass had trained with Sasaki Roshi, so I felt an affinity and a connection. As Ram Dass was aging, I thought, I really want to meet him, so I went to a retreat in Maui. I felt incomplete. A year later I came straight from visiting the original temple in Japan where Sasaki Roshi had been abbot to spend five days on a solo retreat with Ram Dass in his guest house. I didn't have a deep yearning to know Maharajji as a teacher; I just felt an affinity with Ram Dass and wanted to honor him as someone who had taught me indirectly.

In the guest house, I started reading stories in the books there about Maharajji. I would visit with Ram Dass and do sitting practice on my own. On the final night I woke up at 2:15 in the morning because I was heading from there to another retreat. When I woke up, my body was Maharajji's body. I felt a sense of being both Maharajji and myself. I took one hand in the other. When I moved my hand, whose hand was it? And I heard this very distinct message: *divine love comes first.* I had never had a dead teacher before and with such vividness, such aliveness! I was dancing on the edge of being and non-being with a unique partner who could do that dance effortlessly. The experience didn't last that long, but in its wake there was a deep energy flow, an inner choreography that was very rich.

At the beginning of the pandemic, I got into a daily diet of non-dual teachers on YouTube, including video and audio clips of Maharajji. Then my father contracted COVID. Originally, we were planning his 90th birthday. Now he was in a converted nurse's lounge because the hospital had run out of beds. I was in L.A., and he was right in the middle of the New Jersey surge. Eventually, we got him into a rehab center that had a COVID ward, but we were getting texts about the patients and the caregivers there who were falling sick and dying.

My dad's sister died of the virus a week before he did; she had the breathing and oxygen problems and declined very rapidly. He didn't have that breathing problem; he just got increasingly weak and bedridden. I was practicing love at a distance, feeling connected to him, wishing him ease. We finally got the residence to take him back because he really wanted to be there.

A few days later, right around his 90th birthday, I was exercising on a flight of steps. Suddenly, Maharajji was with me. It was like he was holding my hand and he was holding my dad's hand and joining us together. It was so vivid, and he stayed with me. There was this sense of his essence, kind of a heavy perfume in the air. That day, my dad completely shifted from saying don't come anywhere near me to, okay, you can come. I got on a flight that night and spent the next five days helping my dad to die. The caregivers at the residence were completely burnt out, so I was grateful to be there for him. I got to hold the iPad up to dad's face and help him connect with the family.

Maharajji had told me when it was time to be with my dad, even in New Jersey in the middle of the surge. It was just so right that I could be there with him and help the family and his friends let go.

261

The hard part was mourning without physical contact with the people that you love. I didn't get to hug my family.

You wonder what it is that makes Maharajji show up for people. It's a service that he's giving, an act of love. For me he is the obliteration of life and death, the obliteration of any idea about needing a living teacher. And with Ram Dass having passed, I think people need to hear that. How important it is to not be caught in this notion that I am alive and he is dead. It's all one, all one.

ॐ

Lakshman Chandler Moss

I went to a retreat and connected with Rachael, who works for the Love Serve Remember Foundation. Afterward, I kept in touch, particularly when I noticed things about the website, etc. I was elated when she reached out to say they were considering me as a caregiver for Ram Dass. I gave Rachel, Raghu, Ram Dass, and Dassi Ma a solid *yes* to the possibility.

Before I went to Maui, I had a Maharajji photo and was beginning to connect with him. I woke up one morning and came out into the hall; I saw a ball of light go down the hallway and out. Maybe it was just a glitch in my eye, but I told myself that it was Maharajji or someone checking on me.

I wound up being a caregiver for Ram Dass for four years. The internet at the house was always having problems, and I was the "computer guy" (network, computers, graphics, etc.) I do it well, but it can stress me out when things get complicated.

Everybody was already seated at the table one night as I was trying to get the printer online before dinner, which wasn't working. I felt everyone could tell I was frustrated, as I tend to wear my emotions on my sleeve. Then Sita came up to the table, a cute little Maui jungle kitten with a heart on her tabby coat. I love cats, their purrs are a state of pure love. I remember taking a deep breath, scooping her up and putting my face to her loud purring belly, surrendering. All stress seemed to melt into her love. In that moment I thought to myself how love seems to fractal into love.

Suddenly, the printer started working! A mysterious sheet of paper came out and the only thing that was printed on it was: "Love breeds love." Period.

My jaw was on the floor. I asked everyone, "Did anybody here print this?" No. It was wild! I get happy chills up and down my spine just thinking about it.

I don't ever doubt Maharajji. And I find it fascinating to see Maharajji and Spirit in technology. It seems like a natural divide, but it's not. It's all one, right?

॥ ४

Mirabai Starr

I'm one of those people who has had multiple Maharajji dreams over the years that came at times when I needed them most, yet I can't remember a single one! Although the dreams are powerful and vivid and specific, these dreams transcend my thinking mind, my rational mind, so I don't get to hold onto them. I think that's a big part of my spiritual path in general, which has been completely informed by my association with Maharajji: the path of *radical unknowingness*. Maharajji has taught me to "not know" because he's not the kind of Baba that has a fixed belief system that you're supposed to buy into.

I've been comfortable with ambiguity from an early age. My parents were hippies in New York, middle-class Jewish intellectuals and social activists, and they really related to Ram Dass, so *Be Here*

Now appeared in our home when I was a nine-year-old girl. A couple of years later they got swept up in the whole counterculture odyssey and uprooted us from our suburban Long Island life. We lived on a remote beach in Mexico, now known as Cancun, which at the time was total wilderness. We ended up in Taos, New Mexico. Lama Foundation took over this hippie free school we went to. Asha Greer, who's the founder of Lama, was the head of the school.

The two main spiritual mentors of Lama Foundation were Murshid Samuel Lewis from the Sufi tradition, and Neem Karoli Baba. And both of those beings had the same message, which Maharajji called "sub ek"—all is one, all paths mingle in the heart and lead to the same place. Murshid Sam was also about what he called the "meeting of the ways"— that's where the dances of universal peace come from, arising from that one heart. Although Maharajji became more of a direct path for me than Murshid Sam, they both instilled in me this understanding that unknowingness is the path to awakening, and that all the world's wisdom ways carry the distilled essence of the One.

By the time I was twelve, Maharajji was my Baba. The spring I turned fourteen, my first love, my boyfriend Philip, died in a gun accident in Taos and it blasted me open. Then I was in a play at Lama Foundation about the life story of Mirabai; the students wrote the script and the songs, choreographed the dances, directed the production, and I played the part of Mirabai. I very much felt her inhabiting me in that experience. Our teachers were two Maharajji devotees, Surya and Sarada. Soon after the Mirabai play, I went to New York to follow Ram Dass. He officially gave me the name Mirabai at that time.

My relationship with Maharajji grew stronger and stronger; he was like the air I breathed. In my community here in Taos, Maharajji was everywhere. Even though my parents were not devotees, Maharajji's picture was in our home. When I had children, I made my way back in a more formal way to the Neem Karoli Baba satsang. I began leading kirtan and raised my kids at the Taos ashram, where I met my husband and we blended our families. Maharajji is always at the center of all my books and talks. When Ram Dass asked me to lead the first Ram Dass legacy retreat in Ojai a few years ago, it made complete sense.

I take Maharajji's picture with me everywhere. I speak a lot to Christian contemplative communities because I'm a translator of the mystics Saint Teresa of Avila and Saint John of the Cross. I always create a puja table on stage with me and face his picture outward; people rarely ask, but he's always there. When they do ask, I'm always happy to talk about him.

I don't have anything dramatic to share. It's simply that he's my Baba; he lives in my heart.

ᠮ

Nubia Teixeira

In May of 2000, I brought Jai and Geoffrey Gordon[43] to sing kirtan in São Paulo for my community of yoga students and friends. Over the course of ten days in Brazil, Jai and I fell in love, but we couldn't be together at that time in our lives. Jai gifted me *Miracle of Love*, and reading that book first introduced me to Maharajji.

From September 2000 to January 2001, I lived in India to study classical Indian dance, and I had the great fortune "accidentally" to have two encounters with Shri Siddhi Ma—first on her way to

---

43 Geoffrey Gordon was a master percussionist, producer, composer, and kirtan wallah. He drummed alongside Jai Uttal, Krishna Das, Bhagavan Das, and many others, helping to start the kirtan movement in the west. He died suddenly in 2012.

Rameswaram and then, a month later, in the ashram in Virapuram. I believe that my darshans with Siddhi Ma cleared the way for me to be with Jai, and in May of 2001, I moved from Brazil to California to be reunited with the love of my life.

I was not looking for a guru when I was first with Jai, as I had my own guru, T.Y.S Lama Gangchen Rinpoche, a venerable traditional master from Tibet. I met Rinpoche in 1997 and he is a great inspiration in my life to this day. He passed in April 2021 from the coronavirus in Italy. When I first came to Jai's home, I was really intimidated by Maharajji's strong presence in his photos, and a little afraid that he would pop out of the photos and talk to me. When I was a little child, I used to see spirits; I got really afraid of this and shut the door. I began to talk to Maharajji in those photos, saying, "I don't ever want to see you. To me, you are just a picture! Remember, you are just Jai's guru, not mine." Although I felt his magic weaving our lives, somehow I was hesitant to open my heart fully to him.

When I was pregnant with our son Ezra, I started to have many vivid dreams of Maharajji, and in all of them he appeared in picture frames! I felt Maharajji was playfully conversing with me and healing my fear of seeing spirits. In one of the dreams he became a baby in my arms, in another he was wearing Brazilian indigenous tribal feathers. Through a series of dreams Maharajji enchanted me, and my heart's walls melted. I understood Maharajji to be our family guru and, over the years, I have felt that Maharajji is taking care of us and coordinating everything for our family in an amazingly beautiful way. I call him "*vovô* Maharajji." Vovô means grandfather in Portuguese, and I deeply feel his presence and spiritual guardianship.

When I had the idea of Jai offering Kirtan Camp in 2003, I felt like it was a little whisper coming from Maharajji. In those trainings there has always been a strong presence of Maharajji's grace and blessings, and Jai's transmissions became much deeper in that setting. He would talk more and share more intimately about his experiences of Maharajji. I began noticing that the people who were gathering were so inspired by Maharajji and that the space we created was providing a refuge for them to develop love and devotion. I understood that my role in Kirtan Camp was to support Jai's work and the legacy—the sea that is Maharajji's love and its many gifts.

Grandfather and Guru! I feel humbled and grateful to be his.

ॐ

Robin Westen

I was a hippie, so of course I read *Be Here Now*. About a decade later, when I was twenty-eight-years old, I had a spontaneous awakening. The world shattered and I knew where I had come from and where I was going. This undeniable experience began my path. For a while, even though I'm Jewish, I got into Jesus big time. Later, I ended up in a Zen monastery. But years passed and my spiritual longing went dormant. Then in 2011, I came upon the Open Your Heart in Paradise retreat in Maui with Ram Dass. My husband, Howie, said, "Go! Use my frequent flyer miles."

While I was there, I had an unforgettable connection with Maharajji. In the early morning, while it was still dark, I felt a strong push on my back nudging me outdoors—first to the ocean and then towards the pavilion. When I arrived in the vast, silent room, no one was there except Maharajji and me. In an instant, my heart broke open. I fell to my knees and couldn't stop crying.

But once I left the retreat, the feeling didn't last. At home I felt disconnected and terribly sad that the loving feeling was gone. Desperate, I went to see David Harshada Wagner, a meditation and transformational teacher, for a private session. As I was leaving, he said, "Robin, do you have a chair? A chair you can sit in and look at the view, look at the world?" I'm a minimalist, so actually I didn't have a chair! In fact, I'm always in a state of slight discomfort. At first, I thought, *Wow, I just paid $200 for this guy to tell me to get a chair*. But then I thought, *What have I got to lose?*

I live in Brooklyn but own a little house in Vermont, so I decided I'd drive to an antique shop up there. But I had a sudden work deadline and couldn't take the time. Instead, I went on Craigslist. The first advertisement that came up said, "Oak rocking chair $100." I responded right away. The person who posted the ad wrote back immediately and told me I had to get to the apartment by noon. It was already eleven o'clock.

I grabbed my husband, who was quite ill at the time, but I needed him to sit in the car so I wouldn't get a ticket. We drove fifteen minutes to Park Slope. Lo and behold, there was a parking spot in front of the building. A New York miracle! I left Howie in the car and walked up to the top floor.

A young man with a slight build and friendly face greeted me. The apartment seemed empty except for the rocking chair in the middle of the living room. I went straight to it and sat down. While rocking back and forth, my eyes were drawn over my right shoulder. On the mantle above the fireplace was a picture of Maharajji! Over-whelmed, I started to cry. I mean *really* cry.

The man fixed his gaze on me. "Oh, I see. You're an old friend," he said. I stood up and we hugged each other. It felt like a reunion. I knew then he really was my old friend.

"I'm Jeremy Frindel," he said. "I just made a movie about Krishna Das. He's chanting at my yoga studio soon." Then he paused and added, "Funny thing is that there were absolutely no tickets available, but just as you were walking up the steps, a woman emailed me to say she couldn't make it. Now there's an extra ticket. Would you like to come?"

A few minutes later, I was walking down the stairs, schlepping the chair. I told my husband I was going to spend the afternoon at the Brooklyn Yoga Studio where I had never been before. And that was that. Maharajji let me know in no uncertain terms that he had never left. He was still with me. I've never doubted his presence again.

ॐ

Shiva Baum

As far back as I can remember, I was aware of Maharajji. It felt then, as it feels now, nothing less than home. Both my parents were with Maharajji in India, and I was born a year after he left his body. It does fascinate me how natural he's always felt to me. My house was covered with pictures of this old man in a blanket, and I think it's one of his miracles how I wasn't subjected to teasing by my friends. If I do have a regret, it was that I had access to these great devotees—Dada and Tewari, whom I loved and got to interact with—but I was too young to have an inquiry with them. I knew them as sweet grandfatherly figures, although Tewari had an unmistakably powerful presence that even as a boy I could feel. I'd love to be able to go back in time and ask them some questions.

My earliest memories were my parents' Maharajji pictures and the voice of Krishna Das. Krishna Das was Krishna Das then as he is now; the only difference is that now he shares it with more people. He sang with that same tone of reverence and devotion. It's my earliest memory of sound. I've always had this connection with kirtan and mantra, which bring me to the best place in myself. I've been able to do things like emcee for Bhakti Fest because I've had a lifelong relationship with this music and real affection for it.

I grew up with Ram Dass and the whole California family, the Massachusetts family, and the New York family. Ram Dass's influence was the core foundation of the wisdom that I absorbed. The thing that affected me the most from Ram Dass was *Be Here Now*, especially after having my own experiences with psilocybin and LSD when I was sixteen. The book was in my living room my whole life, but then I began reading it like it was the Bible, this holy sacred book.

For years I was resentful that other people seemed to have very vivid experiences of Maharajji, but I never did. He was such a normal part of my day-to-day life, yet I never felt as close to him as I heard other people describe. I would get sad when I thought about it in that way, as I often did. Then in my twenties, he came to me in a dream. He didn't give me the keys to the kingdom, but he let me know it's all cool. Relax a little bit.

Most recently he helped me get past what had seemed an insurmountable rift with my father. I had a lot of anger at my father and I couldn't let it go. The venom was growing in strength, causing a greater and greater separation between us. So Maharajji got involved, and there was a leela that played out that resulted in a healing between my father and me. You realize who could script such an intricate thing, so specific to our individual trips and what we're working with in that moment. This is how I know it's real: now I can be with my father and truthfully tell him I love him. I was given the grace and the gift of forgiveness. I'm deeply grateful.

I feel like Maharajji has given me a backstage pass to watch how real he's been for so many people that I love and care about. I feel like I've been able to be with him the most in that way—seeing his love and his grace and his magic work in the lives of other people as well as in my own. Today, I feel him more than ever.

राम

Sita (Lynnie) Callahan

The handmade knitted shawl had been made by local church women, whom I never met, and was given to me after my husband's passing. With no warning, he had literally dropped dead. It was shocking, and my mind, body, and spirit were numb with grief. I am a long-time yogi and could barely turn to my practice. I wanted to stay numb, not feel the immense grief that shrouded me.

At night I would wrap myself in the shawl and feel cocooned, safe, and somehow loved. The smell of the oils that were infused in the shawl were delicious. I could feel my whole being settle, allowing a little respite from my grief. I wondered how these women could have known that this shawl would comfort me in ways no human could.

As healing began to unfold, bhakti yoga became my medicine. Over the years, the numbness lifted and the true work began: acknowledging my grief, letting it flow in and out like the tides of the sea. Sometimes it was so fierce it took my breath away; other times soft undulations allowed me the grace to heal. I began to hear stories of Neem Karoli Baba and was drawn to the satsang of devotees. I attended workshops, retreats, and immersed myself in the stories. I bought a harmonium, learned to play and chant the names so I could bring the divine love of Maharajji deep into my heart. Ram Dass taught me grief is love, and many many more teachings. I sold the home John and I had had, purged, packed up, and built a new home that I wanted to reflect my spiritual life.

Maharajji was with me from the very beginning after John's death, although I was unaware of that until I returned from my yatra in India. There I had walked the path of Ram Dass, where he had been with his beloved Maharajji, and I truly opened my heart to live fully, to be of service, and to grasp how Maharajji was with me.

One day back at home, I was sitting in my meditation room, and I thought of my shawl, which I had packed away when I moved two years earlier. I removed it from a cabinet, brought it up to my nose to smell the very faint remnants of the infused healing oils. I placed the shawl over my legs as I was getting ready to wrap it around me. I looked down, and there in one small spot was one string of red yarn in the sea of blue yarn. It was as though a piece of red thread from Maharajji's blanket miraculously had been knitted into the healing shawl. When the shawl is wrapped around me, the red thread sits at the back side of my heart.

The threads from his blankets have been woven into the wrist malas that I have received from Ram Dass at the OYHIP Mala Ceremony. Seeing the red thread in this small area of my healing shawl, for me the significance was obvious: Maharajji was and continues to be present in my heart and soul. I knew at that moment, as I wept with joy, that Maharajji had been wrapping his love around me, that he held me in his healing arms before I even knew of him as I navigated my grief.

Now, by his grace, I have opened my heart to life, to joy, to love again. I bow deeply in gratitude.

ॐ

Susan Grant

At the beginning of 1973, I was in Mendocino on a hippie commune. That was the first time I read *Be Here Now*. Then I moved to Boulder, Colorado. Everybody was talking about Maharajji, Maharajji. But they were talking about the thirteen-year-old one, not Neem Karoli Baba, and it just didn't feel right.

When I visited L.A. again in 1976, I met Ram Dass. I felt like a bright light went on, a bright sun, and I started taking the teachings seriously. I went to graduate school and studied psychotherapy, taking some courses at Naropa (and seeing Ram Dass, Hunter Thompson, Allen Ginsberg, etc.) and at the Transpersonal Institute at University of Colorado. I was getting deeper and deeper into what is the mind and what is the heart.

Time went on. I was living in L.A. and going to Maui, where I met Jeff Munoz, who had been with Maharajji and was putting together a Tibetan temple on top of a mountain, and I met Bhagavan Das. That was when my heart was really taken in by Maharajji, though I was still doing my Tibetan studies. The only person I knew to talk to about all this was Jeff, who was doing the Tibetan practices but his heart was with Maharajji. You realize it's not just about emptying the mind and being peaceful, it's about getting it in the heart.

And I started to know that it was Maharajji who lives in my heart.

राम

Swapnil Abrol

I was born into a Hindu family, but we weren't very religious. We did what most Indian families do—a few rituals a year, or a blessing here and there. One of my favorite superheroes growing up was Hanuman. He would fly around carrying mountains, which was pretty cool to a little kid. My mom's father, who died before I was born, was the spiritual counsel of many people. His advice to people was, don't worry about looking for a guru, just find Hanuman.

There came a time in my early twenties when I began to explore consciousness. I was meditating and having profound experiences. When I took psilocybin for the first time, it was a verification that what I was looking for was real. In university, I started taking high doses of psilocybin by myself and going completely inwards. Then the spirit of psilocybin said to me, *I am not your medicine.* I didn't know what medicine the spirit was talking about until I stumbled across a podcast about ayahuasca.

I found an ayahuasca retreat center in Peru, and the retreat itself was unbelievably profound. In the very last ceremony of the retreat, I can only say that I became the One—every single little grain of sand, every single star, every single galaxy. I was the heart of every individual and felt the interconnectedness of everything. At the end, I saw Krishna in front of me adorned with flowers and ornaments. His face changed into my face, and I was looking at myself; there was really no difference between him and me.

After the ceremony the shaman said to me, "If you want to learn, my spirit guides say I can teach you this science." I couldn't think about much else other than this offer.

Shortly after coming home I went to a bookstore, my first time in the New Age section. There was this little blue book almost falling off the shelf. As I was putting *Be Here Now* back on the shelf (I wasn't going to get it), I looked at the back cover and it said Hanuman Foundation. I like Hanuman! So I got the book. When I'd finished reading it, I read it again. The interesting thing for me was the idea of a being who has achieved the perfection of humanity and knows everything. I read *Be Love Now.* I read *Miracle of Love,* which quickly turned into the most sacred text I'd ever read. Then I started having experiences that seemed related to things I was reading in the book. Every time I looked for an explanation, the very first thing my mind would land on was Maharajji. So there was this natural growing faith that he was in my life.

I went back to the Amazon jungle in Peru to begin my apprenticeship and started the training with ayahuasca. At one of the very early ceremonies, the shaman said to me, "Who's that old guy that hangs around you?" I had no idea. "Maybe it's my grandfather?" Even before I realized who it was, someone else could see Maharajji with me.

In training, you learn to diagnose and to heal people, so you have to connect with spiritual beings that specifically guide you and tell you what the illness is. A big part of the art of shamanism is communicating with unembodied beings on different planes; we called them the Maestros, the doctors. In the jungle, I was communicating with the Maestros fairly well, but there was always this other presence there, which didn't seem to be overly concerned with all that was going on. No matter where I went, this presence was there. This being was infinitely wise and unimaginably loving. There would be times when I was beating myself up for not learning well enough or for doing the wrong thing, and this presence would be my comfort.

I started to understand that this presence was Maharajji. In visions he would show me his physical form, the body I recognized from the pictures, or colors from the blanket. When the effects of the ayahuasca would be finished, the visions would be gone. The diagnostic ability, that deep connection would be gone, but that presence was never gone. It stayed intact no matter what I did.

Then the guidance I received from the Maestros in my shamanic lineage started to be different than what I was receiving from Maharajji. At this point I had developed a very deep communication with Maharajji; he was my best friend. I would sometimes listen to Maharajji and sometimes to the Maestros. Every single time, whatever Maharajji said was truth and the wiser guidance. One time in a ceremony, he clearly said, "Listen to *me*."

My shamanic approach changed from traditional Amazonian to a style filled with bhakti and Hinduism. Maharajji became the main focus and guide of the ceremonies. I would often sing to him, to Hanuman, and to other deities. Then slowly the desire to practice shamanism started to fall away. I understood and respected the shamanic methods, but the method of simply praying to God and singing to the divine without ayahuasca was easier, more natural to me, and seemed to still have a great impact on other people too. I really did get to know the truth of my Hindu lineage and how it was so deeply ingrained into my being and in my blood.

My day-to-day experience of life became so enriched with Maharajji's living presence that there was nothing lacking. He's my guru. He's in charge. His messenger, Ram Dass, was a real guiding light through it all. Ram Dass talks about how any true method will chew you up and spit you out the other side. You'll go through the method, extract what you can from it, and then the method self-destructs. Shamanism is a very profound method, but I was able to give up the attachment to it gently with the help and support of Ram Dass.

Maharajji was never that old man in a blanket for me. The only word that I can use for him is *paramatman*, all-pervading Spirit, all-pervading Being. He is that.

गम

Victoria Angel Heart

One day I was at Ram Dass's house in Maui, thinking about how I've never been willing to surrender to the love of the guru because it felt too much like the religion I broke free of. As I stared into Maharajji's picture, Govinda began to recite the Hanuman Chalisa; his dog Leela hung out around us. I surrendered to the beauty of the prayer and came into the place of being that is loving awareness. As the Chalisa ended, a profound silence settled over us. I opened my eyes and with a hint of sarcasm I said to the photo, "Alright Maharajji, I am open to you. Let me feel all the compassion of the universe."

Before that thought had even been completed, Leela dog was upon me, *showering me with kisses*! Kisses going up my nose, in my mouth, on my ears, everywhere. She put her paws on my shoulders as the shower of kisses continued. Eventually, she knocked me to the floor as she gave me every ounce of love she had. I laughed and squealed and surrendered into this immediate manifestation of infinite compassion. I felt Maharajji's love completely wash over me—literally washing me with puppy kisses. In that moment, I experienced Ram Dass's mantra "I am loving awareness" completely. It's no surprise that Roshi Joan Halifax thinks Leela is an incarnation of Maharajji . . . I am certain of it!

The next day I came to the house for kirtan and found Ram Dass alone in the living room. I told him about meeting Maharajji through Leela, and he smiled and said, "Yep. That's Maharajji." After kirtan, out of nowhere Leela knocked me onto the ottoman, climbed on top of me, and again showered me with slobbery kisses. I felt myself become totally universal again. This is what the love of the guru is like! Ram Dass and the caregivers were all laughing. "That's Maharajji," Ram Dass said with a smile, looking at me with an ocean of love. Then as quickly as she came, Leela jumped off me and was gone.

On Christmas Eve 2019 I returned to Baba Ram Dass's house to be in his physical presence one last time, this time to say goodbye. As I took off my shoes, I saw a blur coming at me. Before I could even take a breath, I was overtaken by Leela. She knocked me onto my butt as yet again I was swept away in the ocean of love. Leela put her paws on my shoulders, stopped kissing me, and looked directly into my eyes. I saw in them the same penetrating stare of unbearable compassion that I'd seen in Ram Dass's eyes just two weeks earlier. My heart tore open in a simultaneous tumble of grief and love, and I burst into tears.

राम

Vivian Gold

I lived in a communal house, an old Spanish mansion with a natural pool in the jungle part of Coconut Grove, Florida, behind gated walls. We all ran around naked. Ram Dass came to the house in the late seventies because I think he knew the owner. Every time Ram Dass was anywhere near Florida, I would go see him. He always talked about Maharajji, so I had Baba's picture; I loved him because he was Ram Dass's guru.

Miami was very decadent. I was a smuggler in my teens, mostly of cocaine. I'd go to Peru and Colombia as a mule. I ended up addicted—snorting, basing, shooting. I had tremendous shame. I would try to hang with spiritual people, but I couldn't wait to sneak off to smoke cigarettes and drink and do cocaine. I didn't feel good enough next to them. My pattern was to get a job, then blow it when I binged and move back in with my folks in Miami. In 1986, my sister had her first son. My folks said that with the baby around, if I didn't get help, I'd be kicked out. For no other reason than to get them off my back, I agreed to see a drug counselor.

I went on a terrible binge and didn't sleep for days. I went to the pool because as long as I had a tan, I was healthy, right? I put on some crisp white clothes and walked into his office. He was a hip guy, with pictures of him playing guitar with Eric Clapton. I needed rock star stuff. My biggest fear in life was conforming to boring people. The counselor was clean from heroin for nine years at the time. He said, "Well, if you don't have a problem, you won't have trouble abstaining from drugs and alcohol for ninety days. But if you have a problem . . ."

I went to my first meeting that same night. Thank God I felt the vibration of love and acceptance from the other recovering addicts and alcoholics.

About a year after I got clean, I went to massage school, got my license, and developed a great massage practice in Miami. And

I was always attending kirtan. Then two of my friends moved to Asheville, and I followed in 2004. I needed to go to the mountains to heal. I became friends with a couple that had moved to Ashville from L.A.—Marty and Suzanne Malles—who invited me to their house Saturday night for a kirtan, where I met Robin Saraswati and Raghu. It felt like my Jewish family. When we had food and did the blessing, they also did a *baruch atah*[44]. I really did feel the love of Maharajji coming through everybody.

Maharajji changed from being Ram Dass's guru to being mine in a slow process—a natural shift that happened over the years of being in the presence of devotees and hearing their stories. You could say I fell in love with Maharajji's people first.

When I look back on my life, I realize guardian angels were watching over me. There were so many instances when I could've died or gotten AIDS from the way that I used drugs. Now I look at everything I went through as a blessing. I'm clean and sober thirty-five years. Besides doing massage and wellness, I am a clean and sober Recovery Coach/Companion; I go into people's houses and stay with them and show them how to be happy without getting high all the time. I can help somebody else only because I had experienced all those things.

And that's the purpose, isn't it? The purpose is compassion.

---

44 *Baruch atah Adonai Eloheinu*—the start of a Hebrew prayer, translated as "Blessed are You, Lord our God, King of the Universe…"

Acknowledgments

It takes the proverbial village to put together a collection of stories from more than a hundred and fifty people.

First, I must thank all those who shared their personal stories with such open hearts. Your faith in a being you didn't meet in person will inspire others to go beyond their own doubts.

Special thanks to those at the Love Serve Remember Foundation—in particular Rameshwar Das, Raghu Markus, and Rachael Fisher—who supported and gave input on the project. And great appreciation to the wonderfully helpful staff at Mandala Publishing: Katie Killebrew, Phillip Jones, Ashley Quackenbush, and Amanda Nelson. Kudos to HR Hegnauer for the book's interior design.

A big thank you to Pete Holmes for taking the time to write the foreword while in the midst of shooting a new television show.

Another very big thank you goes to Annie Levitt for her tireless work on everything from interviews and emails to the dreaded database that contained multitudes of changing names, information, and permissions.

Next comes Radha Baum, my bhava analyst, with many thanks. If a story didn't touch her heart and have her shedding a tear or two, it was revised or eliminated.

Heartfelt gratitude to the readers of early versions—Mary Godschalk, Gayatri Wagle, Annapurna Sydell, Melinda Edwards, and Jill Fineberg—and to those who contributed early reviews—Krishna Das, Mirabai Starr, Duncan Trussell, Nina Rao, Rameshwar Das, Trudy Goodman, Ramananda John E. Welshons, Trevor Hall, and Lama Tsultrim Allione.

Special thanks to Robin Alexis for eliminating obstacles and providing healing energy.

And, of course, my forever gratitude to Neem Karoli Baba, the heart whisperer.

Photography Credits

© Balaram Das (Dedication)
© Balaram Das (Appearances, p. 1)
© Mohan Baum (Books, p. 39)
© Unknown (Kirtan, p. 65)
© Balaram Das (Photos, p. 99)
© Balaram Das (Temples, p. 119)
© Rameshwar Das (Ram Dass, p. 135)
© Mary Godschalk (Retreats, p. 155)
© Balaram Das (Cry for Help, p. 193)
© Balaram Das (Dreams, p. 209)
© Balaram Das (Many Roads Home, p. 249)
© RamRam (endsheet)

Glossary

AARTI – from the Sanskrit *aratrika*, meaning something that removes darkness. It can be a ritual part of worship that includes waving a light and offering it to the deity or guru, as well as the song itself that is part of the puja.

ASANA – from the Sanskrit, referring to the place and the pose in which a yogi sits. Today, the body postures are taught in yoga classes as exercise.

ASHRAM – a spiritual hermitage or a Hindu monastic community

BHAKTA – one who follows the path of devotion

BHAKTI YOGA – the path of devotion

BHANDARA – a free meal served to people during a religious festival or as an offering for a blessing received

BHAVA – a Sanskrit word indicating a spiritual emotion or attitude of devotion, generated through sadhana and an intense yearning for God

DARSHAN – Sanskrit term meaning "sight of," as in seeing or having a vision of the divine or being in the presence of a holy person.

GURU – the one who removes the darkness (ignorance) and brings the light of illumination and knowledge. From Sanskrit *Gu*, darkness, and *Ru*, light.

HANUMAN – an incarnation of Lord Shiva in the form of a Vanara (the monkey race) who serves Lord Rama. Hanuman's exploits are told in the *Ramayana*. The HANUMAN CHALISA is a hymn of 40 verses in Hindi in praise of Hanuman.

JAPA – a spiritual practice that involves repeating a mantra or a Name of God. From the Sanskrit *jap*, meaning "to utter in a low voice, repeat internally, mutter." Japa is often done on a MALA, a string of 108 beads that carry a spiritual vibration.

KARMA – Sanskrit for the concept of the cycle of cause and effect, where the effects of our words, thoughts, and deeds are seen as shaping all our past, present, and future experiences.

KARTALS – small cymbals played during kirtan.

KIRTAN – chanting the Divine Name. from Sanskrit, meaning "to repeat."

KIRTAN WALLAHS – the singers/musicians who lead kirtan.

KRIPA – divine grace, a central tenet of bhakti yoga.

KRIYAS – a series of postures and breath that produce physical and mental changes in body, mind, and spirit

KUNDALINI – translates as "serpent power"—the current of divine feminine energy that is coiled at the base of the spine until awakened, when it climbs the spinal channels like an electric current and merges with the divine consciousness in the crown.

LEELA – Sanskrit, meaning "sport" or "play"—the activities of God and his devotees.

MAHAMANTRA – the "Great Mantra" from the Upanishads, also known as the Hare Krishna mantra.

MAHASAMADHI – the "great" final samadhi, which means consciously leaving the body at the time of physical death by an awakened being.

MANTRA – a sound, syllable, word, or group of words that are repeated to bring about a spiritual transformation.

MURTI – Sanskrit for form or embodiment, the image of God used during worship

PARIKRAMA – the clockwise circumambulation of a sacred area, like Vrindavan; the path around sacred entities

PRANAM – respectful or reverential salutation or prostration with hands in prayer position; *danda pranam* is a full-length prostration before the guru

PRASAD – literally means "mercy," and refers to anything that has been blessed by being offered to the guru or deity.

Puja – Sanskrit term for worship or adoration performed at home or at a temple or shrine to a murti or person. The inner purpose is to purify the atmosphere, connect with the inner world, and invoke the presence of God or guru.

Rinpoche – from the Tibetan, an honorific given to masters in Tibetan Buddhism, literally means "precious jewel."

Sadhana – spiritual practice

Sadhu – common term for a wandering monk, yogi, or ascetic.

Samadhi – Sanskrit term for the higher levels of consciousness reached through concentrated meditation or grace. For bhaktas, samadhi is the absorption into the object of one's love.

Satsang – from the Sanskrit *sat*-true and *sanga*-company. The assembly of people who come together to share spiritual teachings.

Shakti – dynamic spiritual energy

Siddhi – Sanskrit term for spiritual power or ability, literally means "a perfection."

Sub ek – All one

Takhat – wooden platform that Maharajji sat upon

Yatra – pilgrimage to spiritual sites

RESOURCES

For more teachings from Neem Karoli Baba and Ram Dass, visit
https://RamDass.org
https://NKBAshram.org
https://BeHereNowNetwork.com
https://hanumanmaui.org

Books

Some of the following books are specifically about Maharajji, while others are spiritual memoirs by Neem Karoli Baba devotees that include personal stories about Maharajji. Many are available either from the Taos Ashram (www.nkbashram.org) or from www.ramdass.org, and most can be found on Amazon.

All Roads Lead to Ram: The Personal History of a Spiritual Adventurer by Sruti Ram (Monkfish Book Publishing, 2021)

Barefoot in the Heart: Remembering Neem Karoli Baba by Keshav Das (Sensitive Skin Books, 2011)

Be Here Now by Ram Dass (Lama Foundation, 1971)

Be Love Now by Ram Dass with Rameshwar Das (HarperOne, 2010)

Being Ram Dass by Ram Dass with Rameshwar Das (Sounds True, 2021)

By His Grace: A Devotee's Story by Dada Mukerjee (Hanuman Foundation, 1990)

Chants of a Lifetime: Searching for a Heart of Gold by Krishna Das (Hay House, 2010)

Deva Bhumi: The Abode of the Gods in India by Krishna Kumar (K.K.) Sah (Love Serve Remember Foundation, 2016)

HeartSourcing: Finding Our Way to Love and Liberation by Ramgiri Braun, Ph.D. (Annapurna Institute Inc., 2014)

I and My Father are One: The Grand Unification by Rabbo Joshi (Bibliophile South Asia, 2011)

It All Abides in Love: Maharajji Neem Karoli Baba by Jai Ram Ransom (Taos Music & Art, Inc, 2014)

It's Here Now (Are You?) by Bhagavan Das (Broadway, 1997)

Love Everyone: The Transcendent Wisdom of Neem Karoli Baba Told Through the Stories of the Westerners Whose Lives He Transformed by Parvati Markus (HarperOne, 2015)

Milagro de Amor: Historias sobre Neem Karoli Baba (Spanish Edition) by Ram Dass (translated by Durga Julia Sanchez and Maria Clara Herrera, 2021)

Miracle of Love: Stories About Neem Karoli Baba by Ram Dass (E.P. Dutton, 1979)

Neem Karoli Baba: An Indian Incarnation of Lord Hanuman by Vishnu Ratna (Notion Press, 2019)

Sometimes Brilliant: The Impossible Adventure of a Spiritual Seeker and Visionary Physician Who Helped Conquer the Worst Disease in History by Dr. Larry Brilliant (HarperOne, 2017)

The Divine Reality of Sri Baba Neeb Karori Ji Maharaj by Ravi Prakash Pande Rajida (Sri Kainchi Hanuman Mandir & Ashram, 2005)

The Near and the Dear by Dada Mukerjee (Hanuman Foundation, 2000)

PHOTOS

There are photos of Maharajji available to download for free: https://imageevent.com/neemkarolibabaphotos

You can get photo prints, postcards, and posters from the Taos Hanuman Temple: https://pujadukan.myshopify.com/collections/photos-and-posters

CHANTING AND HANUMAN CHALISA

There is a lot of good music out there for opening hearts and deepening devotion, as well as instruction in the Hanuman Chalisa and fellowship in chanting. The following chant masters may have different styles, but they are all singing the sacred Names!

https://ambikachant.com/
https://bhagavandas.com/
https://bhaktiyogashala.com/
https://davidnewmanmusic.com/
https://iamadambauer.com/
https://jaiuttal.com/
http://keshav-music.com/keshav-das-music/
https://krishnadas.com/
https://ninaraochant.com/
https://shubalananda.com
https://shyamachapin.com/
https://shyamdasfoundation.com/
https://umareed.com/

MANDALA

An Imprint of MandalaEarth
PO Box 3088
San Rafael, CA 94912
www.MandalaEarth.com

Find us on Facebook: www.facebook.com/MandalaEarth
Follow us on Twitter: @MandalaEarth

CEO: Raoul Goff
Associate Publisher: Phillip Jones
VP Creative: Chrissy Kwasnik
VP Manufacturing: Alix Nicholaeff
Editorial Director: Katie Killebrew
Associate Art Director: Ashley Quackenbush
Production Manager: Joshua Smith
Sr Production Manager, Subsidiary Rights: Lina s Palma-Temena

Visit BeHereNowNetwork.com for insightful and entertaining podcasts. Follow @babaramdass on Instagram, Facebook, Twitter & TikTok.

Every good faith effort has been made to obtain permissions for letters that were written many decades ago and adapted in this work. If you are, or know of, our "missing" letter authors, please email info@ramdass.org.

ISBN: 978-1-64722-668-8
Manufactured in India by Insight Editions
10 9 8 7 6 5 4 3 2 1

ROOTS of PEACE   REPLANTED PAPER

Insight Editions, in association with Roots of Peace, will plant two trees for each tree used in the manufacturing of this book. Roots of Peace is an internationally renowned humanitarian organization dedicated to eradicating land mines worldwide and converting war-torn lands into productive farms and wildlife habitats. Roots of Peace will plant two million fruit and nut trees in Afghanistan and provide farmers there with the skills and support necessary for sustainable land use.